CAMPING
WASHINGTON

Mount Rainier from Paradise

The blue-green waters of Ross Lake, near Colonial Creek Campground in North Cascades National Park

A fir buds in springtime.

Wild berries collect dew.

A great blue heron wades near the shore in Birch Bay State Park.

Pileated woodpeckers are frequent visitors to Northwest campgrounds.

Bald eagles watch over the Nooksack River.

A yearling black bear cub emerges from hibernation near Mount Baker.

A visitor scans the spectacle of Dry Falls near Sun Lakes State Park.

Bumping Lake reservoir bursts into golden larch-tree splendor in autumn.

A historic shelter awaits campers at Soda Springs, in the South Cascades.

A glider pilot lands in the Cowlitz Valley, near Taidnapam Campground.

Getting wet is a prime activity at Kopachuk State Park on South Puget Sound.
(Photo by Janice Ohlsen)

Views are stunning from atop Mount Constitution in Moran State Park.

A suspension bridge spans the Spokane River in Riverside State Park. (Photo by Seabury Blair Jr.)

Autumn leaves brighten the banks of the Icicle River near Leavenworth.

CAMPING WASHINGTON

**The Best Public
Campgrounds
for Tents and RVs
—RATED & REVIEWED**

Ron C. Judd

THE MOUNTAINEERS BOOKS

THE MOUNTAINEERS BOOKS
is the nonprofit publishing arm of The Mountaineers,
an organization founded in 1906 and dedicated to the exploration,
preservation, and enjoyment of outdoor and wilderness areas.

1001 SW Klickitat Way, Suite 201, Seattle, WA 98134

© 2009 by Ron C. Judd

Disclaimer: A guidebook to outdoor recreation is a slice in time. The information herein is the latest and most accurate available to the author and publisher at press time. However, neither can control the forces of nature, or bureaucracies, that shape the status, open and closing seasons, general welfare, rules, or availability of campgrounds, which tend to open and close unexpectedly from one year to the next. Please see contact information for each campground listed, and check for updates before embarking on a camping trip.

First edition: first printing 2009, second printing 2011, third printing 2013, fourth printing 2015

Manufactured in the United States of America

Copy Editor: Susan Hodges
Cover, book design, and layout: Peggy Egerdahl
Cartographer: Pease Press Cartography
All photographs by the author unless otherwise noted
Front cover photograph: *Point of the Arches, Washington* © Rene Frederick, Age fotostock
Back cover photograph: *Pearrygin Lake State Park often books up on summer days.*
Photograph, page 1: *A tent-camping site on the shores of Lake Wenatchee at Glacier View
    Campground*
Photograph, page 8: *A hiker takes in the old-growth forest on the Hall of Mosses Trail in the Hoh River
    Valley of Olympic National Park.*

Library of Congress Cataloging-in-Publication Data
Judd, Ron C.
  Camping Washington : the best public campground for tents & rvs / Ron C. Judd.
    p. cm.
  Includes index.
  ISBN 978-1-59485-092-9 (ppb)
1. Camp sites, facilities, etc.—Washington (State)—Guidebooks. 2. Camping—Washington
(State)—Guidebooks. 3. Recreational vehicle camping—Washington (State)—Guidebooks. I. Title.
  GV191.42.W2J298 2009
  917.9706'8—dc22
                      2009015643

ISBN (paperback): 978-1-59485-092-9
ISBN (ebook): 978-1-59485-504-7

CONTENTS

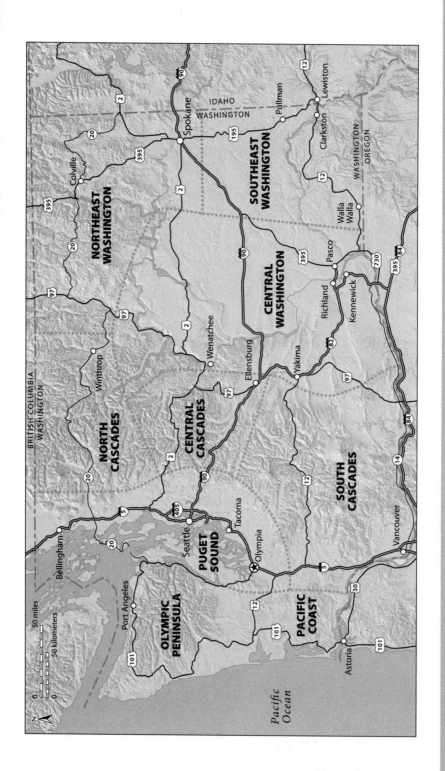

INTRODUCTION

Life tastes better outside.

This is a universal truth in the Evergreen State—assuming, of course, that said taste is not unduly influenced at a given moment by diesel fumes from a broken-down Metro bus on the parking lot formerly known as Interstate 5.

The idea here is to get away from all that, and it used to be quite simple. Back in the days before pant legs flared out, then sucked back in again, you could arrive home from work on a Friday evening; pile the kids, dogs, blue tarps, broken-down canvas tent, cooler, matches, Oreos, six-packs of Tab (remember Tab?), and piles of Tupperware with ill-fitting lids into the back of the Buick Roadmaster; and head to the hills (and a waiting campsite) before dark. Nowadays, you'd be lucky to get out of the Mount Baker tunnel by dark; and if you did, all the good campsites would have been long-ago occupied by retirees, encroaching Californians in Greyhound-size motor homes, tent-squatting guidebook authors, and other miscreants who, for some reason, don't live on normal schedules.

Like any other form of outdoor recreation, camping now requires a bit more strategizing. Campground reservation systems today are more norm than exception—even more so than when we put out the first edition of this camping guide almost a decade ago. Ignore them at your own peril: they're the key to locking up that gorgeous site you used to claim first-come—before most of the rest of the planet started coming first.

Granted, this excises some of the spontaneity from getting out and away ("spontaneity" all too often translating to "sleeping in the car in the parking lot of the Forks Motel after finding every camping space on the Olympic Peninsula full"). But it also eliminates much of the guesswork. Somehow, heavy traffic on the way over Snoqualmie Pass seems a lot less stressful if you know an open site is waiting, with your name on it, at Steamboat Rock State Park.

In that sense, camping in Washington is better than it used to be. You fellow natives (defined by the author as people who remember when Bumbershoot, the big Seattle Labor Day arts festival, was free) might chortle over this. But think about it: As with other forms of outdoor recreation, the numbers of campers have exploded in recent years, especially as Baby Boomers reach the Mandatory Winnebago-Acquisition Age. But unlike other cherished outdoor activities, such as hiking, boating, skiing, et al, campgrounds come with their own built-in restrictions. Witness: Kalaloch Campground has the same 170-odd (a few of them very odd, indeed) sites it's had since the author was in diapers. True, some little things have changed—you can pay by credit card now, and reservations (!) are now a normal part of oceanfront camping life. But otherwise, once you pitch the tent or drop the RV jacks, you're set. Time warped. Grandfathered. Why? Because, in the same fashion as a person can only get so wet while hiking in the rain forest, a campground can only get so crowded. Latecomers don't muscle in; they go home. The same cannot be said of hiking a trail or fishing a stream, where bodies just pile up until it's unbearable.

Stairs lead to Tongue Point, a prime tidal pool viewing area, at Salt Creek Recreation Area on the Strait of Juan de Fuca.

And camping is better in still other ways: Once at your coveted site, you'll probably be a lot more comfortable today than ever before—at a lower cost, thanks to the abundance of imported outdoor gear. Technical innovations—camp stoves; heaters; lightweight, waterproof tents and clothing; synthetic insulations; and inflatable sleeping mattresses—have turned Washington camping from a wet, cold Navy SEAL survivalist experience into something bordering on living-room cozy. And this applies equally to those in 3-by-6-foot tents and 48-foot motor homes.

You know what all this means. It means you no longer have a good excuse. Can't ever get a site? Find an obscure one (plenty await herein). Or plan ahead six months and reserve one. Don't have the gear? Buy it. Borrow it. Rent it. You don't have to spend a fortune—or even a lot of money—to have fun camping in Washington.

Camping, quite simply, is the best adventure you can still undertake on a shoe-string budget. It's a never-fail memory maker. It's as close as modern people come to pulling off a Columbus-style voyage of discovery—at least without enlisting the aid of a queen and fretting about dying of scurvy. It is the perfect personal "reboot" button for souls too cluttered by computers, deadlines, and corporate buyouts.

And it's difficult to imagine a better place to do it than the aptly named Evergreen State. From the sparkling beaches of Puget Sound to the pounding surf of the Olympic Peninsula, from the crisp, sweet alpine air of the Cascade highlands to the warm, sprawling lakefront lawns of the Columbia Basin, Washington is the Disneyland of American camping. Few states—or other similarly sized regions of the planet—offer the campsite diversity found between Bellingham and Walla Walla, Vancouver and Metaline Falls.

It's all here, campers. The trick is to put yourself in the midst of it and let fate have its way. We've spent a lifetime doing just that, learning a lot in the process. Camping was such a normal part of life in the Judd household, in fact, that it wasn't until my two sisters and I were college-aged that we realized a family camping could consist of something *other* than camping.

Most of that accumulated campground knowledge is capsulated in the pages that follow. Use it in good health, and be prepared to get hooked.

For most of us, one taste is never enough.

Ron C. Judd

A viewing platform overlooks Dungeness Spit National Wildlife Refuge.

HOW TO USE THIS BOOK

The easy-to-read format of this guide should make using *Camping Washington* fairly self-explanatory. But a few notes on its construction, as well as on our philosophies in describing and rating each campground, should make it even more helpful. Here's a look at how each campground listing is set up.

Sample Listing

3 Lincoln Rock State Park ★ ★ ★ ✦

SITES	RESERVATIONS	CONTACT
🏕️ 🚐	(888) 226-7688 or www.parks.wa.gov	Washington State Parks (360) 902-8844
	OPEN	Lincoln Rock State Park (509) 884-8702
94 sites, 32 full hookups, 35 water/ electrical hookups, RVs to 65 feet	March to mid-October	

Lincoln Rock has long been one of our favorite state parks, mostly because of the amount of local character revealed by its namesake. History records that somewhere back around 1889, a local man, Billy Schaft, photographed a large rock outcrop across the river from this park and remarked how much it looked like a profile of Abraham Lincoln. Plenty of other local people who—let's face it, living in Wenatchee and all—had plenty of time to consider such things, agreed. Someone sent the picture to a photo contest in *Ladies' Home Journal*, and it won first prize. Voila! Lincoln Rock went on the maps, and public gatherings soon followed. The park, on a broad, flat Columbia River shoulder across the river from the rock, now bears its name. If you look through the little fixed pipe near the Lincoln Rock upper restroom, you can see it. By George, it does look like Abe. Wake the kids. The campground here is worthy of a visit on its own, however. It's the prototype for a series of Washington State Parks on the middle Columbia, all of which follow a wildly successful formula: sprawling grassy playfields; boat launches; a swimming area; and flat, open trailer and tent sites separated by young shade trees. All these parks are popular with boaters, who flock here in summer months to water-ski and soak up the sun. Lincoln Rock, on the Columbia's Entiat Lake behind Rocky Reach Dam, has all of these pleasures and more, including two boat launches, multiple moorage docks, tennis and basketball courts, coin-op showers, horseshoe pits, a large kitchen shelter, and an amphitheater. It's a very pleasant spot—too hot for some tastes in the summer, but just right for the lizard people among us. Just across the river is the popular Rocky Reach Dam Visitor Center, which you can only get to by driving back south to Wenatchee, crossing the river, and driving up U.S. Highway 97A.

Getting there: The campground is 7 miles north of East Wenatchee on U.S. Highway 2, on the east side of the Columbia River.

Here's an explainer for the individual categories in the Lincoln Rock listing above:

Ratings

Each campground is rated on a scale of one to five stars—one being lousy, five being tops. These ratings are based on personal visits and camping experiences of the wildly opinionated author and his mildly opinionated associates. In other words, even though they are based on what I believe to be sound knowledge from well-informed campers, like any ratings they remain *completely subjective*. Please understand that they have no underlying mathematical equation that takes into account distance from home, number of spaces, weather, or the likelihood that a garage band called "Used Food" will set up camp in the space next door. Rather, the ratings reflect each campground's overall feel, natural beauty, quality of facilities, ease of use, and other intangibles. It's important to understand that campgrounds, being out there in the wild and all, can change dramatically from one season to the next—or even from one week to the next, if disaster strikes or uncouth irritants happen to occupy the sites on either side of you. That Forest Service campground we rated a solid "4.5 stars" might be a lot less attractive once you arrive and find that a November blast has leveled every tree in the place. Because of this, not to mention variations in taste, your camping experience may, and likely will, vary. If it does so markedly, please write and tell us about it, or post a note to the Camping Washington section of the author's blog, found at www.ronjudd.com. We'll consider your opinions as valuable contributions to the next edition of this guide.

OK, that said: The ratings system is somewhat stingy. You'll find, for example, only a handful of campgrounds rated "5 stars" in this book. That's an honor, and a deliberately high standard that we take quite seriously. Campgrounds designated as such are those we consider essential to the serious Washington camper's resume. (You also might be surprised at some of the lesser-known campgrounds we rate "4 stars" or better: Many of these are places outside the camping "mainstream" that we've come to love and appreciate during a lifetime of camping in the state.)

Conversely, you'll find few campgrounds herein rated lower than "2 stars." Most "1-star" campgrounds were either purposefully left out of this guide (why would we send you there?), or listed under "Other Campgrounds" at the end of each section. Why include them in the guide at all? To help you know what you're getting into when you see the name on a map and it's your only option, or when you get steered toward it by someone who doesn't know better. We've attempted, in other words, to make a lot of your mistakes for you. You're welcome.

THE CAMPING WASHINGTON RATINGS KEY

★ ★ ★ ★ ★ The crème de la crème. A can't-miss Northwest classic. You haven't truly camped until you've camped here.

★ ★ ★ ★ A stunner. Among the best. Bring a lot of film and site-finding patience.

★ ★ ★ Very nice. A pleasant, occasionally beautiful getaway—but don't set aside two weeks.

★ ★ Passable. It'll do for an overnight spot on the way to somewhere else.

★ A stinker. We spent the retirement money on a Winnebago—and guidebook—for this?

Sites

Total numbers of sites are listed for each campground. Unlike some other guides, we've chosen not to distinguish between "tent" sites and "RV" sites, for a simple reason: Experienced campers know that tents usually can be pitched comfortably in sites that are designated as "RV" sites simply because they have some sort of utility hookup. Designating these sites strictly as "RV" is misleading, because it suggests tents aren't welcome. Not so. Some of the nicest Washington State Parks tent sites, in fact, are listed as "RV" sites in most guides. That doesn't mean you could not or should not pitch a tent there. Example: All except three of sixty-three campsites at Grayland Beach State Park, one of the most pleasant state parks on the Washington coast, are designated "RV" sites because they have full hookups. But all sixty-three sites also are spacious, grassy, flat— and extremely popular with tenters. Tent campers who overlooked this camp because of the RV designation would be making a mistake.

We've tried to work around this problem: Listings include the total number of campsites, "RV" and "tent" inclusive. To assist the RVer or trailer owner who's interested in utility hookups and campsite lengths, we list both the number of sites with utility hookups and the overall length available to RVers. Thus, our sample park above, Lincoln Rock, contains this listing: "94 sites; 32 full hookups, 35 water/electrical hookups; RVs to 65 feet." Savvy tenters who read between the lines will note that all sites are available to them, but twenty-seven of them don't have any sort of utility hookups, and thus are probably either designed for tents, or available to tenters at a lower price than the RV sites.

Tent, RV, Cabin, and Yurt Symbols

Each campground is marked by a tent and/or RV symbol. Parks that offer permanent cabins or yurts carry these symbols, as well. Those with both tent and RV symbols have sites catering on some level to both tenters and RVers. Those with only a tent mean that literally: Tents only. Most of these are smaller, difficult-to-access campgrounds in the mountains, where RVs of any size cannot reach. They might not all be *technically* off-limits to RVers, although some are. We're just giving you our best judgment here. The rules are slightly different for campgrounds marked only by an RV symbol. These typically are paved, cramped RV quarters where only the most desperate tenter would dare pitch his or her abode. You'd probably be *allowed* to pitch a tent here. You just wouldn't want to.

Open (the Camping Season)

Each listing indicates the campground's scheduled opening and closing dates. This is a matter of increasing importance to Washington campers, particularly RV owners, who are fighting the jam-packed madness of summer camping by extending their outdoor seasons all the way through the winter. Even tenters often can find shoulder-season camping in the early spring or late fall a pleasant switch from the crowds of summer.

Stone "hoodoos" are a unique feature of the Okanogan Highlands.

Latch onto a down sleeping bag, and give it a shot. You just might get hooked. Or get frostbite.

Opening and closing dates vary widely, and they're all subject to change with little or no notice to hapless guidebook assemblers. But some trends can be noted. Washington State Parks, the vast majority of which are in low-elevation locations less affected by snow or unseasonable weather, usually open and close precisely on the dates listed. You can see a full winter schedule for Washington State Parks on the agency's website, www.parks.wa.gov. It's where we go for the latest info; you should, too.

U.S. Forest Service and national park campgrounds, which are often found in high-elevation areas, are less consistent. That's why some of those campground listings will be more vague: "mid-September" as a closing date as opposed to "September 15." National Park and Forest Service operating dates can vary by as much as three weeks from year to year, because of unusually heavy or light winter snowfall. For these campgrounds, consider the listed dates a mid-range target. Then call the contact number listed to get exact dates as your trip approaches.

Persistent campers will find that camping is possible in some places even after the campground officially "closes." This is particularly true of some Forest Service campgrounds. Many ranger districts will close and gate most of their campgrounds, but leave one or two open for hardy late-season campers, hunters, and other warm-blooded outdoor lovers. Generally, if the campground gate is open in the fall, you can camp there, usually free of charge, until snows close the campground for good. Note that water and garbage services probably won't be available after seasonal "closings." You'll need to pack everything in and out. Again, check with the contact agency about off-season camping. Opening and closing dates also can change from one year to the next because of budget shortfalls and other unnatural factors.

Reservations

You already know "why." This guide should help you with the "where" and the "when." Unfortunately, campers in people-clogged Washington keep getting tripped up by the "how."

Just knowing where you want to go and during what season no longer cuts it in the Evergreen State, where landing a non-reservation campsite on any given summer

Friday night ceased being simple about the time the Seattle Mariners came to town (for you newcomers: 1977). It's increasingly a good idea to take advantage of campgrounds that accept reservations. Doing so removes much of the uncertainty (also known in some old-fashioned circles as "fun") from camping. You'll know before you ever leave home whether your favorite campground is booked. If it is, reservation operators usually can help you choose a guaranteed alternate site in the same area.

The bulk of Washington's reservation campgrounds use one of two systems:

State Parks

A web-based reservation system, run by a contractor, accepts online and telephone reservations for Washington State Parks and Tacoma Power Parks. At this writing, sixty campgrounds accept reservations online at www.parks.wa.gov or by phone at (888) 226-7688. Phone lines are open every day of the year, 7:00 AM to 8:00 PM (PST), except Christmas Day and New Year's Day and with shortened hours on Christmas Eve and New Year's Eve. Campers can reserve sites up to nine months in advance (or as little as one day in advance). Holiday weekends usually require a two-night minimum. State Parks yurts, cabins, rental houses, group sites, and other facilities also can be reserved through this service.

Credit cards are the preferred payment method, and they speed up any refunds. But you can pay by check if you can get it to the agency within seven days of making your reservation for a site booked at least twenty-eight days in advance. See the agency website for information. A non-refundable reservations fee is charged for the service. At this writing, it's $8.50 for phoned-in reservations and $6.50 for those made online. If you have to cancel, the earlier you do it, the more of the fee you get refunded.

Some things to keep in mind:

The nine-month advance window is crucial. If you're looking to get a site in, say, Steamboat Rock on the Fourth of July, you'd better be punching up "redial" on the preceding fourth of October.

While a growing number of state parks (Deception Pass, Cape Disappointment, Dosewallips, Grayland Beach, Kitsap Memorial, Ocean City, Pacific Beach, Ike Kinswa, and Steamboat Rock) now operate under the reservation system year-round, most use it only between May 15 and September 15. These parks revert to first-come, first-served during the winter. If you're frustrated at trying to get into your favorite park during the reservation season, try it in the early spring or late fall. Some very pleasant camping conditions often can be found in October, in particular.

Don't overlook the fact that the majority of Washington State Parks still are not on the reservation system. Sites there can still be nabbed the old-fashioned way: showing up early. Call the Washington State Parks information line, (360) 902-8844, for information on campgrounds that are not part of the reservations system.

Federal Campgrounds

The former National Recreation Reservation System, which booked campgrounds for the U.S. Forest Service, and the National Parks Reservation Service, which did the same for national parks, have been consolidated into a single agency. Actually, NRRS now handles all federal reservations (including the U.S. Army Corps of Engineers and the Bureau of Reclamation), either online at www.recreation.gov, or by phone at (877) 444-6777. Many of Washington's 500-plus Forest Service and National Park Service campgrounds now use this system. Individual campsites, cabins, and lookouts can be reserved six months in advance; group sites can be reserved a year in advance. Online reservations can be made at any time. The call center operates from 7:00 AM to 9:00 PM (PST) from March 1 to October 31, and from 7:00 AM to 7:00 PM (PST) from November 1 to February 28. Credit card payment is required. See the website for cancellation and refund information. A reservation fee of $9 is charged for this service.

The website is fairly intuitive and has a nice search feature; you can specify a region you're seeking to camp in, or just name a campground you already know you want. Campsite listings include a locator map and much useful information, such as how big of an RV or tent(s) the site will accommodate, whether it's shady or sunny, etc. The site also will inform you that many campsites—particularly those in national parks—cannot be reserved online, and must be booked by telephone. Note that you'll need to reserve a minimum two nights at most campgrounds on weekends, and three nights at many sites on holiday weekends. Unlike Washington State Parks, most Forest Service campgrounds offering reservations still set aside about half their sites for first-come, first-served campers. Call the contact number listed with each campground for advice on site availability.

Note: The former, separate reservations services for national park campgrounds including Kalaloch in Olympic National Park and Cougar Rock and Ohanapecosh in Mount Rainier National Park, thankfully, are no more. Gone also is the former requirement to have a reservation during summer months at Mount Rainier campgrounds. It's still a good idea to get a summer reservation for all these campgrounds, however.

Contact
Numbers listed reflect the closest and best information source for each campground. We strongly recommend phoning before you go, no matter where you're going or when.

Campground Descriptions
We've attempted to describe the campground, its surrounding area, local attractions and interesting history, individual campsite recommendations, and things to look out for in the main text of each listing. Generally, the more noteworthy the campground, the more long-winded we become—a handful of top-rated campgrounds are described in far more detail than standard listings. At the end of each chapter, under "Other Campgrounds," unrated campgrounds are noted with just the barebones facts.

The main text is also the place to pass on vital information about the campground's facilities. For brevity's sake, we've made the assumption that a basic Washington campground is minimally equipped with a picnic table, fire pit, piped water, and flush toilets. If facilities aren't discussed in the text, you can assume the camp will offer those services. Any variances—the lack of piped water or flush toilets, the presence of hot showers, and so on—are noted in the description. Of course, we can't be everywhere at once, and piped water at some National Forest campgrounds, in particular, can come and go. This is why it's a good idea to use the provided contact numbers before you set out.

Facilities vary widely from campground to campground, but these trends generally hold true: **Washington State Parks** are the most creature-comfortable public campgrounds. All are equipped with fire pits, picnic tables, piped water, and flush toilets; most also offer a true nicety for tent campers: coin-op showers (although sadly, some of these are in a sorry state of repair). Many state parks also offer full hookups (water, sewer, and electricity) for RV campers. The vast majority also have RV dump stations, while many feature picnic facilities, boat launches, group camps, historic buildings, and other amenities. Most **U.S. Forest Service** campgrounds in Washington have picnic tables, fire pits, piped or hand-pumped water, and pit toilets. (True loo aficionados take note: Yes, some modern Forest Service toilets are technically "vault" toilets; we've used the term "pit toilet" to describe all non-flushable commodes.) None offer utility hookups, and only a small number have flush toilets, RV dump stations, picnic areas, boat launches, or other services. As a general rule, Forest Service camps do not have showers. Campsites in Mount Rainier, Olympic, and North Cascades **National Parks** are equipped with picnic tables, fire pits, and, with only a couple exceptions, piped water and flush toilets. Some have RV dump stations, picnic areas, and other facilities. None of them offer showers, and one in particular (not to mention any names, but it's Mount Rainier) has gone so far as to tell us that even portable solar showers are forbidden. Please join us in writing your congressional representative. Pretend he or she has nothing better to do.

Getting There

Each campground listed includes detailed road directions, most of which begin at the nearest sizable town or landmark. To make your travel and camping plans easier, campgrounds in this guide generally are arranged according to common highway travel from the Puget Sound area. For example, listings in the Stevens Pass and Lake Wenatchee section begin at Gold Bar and proceed in a west-to-east order along U.S. Highway 2. If you're traveling in the opposite direction, start at the end of the section and work your way back to the beginning. (The alternative is turning the book upside down, which is not recommended, particularly if you are piloting a large motor home.)

Some additional information that you should know about, in general, and that may help you navigate this guidebook:

"Best" Lists

Sprinkled throughout this guide you will find "Best" lists for campgrounds divided by prime features, e.g., best riverfront camps, best hiking camps, or best oceanfront camps. Two things to keep in mind: like our rating system, these are somewhat subjective. Under "Best Fishing Camps," for example, we could have easily listed a top twenty, but went with the first five that came to mind. Also: each list's 1–5 numbering system is not meant to imply that number 1 is five times superior to number 5. They're just five campgrounds we find particularly attractive for the activity in question, in no particular order. We hope the lists will be of assistance when trip-planning for specific purposes.

Fees

Because campground prices often change, individual campsite prices are not listed with campground descriptions in this guide. There are a few exceptions: If we're describing a camp that's run by an unusual agency, such as a city government or a public utility district, we'll include current pricing because that information is typically harder to come by. For most campground listings, however, the following rules apply.

In **Washington State Parks,** primitive campsites (no tables, sometimes no fire pits) cost $12 to $14 per night; standard sites (tables and fire pits, but no hookups) are $19 to $21 per night; and utility sites (tables; fire pits; and sewer, electrical, and water hookups) are $29 to $36 per night. A summer surcharge is added at some popular parks. Also note that fee-paying campers are exempt, for that visit, from the State Parks day-use fee, initiated in 2011. Other fees: $10 for a second vehicle, unless it's towed by an RV; $5 to $7 for trailer dumping and boat launching (annual permits available for $70 for you frequent dumpers/launchers). **National Park, city,** and **county park** campgrounds range from $12 to $24 per night for standard sites. Add about $5 more per night for hookup sites. **U.S. Forest Service** campsites average $14 per night. A few are pricier, but many, especially those without piped water, are free. **State Department of Natural Resources** (DNR) campgrounds also tend to be free and usually offer very primitive facilities; some are hike-in or boat-in campgrounds.

Private Campgrounds

Observant campers, particularly those in RVs, will notice that with a few exceptions, we haven't listed private campgrounds in this guide. The reasoning is simple: There are far too many of them to make listings practical, and private campgrounds can change ownership so often it's difficult to vouch for their quality or level of service. We've also omitted them for philosophical reasons: while we on occasion enjoy a hot, clean KOA shower as much as the next person, we sought to create a guide that fully explores the "wild" camping experience more commonly found at public parks. A few exceptions crop up. In areas that receive heavy summer traffic, but offer few public campgrounds, we've listed phone numbers and locations for the most popular private parks. Examples include the San Juan Islands and the area around the Gorge Amphitheater summer concert venue near George in central Washington. Comprehensive "Yellow Page" listing books are available, and they make nice companions to this volume.

Pets

Pets are allowed—on leashes—in nearly all Washington public campgrounds. Any exceptions are noted in the text. They are *not* allowed, however, in Washington State Parks yurts or cabins. Even in national parks, where pets are strictly prohibited on trails and other wild lands, pets are permitted within campgrounds, provided they're kept leashed or caged, quiet, and under control. Check with administering agencies for local regulations regarding pets on beaches, in playfields, and in other areas adjacent to the campground. As a general rule, however, no public campground is a suitable place to let your dog roam. Earn the right to bring along your pooch by picking up after it and being courteous of non-pet-loving neighbors. It's common sense—and common courtesy.

More Information

The contact numbers listed with each campground are, for the most part, year-round numbers. They're usually your best source for specific information. More general questions about campground choices, or recreation on surrounding public lands, can be addressed to the Outdoor Recreation Information Center, located in REI's Seattle flagship store, 222 Yale Avenue N. Call the center at (206) 470-4060. For current road construction

A young bald eagle checks out a visitor to his streamside roost.

and winter weather information, reach the Washington Department of Transportation hotline by simply dialing 511 on your home or cell phone. (You can link in to the same system from pay phones or if you're calling out of state by dialing 800-695-7623.) This system is supposed to be updated every five minutes, and includes links to traffic reports, mountain pass reports, ferry system information, weather, phone systems for passenger rail and airlines, and connection to Oregon's similar 511 system.

Special Note on Washington State Parks

When this book went to press, the state of Washington, as is too often the case, was reacting to yet another budget crisis by mulling the idea of "mothballing" or closing a number of parks. The park service first issued a list of fifteen parks, most of them day-use parks not included in this guide. But also on the table was a proposal to close or, preferably, find other public agencies to assume control of about a dozen other parks to save money. These parks include Osoyoos Lake, Brooks Memorial, Bogachiel, Fay Bainbridge, Wenberg, Joemma Beach, Kopachuck, Lake Sylvia, Schafer, and Old Fort Townsend, all of which have camping areas and are included in this guide. These parks are not necessarily expected to close, but there are no guarantees, and the parks may be operating as something other than Washington State Parks when you arrive. Consider them first in line on the "hit list" of possible state budget cuts.

Soon afterward, the park system, responding to a call for even deeper reductions, issued a separate list of parks that stood to be "mothballed," i.e., closed to public use, unless more secure financing, such as higher user fees, revenue from auto license plates and other means, or some combination thereof was authorized by the state legislature. Parks on that list include all of those on the list above, plus: Fields Spring, Rainbow Falls, Beacon Rock, Lewis and Clark, Alta Lake, Wallace Falls, Lake Easton, Yakima Sportsman, Maryhill, Illahee, Dash Point, Potlatch, Twin Harbors, Ginkgo/Wanapum, Saltwater, Ocean City, Fort Ebey, Wenatchee Confluence, Lake Wenatchee, Fort Flagler, Millersylvania, Sun Lakes, Larrabee, and Fort Casey. A mothballing of some or all of those parks would constitute such a gutting of the Washington State Parks system, one wonders why the state would even bother to pretend to have a legitimate parks system. Yet we offer it up as a possibility in a state that cannot seem to see fit to reform its tax structure to eliminate or soften the roller coaster ride inherent with reliance on a sales-tax-revenue model subject to the whims of consumer spending.

Also, as in past budget crunches, the parks system is considering a rollback of winter operations in many parks, or perhaps shortening the camping season. See the agency's website, www.wa.parks.gov, for the latest information about these possible closures.

A NOTE ABOUT SAFETY

Safety is an important concern in all outdoor activities. No guidebook can alert you to every hazard or anticipate the limitations of every reader. Therefore, the descriptions of roads, trails, routes, and natural features in this book are not representations that a particular place or excursion will be safe for your party. When you follow any of the routes described in this book, you assume responsibility for your own safety. Under normal conditions, such excursions require the usual attention to traffic, road and trail conditions, weather, terrain, the capabilities of your party, and other factors. Keeping informed on current conditions and exercising common sense are the keys to a safe, enjoyable outing.

—The Mountaineers Books

RON JUDD'S FAMILY CAMPING GUIDE

The bad news: You could get cold. You might get wet. There's probably no cable—and definitely no Wi-Fi.

The good: Aside from an angry nest of hornets or two, that's pretty much the worst-case scenario.

Entire generations of people—a minority, for sure, but a vocal one—have grown up successfully avoiding campouts, due mostly to the "Yick" Factor. You know: Ants and bugs. *Yick*. Mildew. *Yick*. Sleeping on the ground, which God clearly intended only for animals. *Yick*. Noisy college students and their boom boxes camped 5 feet away. *Yick!*

OK, so they're on to something. But clearly not the whole story. Things have changed out in the woods. So much so that even the most serious campophobe owes it to him- or herself to look around and see the new truth: This is not your father's camping these days.

The fact is that modern technology, coupled with decades of lessons learned by our admittedly hardier forebearers, have made spending a night outside in fresh air easier and, arguably, more economical than ever.

And this is a good thing, because camping out is a vacation that's cheap, relatively easy, and more important, actually good for you and the kids. (You should keep repeating this to yourself, even after the kids have set the local vault toilet on fire, and your dog has done its business right in the children's wading area.)

Without family campouts, those keen watermelon tablecloths would all be homeless.

Seriously: campouts today don't have to be complicated, particularly well-organized, or costly. In fact, most people can probably spend one afternoon rummaging around the garage or basement and the local discount store, and compile everything needed for a first-time fresh-air escape.

It's really not difficult at all, unless you, like certain people we would never publicly identify (you're welcome, Mom) choose to turn every camping trip into a Major Expedition, requiring days of pre-camping engagement in a horrible, scarring experience known as "loading the trailer," which I recall being just a little bit more fun than the Bataan Death March.

But I digress. The important thing to remember about surviving a multi-day period in which you move your entire life outside is that compromising and getting by with what you have on hand is half the fun of camping. (Rubbing calamine lotion on the poison oak rash is the other half.)

Trust me: Anyone can survive a few happy days in the woods or mountains or on the lakeshore. Newbies just need to remember to be flexible, expect to make some mistakes, and stick to some basics, which I'm happy to spell out for you below.

It's the product of lessons learned over a lifetime of doing things outside, usually in the wrong way. Read and learn.

Gearing Up

First things first: shelter. Unless you're bound for a state park with a rental cabin or yurt, you'll need a basic roof over your head. Emphasis on **basic**. A lot of campers make the rookie mistake of tooling down to REI and dropping 400 clams on a two-room tent with enough space and frills to serve proudly for four years at Everest base camp. Don't do it. Because you should assume two things right off the bat about your first tent:

—It's likely to be destroyed, through unintentional misuse, before it lives to see its second birthday.

—It almost certainly will not be the tent you want to spend the rest of your life camping in, because this is an activity where you won't learn what you really need until after you've done it for a while.

So, if you're just dipping one toe into camping waters and are not certain it will become a family tradition, don't invest a lot of money here. Borrow a tent if you can, or rent one from a gear dealer such as REI. If you think you might get at least a couple seasons' use out of it, though, go ahead and buy one. They're a lot cheaper than they used to be.

Thanks mostly to mechanized sewing processes and cheap goods from Asia, you'll get more tent for your money these days than ever before. Tents of decent quality can be found at discount stores for less than $75—a small investment for years of fun. Well, a couple years, at least.

You don't want to spend hours and hours setting up a Tent Mahal (the name I applied to a mammoth Costco tent I purchased some years ago), but bigger really is better for families, especially while you're learning to camp. Get a tent with a rain fly that comes down far enough on the sides to cover the windows. It also should have a waterproof (coated nylon) floor and—and this is important—good ventilation.

Two doors is a major plus—one you won't appreciate until the kids have stampeded over the top of you to get out through a single one in the morning. Free-standing tents (those that stand without stakes and guy ropes) are also very beneficial because you can move them around your campsite once they're struck.

Now prepare to fill that baby up. Sleeping bags are a requirement. Again, don't bust the bank on one: Borrow bags from friends who already camp, or rent on your first trip. Or buy one: Like tents, they're cheaper and better today than ever. Get a synthetic-fill bag. It'll keep you warm even if your tent fails to keep you dry. Which, at some point, it probably will. (Once you become a certified expert camper, buy yourself a fluffy down bag as a graduation present.)

Remember: Even the best sleeping bag will be torturous without a decent sleeping pad. Inexpensive, closed-foam pads (they're usually blue) at many retail outlets will do the job fine. They provide ample cushion for the bod and insulation from the cold ground. However, if you have a friend with a Therm-a-Rest or other inflatable foam pad, beg, steal, or borrow it. They're the warmest and most comfortable pads available. One warning: Those big inflatable air mattresses, with no foam core, are an absolute no-no. All that air inside might feel soft, but it takes on the same temperature as the ground, making you feel like you're sleeping on a pillow of ice.

Other basics: A cook stove, preferably one that runs on bottled propane (white gas is fine, but it's more difficult to handle, store, and use safely). Basic cookware, which you can probably find in the basement—or for two bucks at a garage sale (a couple old aluminum pots, basic utensils, soap, and a sponge are all you really need). A couple good flashlights with extra batteries. Candles are nice. Games, a deck of cards, or other things to keep the kids amused can be a godsend.

Also, wool blankets for extra warmth on top or beneath your bed are always a good idea. If you plan to bring any fresh foods or cold drinks, get a cooler, even if it's a cheap Styrofoam job. Another essential: Something to sit on. This can be one of those ubiquitous, collapsible camp chairs, simple blanket-pads for picnic table benches, or something as simple and inexpensive as an upside-down five-gallon bucket used to bring other goods.

Other things you won't think about until it's too late: A small doormat or scrap of rug to wipe off muddy feet before entering the tent. A multipurpose tool, such as a Leatherman. A five-gallon water jug, preferably with a spigot, so you don't have to troop to the faucet every five seconds while cooking. (We have a spiffy new one that holds seven gallons and has wheels, so you can roll it from the faucet.)

Some other niceties: A big blue tarp and clothesline to rig a cover for a table or campfire in the event of rain—or perform a hundred other tasks that nothing else works quite as well for. A couple rolls of paper towels. Bug dope. A decent pillow or facsimile, such as a soft stuff-sack that can be stuffed with a fluffy jacket or sweater. A transistor or shortwave radio, which you will learn to love with nothing else around to entertain you. Oh yeah: duct tape!

Proper Attire

Bring clothing appropriate to the time and place. For most Northwest campouts, a basic layering strategy is best. Make your base layer synthetic long underwear, even in summer. A mid layer can be a warm sweater or pants made of wool or polyester fleece. An outer-layer wind/rain shell seals the deal (for sitting around camp, a $25 discount coated-nylon anorak works just about as well as a $325 Gore-Tex or E-Vent parka). Basic sneakers or light hiking shoes make fine camp footwear. A pair of clogs, such as Crocs, are quite handy, too: You can slip them off whenever you go in and out of your tent without needing to bend over and retie them.

Never—never, ever, ever—go camping without wool socks, or a stocking cap, even in summer. Slipping both on at night is a surefire way to warm up a cold sleeping bag.

Grub

This is a universal rule: Your campout will only be as good as your camp food. The easy—and cheap—way to go is canned foods. Soups, stews and canned meats (yes, even Spam) taste better outside than you might think, and prep is very easy. But a little home cooking goes a long way. A large Tupperware container full of chicken and noodles or homemade chili—made at home and frozen ahead of time—is a sure winner. And it serves a dual purpose: Your block of homemade delight will keep the rest of your food cold in the cooler until you eat it.

If you want to get fancy, bring an old (or new) cast-iron Dutch oven for some real campfire-coal cooking. Or pick up a contraption often known as a "pie iron." These are essentially sandwich cookers made of a metal chamber split horizontally, with each half attached to a long metal handle. Put a slice of bread, buttered on the outside, on the bottom, pile it with sandwich or pie filling, add another slice of bread on the top, seal and insert into the fire. After about five minutes, open it up and find a blazing hot, nicely toasted (you hope) sandwich or dessert item.

You can also get campfire popcorn poppers, corn-cob roasters, and any other manner of camp-cooking paraphernalia. It's fun, but not really necessary. A box of graham crackers, stack of Hershey bars, bag of marshmallows, and a few roasting sticks go a long way.

Remember: *Simplicity is key.* Bagels (they won't crush in the food box like bread) and fruit or instant oatmeal for breakfast, sandwiches for lunch, a hot meal for dinner. (One cheap-and-easy standby: A packaged noodle mix and a can of chicken or tuna. Add water, mix, heat, and serve!) Energy bars and other wet-proof, non-crushable items are great for hiking or snacks. Instant hot chocolate is a favorite of kids from four to ninety-four.

A word of caution: Those fancy, freeze-dried backpacking dinners are convenient, but frankly don't taste that good and cost five times as much as comparable packaged or canned food. They're also prone to giving diners severe cases of the…how do we say this in a family camping guide…freeze-dried trots. No fun. No fun at all. (Especially given that said trots often are so severe that they necessitate the need to use nearby facilities within about, oh, fifteen seconds of first notice. Given that this is less than half the time it takes a normal human to extricate him/herself from a mummy bag, the math is not on your side here.)

Finally, bring heavy-duty aluminum foil for cooking on the fire and storing leftovers.

Storing It All

Two words of advice to keep campers sane: Plastic bins. Those big, blue plastic containers with snap-tight lids, made by Rubbermaid and others, have revolutionized camping for most of us. The advantage: They allow modular packing,—even in your truck bed or on your roof rack—in weatherproof, mostly critter-proof, containers. It's important to remember that any gear that can't fit back in your vehicle—and you don't want in your tent—needs to go somewhere. And a lot of it can't be left out in the wet. This is where plastic bins are lifesavers. Just leave them outside and worry not. (Don't leave food in them, however. Bears and raccoons will be inside them in no time.)

Establish one gear box for food (lock this one in the car at night), one for cookware, one for coats and parkas, one for other camping essentials, etc. Mark them on the lids and sides with a permanent pen. They're a godsend. Plus, you can leave your gear in them, stored in the garage and basement, when you get home. Just remember to give that food box a once-through when you get home, and make sure the others are dry. No matter what they say about shelf life, two-year-old Hostess fruit pies are a disaster.

Clothing, pillows, toiletries, and other soft goods that you'll want in the tent with you at night are best stored in duffle bags, one per person. Nylon stuff-sacks are great for compacting bulky sleeping bags and jackets (those with compression straps are even better for downsizing bulk). Gallon-size Ziploc bags are great for storing personal items, books, playing cards, and anything else you don't want to get wet or damp. A couple of big, industrial trash bags are always great to stash all your wet stuff in if you're bailing out in a rainstorm, which, at some point, you very likely will.

Planning Ahead

The two other items you're likely to need before you head out the door are crucial, and often overlooked: Recommendations and a reservation.

This guide should help you with both. It contains personal reviews of campsites, including information on local attractions, things to do with the kids, and other info. But there's no substitute for word-of-mouth wisdom. Ask other people who camp where they go, when they go, and why. You can take a quantum leap forward by avoiding all those places the rest of us learned to stay away from the hard way.

Once you know where you're bound, get a reservation. It's especially helpful for beginning campers to arrive at a place without having done a Speed Racer imitation, for fear of not finding a spot. Having one there, literally with your name on it, provides for a much more relaxing start.

Many of the campgrounds in this guide accept reservations, usually six months to a year in advance, and reservation information is included in campsite write-ups herein. Naturally, the best campgrounds book up far in advance. It's to your advantage to start thinking about a family camping trip not during camping season, but during the winter before.

Those are the basics. The rest is up to you. Take it from an expert: Quality camping is more of a trial-by-error process than a science or fine art. The best camping trips are the simplest, and the idea is to have fun.

Just remember, no matter where you're headed or when, take every outdoor professional's secret little helper: A Duraflame log!

Nobody will ever need to know it's there, underneath all that wet, smoldering wood, keeping the campfire going.

Opposite: *Campers negotiate a log crossing at Washington Park in Anacortes.*

1. PUGET SOUND

They turned us into campers.

No, not our parents. Not Boy Scout or Brownie leaders. Not even friends and relatives, although the co-conspirators who taught generations of Puget Sound natives to be nature fans almost qualify as such. We're speaking of the magically comforting old-growth trees of Whidbey Island; the taffy-sweet saltwater breezes rising from warm, rocky San Juan Island beaches; those unforgettable sunsets over Samish Bay.

All of this came—and still comes—to us at campgrounds around Puget Sound, an inland sea blessed by hundreds of miles of calm saltwater beaches, patches of old-growth forest, and grand places to pitch a tent and breathe it all in.

Not surprisingly, the best campsites around Puget Sound, from the rocky beaches and stiff breezes of Birch Bay to the maritime splendor of Penrose Point, are on the

Sound itself. A series of majestic Washington State Parks, nearly all of them abandoned World War II military sites on prime, waterfront property, stand guard over this natural heritage, allowing the region's ever-inflating population to stealthily bow out of the urban rat race for overnight splurges in fresh air.

These parks are the highlights of Puget Sound camping, and they contribute much to the area's vaunted reputation for a high quality of life. While campsites within a short drive of downtown Seattle are relatively scarce, an abundance lie on the Sound within a two-hour drive of the metro area. They're ample in quantity and perhaps unparalleled in quality, thanks mostly to a fortuitous topography that mixes tall forests, saltwater beaches, and million-dollar views.

Many of us natives have come to take them for granted (Witness: Washington State Parks' seemingly never-ending battle to remain solvent). We're jolted from this complacency only during those odd years when out-of-town visitors make the trip to Moran, Larrabee, Deception Pass, or Scenic Beach State Park, and return agog. Why, they always want to know, aren't you out there all the time?

It's hard to explain to them but, in our own way, we are. The body of a Puget Sound resident might be chained to a keyboard. But the spirit can always smell the saltwater.

North Sound and Islands
1. Camano Island State Park
2. Cama Beach State Park
3. South Whidbey State Park
4. Fort Casey State Park
5. Fort Ebey State Park
6. Staysail RV Park
7. Deception Pass State Park
8. Washington Park
9. Spencer Spit State Park
10. Odlin County Park
11. San Juan County Park
12. Moran State Park
13. Shaw Island County Park
14. Bay View State Park
15. Larrabee State Park
16. Birch Bay State Park

Greater Seattle and Cascade Foothills
17. Wenberg State Park
18. Kayak Point County Park
19. Flowing Lake County Park
20. Saltwater State Park
21. Dash Point State Park

South Sound and Key Peninsula
22. Kopachuck State Park
23. Penrose Point State Park
24. Joemma Beach State Park
25. Jarrell Cove State Park
26. Millersylvania Memorial State Park
27. Kanaskat–Palmer State Park

West Sound and Kitsap Peninsula
28. Fay Bainbridge State Park
29. Kitsap Memorial State Park
30. Scenic Beach State Park
31. Illahee State Park
32. Manchester State Park
33. Blake Island State Park
34. Belfair State Park
35. Twanoh State Park

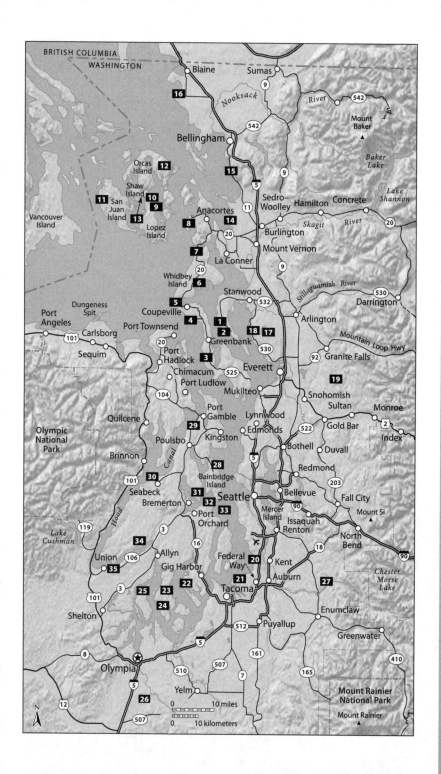

1 Camano Island State Park ★ ★ ★ ★

SITES	RESERVATIONS	CONTACT
 88 sites, no hookups, RVs to 40 feet, 5 cabins	Group camp only, (360) 387-3081	Washington State Parks (360) 902-8844
	OPEN	Camano Island State Park (360) 387-3031
	Year-round	www.parks.wa.gov

The squiggling toes of many a Puget Sound tyke got their first dip into the world of camping at Camano, a sprawling park with 6700 feet of rocky waterfront on sparkling Saratoga Passage. The 134-acre park's unusually good weather (it's at the far end of the same Olympic Mountain "rain shadow" that keeps Sequim and the Dungeness Valley dry), exceptional beaches, and plentiful wildlife make it a grand family spot. Campsites are snuggled nicely among the madronas on a high bluff. Trails lead a couple hundred vertical feet (and a mile or less) down to the gravelly beach, which is the real highlight here, with grand views of sunsets behind the Olympic Mountains. Look to the south on clear days for striking views of Mount Rainier.

A two-lane boat launch makes the beach area a high-traffic boating venue, particularly during summer salmon-fishing season. Surf fishing for bottomfish (perch, flounder) can be decent here, crabbing is conducted offshore (in season), and clams are found at very low tides (check Washington Department of Fish and Wildlife for

The gravel beach at Camano Island State Park is a peaceful escape.

availability; in recent years temporary closures have been enacted to preserve dwindling clam populations here).

About 3 miles of hiking trails (including a pleasant, family-friendly nature trail) run through the park's upper, woodsy area, connecting the three main campground loops, the beach area, and the picnic area, which is one of the largest on Puget Sound, with a picnic shelter for up to 100 people, a smaller one for 12 people, and 108 unsheltered picnic tables throughout the park. Another path now connects the park to adjacent Cama Beach State Park, just over a mile away.

The park has a trailer dump station, coin-op showers, and a group camp for up to 100 people in a shady, wooded area. The group camp, which has its own restroom and showers, can be reserved. Note that the park also offers five rental cabins, clustered together in a densely wooded area in the park's upland sector. Not exactly the most scenic locale, but a bonus for campers who don't want to deal with all the gear of outdoor camping. Some campsites in this older, somewhat timeworn campground are small; RVers are advised to stick to the roomier upper loop. The lower loop, though, offers the most sunlight and some peekaboo views of Puget Sound.

Some park history: The site's early inhabitants, the Kikalos and Snohomish Indians, used the beach much as we do today—as a place to live during the summer and gather seafood and berries. The Native name for the park is *Kal-lut-chin,* which means "land jutting into a bay." The island was renamed Camano in honor of Jacinto Camano, an early Spanish explorer. The park was established in 1949.

Getting there: From Interstate 5, about 18 miles north of Everett, take Exit 212, Stanwood, and proceed west on State Route 532. About 4 miles west of Stanwood, bear left at fork (road is now East Camano Drive and no longer SR 532). Bear left onto East Camano Drive, which becomes Elger Bay Road. Just after Elger Bay Grocery, take a right onto Mountain View Drive. Travel 2 miles, climb a steep hill, then turn left onto Lowell Point Road. The road will dead-end at the park entrance. (The route is well marked.)

2 Cama Beach State Park ✦ ✦ ✦ ✦

SITES	RESERVATIONS	CONTACT
🏠	(360) 387-1550	Washington State Parks (360) 902-8844
24 cabins	**OPEN**	Cama Beach State Park (360) 387-1550
	Year-round	www.parks.wa.gov

First things first: Cama Beach is not a true campground per se, as all its overnight guests are bunked in vintage cabins that sit in two rows facing the saltwater of Saratoga Passage, mere feet from the gravelly beach. But Washington's newest state park, opened in June 2008, provides such a unique camping experience, we believe it warrants inclusion in any serious camping guide. It is a camp, after all—a fishing camp. Cama Beach was run from 1934 to 1989 as a fishing resort by its original owners, Murl and Lee Risk. Through a sale and donation process, their daughters passed the stunning property on to Washington State Parks.

What a gift. The state, over a long period of time, secured funding to renovate the resort's cabins, store, boathouse, and other buildings, creating, in effect, a fishing resort that seems to have been pulled intact from a time capsule. The camp's twenty-four standard cabins lie in two rows, with only a short seawall separating them from the waters of Puget Sound. Most cabins are 14-by-20 feet, with a small living room, kitchen area, and bedroom, and sleep up to six people. The original cedar-plank construction has been maintained, and modern amenities—electric heat and lights, a refrigerator, microwave, and sink—have been added. Restrooms and showers are in adjacent buildings nearby. Campers need only to show up with their own bedding, pillows, towels, cookware, dishes, and utensils. The camp also has a variety of larger cottages for bigger groups. Rental rates for the standard cabins in 2009 ranged from $23 to $62 per night, depending on the cabin and the season. Larger cabins rented from $41 to $129.

Guests feel like members of a small, seafront community of sorts. Cama Beach is 435 acres of wooded uplands and beachfront. But the waterfront camp itself is centered around a large boathouse, where wooden rowboats once were launched down a ramp into the Sound. The boathouse is now staffed by members of the Center for Wooden Boats, which uses it to restore boats and teach about the region's seafaring history. Guests get a chance to relive that history by renting their own watercraft.

The camp also has a quaint snack-and-staples-stocked country store at its north end—a gathering spot, with a playground, grassy picnic area, horseshoe pits, and campfire circle nearby. The store's original, vintage gas pumps remain out front. No need for those—all auto traffic at Cama Beach is contained in the upper, wooded area of the park, where a series of parking lots are available. Guests catch a shuttle down to their cabin, where they're dropped off at the front door.

What's to do here? It's up to your level of energy. It's a great place to simply curl up with a book and listen to the waves. But the park also has several miles of new hiking trails circling its upper wooded regions. They connect to a trail network of about 15 miles in the area. One path leads just over a mile to Camano Island State Park. Boat rentals are available, and cyclists will find the short ride to nearby Camano Island State Park pleasurable on the island's lightly traveled roads. Fishing from the beach or rental boats is another popular option. Whatever your pleasure, be prepared to be thrown back in time on your visit to Cama Beach. It's an especially pleasant getaway in the off-seasons of spring or autumn.

Getting there: From Interstate 5, about 18 miles north of Everett, take Exit 212, Stanwood, and proceed west on State Route 532. About 4 miles west of Stanwood, bear left at fork (road is now East Camano Drive and no longer SR 532). Bear left onto East Camano Drive, which becomes Elger Bay Road. Just after Elger Bay Grocery, take a right onto Mountain View Drive. Travel 2 miles, climb a steep hill, then follow the road as it curves to the right and becomes West Camano Drive. The park entrance is about a half mile on the left. (The route is well marked.)

A fire ring awaits campers at Cama Beach State Park, a converted old-style Puget Sound fishing camp.

3 South Whidbey State Park ✦✦✦

SITES	RESERVATIONS	CONTACT
 54 sites, 8 water/electrical hookups, RVs to 50 feet	(888) 226-7688 or www.parks.wa.gov	Washington State Parks (360) 902-8844
	OPEN	South Whidbey State Park (360) 321-4559
	February through November	

A quiet park tucked onto the southwest shore of the island, South Whidbey is a pleasant, close-to-home getaway for anyone and everyone sick of all the Seattle metro-area bustle. This is not a park for sun worshippers; the campsites are found in mature second-growth forest (no water views), with trails leading down to 4500 feet of gravel beach and saltwater shoreline on Admiralty Inlet. The beach is the star here, but alas, major bluff erosion caused the park to close access to the beach area in 2007; it's uncertain whether or when it will be reopened.

For another major attraction, look upland to find a 347-acre stand of old-growth forest, mostly Douglas fir, that's unique in this area. The trees, which include some grand western red cedars, are best seen by following the Wilbert Trail (easy, 1.5-mile loop) on the east side of Smuggler's Cove Road, opposite the developed park area. Cyclists should take note of an additional six walk-in campsites on the south side of the park. The park has an RV dump station and coin-op showers. Off-season day-users will find the forested picnic area a relaxing, though shady, retreat with a shelter to flee to in bad weather.

Getting there: From the ferry terminal at Clinton on Whidbey Island, drive 9 miles north on State Route 525, turn left (west) onto Bush Point Road and follow signs to the park, on Smugglers Cove Road.

4 Fort Casey State Park ★ ★ ★ ★

SITES	RESERVATIONS	CONTACT
35 sites, no hookups, RVs to 40 feet	None	Washington State Parks (360) 902-8844
	OPEN	Fort Casey State Park (360) 678-4519
	Year-round	

Here's a Puget Sound classic. Old Fort Casey, on Whidbey's west shore across Admiralty Inlet from Port Townsend, truly is one of the most picturesque spots in the Northwest. The lineup is formidable: 467 sunny acres, much of which are wide-open, grassy uplands with stunning views of the North Sound and Mount Baker. More than 10,000 feet of saltwater shoreline for uninterrupted beach strolling, surf fishing, or lounging. Gun emplacements with restored cannons—always a hit with the kids. And a beachfront campground that's highly sought after year-round, particularly by RV owners.

Most day visitors and campers flock to the day-use area, high on a bluff near the old gun mounts. Frisbees, softballs, stunt kites, and enthusiastic dogs share the airspace over the lush, spacious grass here. Trails lead along the bluff to several grassy viewpoints (unfenced; be careful with kids), all grand sunset-watching perches. Back by the gun mounts, interpretive signs describe the fort's history as a World War I–era gun emplacement and World War II–era training facility. A large picnic area is nearby.

Don't miss the grand old lady back in the woods. The Admiralty Head Lighthouse, built in the 1860s and literally hidden at the north end of what's now the day-use area, is a graceful beauty, one of the stateliest light stations in the West. The light was intentionally obscured from water view after the military moved in. The building now contains an interpretive center filled with park history. The park also has coin-op showers, a boat launch, a couple miles of hiking trails, and an underwater park for scuba divers. The beach is a popular spot for surf fishing for bottomfish, salmon, and steelhead.

Unfortunately, Fort Casey's campsites don't keep up with the park's crowds, at least in terms of numbers. The thirty-five sites are almost literally on the water, on a sand spit below the blufftop gun emplacements, adjacent to the Keystone ferry terminal. The waters of Admiralty Inlet lap just outside your tent flap or doorstep, and a ferry plies the waters from Port Townsend to a landing right next to the campground. Needless to say, it's a popular spot—particularly among RVers, who are less troubled by the persistent winds on the mostly exposed beach.

Getting there: Following signs for the Keystone ferry terminal, turn west off State Route 20 near Coupeville and proceed about 3 miles southwest to the park, near the Keystone ferry terminal.

5 Fort Ebey State Park ★ ★ ★ ★

SITES	RESERVATIONS	CONTACT
⚠ 🏕🚐	(888) 226-7688 or www.parks.wa.gov	Washington State Parks (360) 902-8844
50 sites, 10 water/electrical hookups, RVs to 70 feet	**OPEN** Year-round	Fort Ebey State Park (360) 678-4636

Another of Whidbey's abandoned military sites, Fort Ebey is much smaller, more secluded, and a lot less famous than its North Whidbey cousin, Deception Pass State Park, just a ways up State Route 20. But it offers a similar saltwater beach experience, and its camping area is actually brighter, tidier, more private, less congested, and more relaxed. Sites in this treed, blufftop campground are nicely spaced in two loops. Many are flat, very spacious pull-throughs. Trails lead to old gun mounts, a quasi-lighthouse (it's more "light" than "house"), fine saltwater views from the nearby bluffs, and to the lovely 3-mile-long sandy beach below Point Partridge. None of the campsites have actual views out into Admiralty Inlet, but some are separated only by a thin wall of low trees. This is a particularly nice place to visit in the spring, when wild rhododendrons are out in pale pink splendor. And if you can muster fifty-nine friends who want to qualify as a "group," don't hesitate to check out Ebey's group campsite. It's one of the nicest we've seen, with green lawn for tents right at the blufftop, plus a grand, covered cooking and eating area. Reserve it through the reservations number above.

Also note that this park is home to the "Kettles" trail system, a series of 25 miles of mostly single-track mountain bike paths through the region's hilly geologic formations, left by receding glaciers about 15,000 years ago. And in recent years, the beach at Fort Ebey has become a popular beginner's surfing area.

Historical note: Unlike nearby Forts Casey, Worden, and Flagler—all built early in the twentieth century—Fort Ebey was a "second-generation" Puget Sound fortress, part of a triad of 16-inch cannon emplacements built during World War II. Ebey's sister installations were built at Cape Flattery and at Striped Peak west of Port Angeles (see Salt Creek Recreation Area, in the Olympic Peninsula and the Pacific Coast section). The park has coin-op showers, but mysteriously lacks an RV dump station.

Getting there: From State Route 20, about 8 miles south of Oak Harbor and 2 miles north of Coupeville, turn west onto Libbey Road, proceed 1.5 miles to Hill Valley Drive, turn left and follow signs to the park.

6 Staysail RV Park ★★

SITES	RESERVATIONS	CONTACT
▲ 🚐🚙	None	City of Oak Harbor Parks Department (360) 279-4756
	OPEN	
82 sites, 56 full hookups, RVs to any length	Year-round	

This mid-Whidbey spot in downtown Oak Harbor is basically an RV stopover, although the park now advertises twenty-six tent sites on the grass behind the flat, gravel spaces for big rigs. It's not exactly a back-to-nature experience, but it is close to a saltwater beach, the city marina, downtown shopping, and parks. And it's a short drive from both Deception Pass and Fort Ebey State Parks—making it a dependable backup for campers who can't get into one or the other. (Can't imagine choosing this park over one of the nearby state parks unless you have some reason to be close to downtown Oak Harbor.)

The park has an RV dump station and coin-op showers. In 2009 sites were $20 for RVs and $12 for tenters.

Getting there: The park is on 80th Street Southwest in downtown Oak Harbor, a short distance from the intersection of Pioneer Way and State Route 20.

7 Deception Pass State Park ★★★★★

SITES	RESERVATIONS	CONTACT
▲ 🚐🚙 🏠	(888) 226-7688 or www.parks.wa.gov	Washington State Parks (360) 902-8844
	OPEN	Deception Pass State Park (360) 675-2417
320 sites, 143 full hookups, RVs to 60 feet, 1 cabin	Year-round	

It's all here. And then some. Washington's flat-out most spectacular state park (if not single chunk of real estate), Deception Pass is a showcase for all the elements that make the Northwest magic: sprawling saltwater beaches, jutting cliffs, deep forest, freshwater lakes, and great views. As a bonus, they threw in a magnificent bridge that might be the most artful assemblage of steel in the country. All told, it's a magnificent package—one that every Washington nature lover must unwrap at least once in his or her outdoor career.

Plan to stay a while. This is a park that can't be fully explored in a single day. Deception has an impressive 4134 acres of wooded uplands, a remarkable 77,000 feet of saltwater shoreline, three campgrounds, multiple day-use areas, five saltwater and three freshwater boat ramps, 710 feet of saltwater and 450 feet of freshwater docks, and 34,000 feet of shoreline on four freshwater lakes.

If you only have time for the highlights, park in one of the State Route 20 pullouts and, if you dare, walk out on Deception Pass Bridge, which spans one of the most treacherous, tumultuous saltwater channels in the Northwest. After you catch your breath, get back in the car and follow the winding road from the park's main entrance (a short distance south of the bridge) downhill to the beach day-use area. From here, trails lead along North Beach to viewpoints of the impressive bridge—actually two steel spans linking Whidbey and Fidalgo islands—over the turbulent, swift current coursing through Deception Pass. The southern end of the main day-use area fronts on both Rosario Strait and Cranberry Lake, offering fine salt- and freshwater swimming in the summer. A separate, splendid picnic area on the opposite shore of Cranberry Lake has a boat launch and a dock, where trout fishing is often good. The park also has an RV dump station and coin-op showers.

Even more of the park is found on the opposite (north) side of the bridge. Pass Lake, a productive fly-fishing venue, is right off SR 20. Nearby, a road leads steeply downhill to Bowman Bay, where a saltwater fishing pier, small (eighteen standard, two utility sites) campground, and boat launch are found. The park's Cornet Bay area to the east offers 1980 feet of saltwater moorage. All of this is tied together by an astonishing 38 miles of well-worn hiking trails, 3 miles of bike trails, and 6 miles of trails for horses. New trails are being developed on Hoypus Hill, near Pass Lake, and other places.

The vast majority of campsites (147 standard; 83 utility) are found in three loops in the southern Cranberry Lake sector, which has been substantially upgraded with utilities, regrading, and other major work in the past half decade. Compared to the park's overall grandeur, the main campground is still found somewhat wanting: the sites are close together, with little privacy. But if you scout around, you can find a good one. And you can't argue with the location. Many sites are within a short walk of the park's scenic, sprawling North Beach day-use area. If you have a choice (which you probably won't), go low and get one of the open-air sites closest to the water, thus farthest away from busy SR 20. The recent addition of the park's Sunrise camping area brings its total site count to 320—second largest in the state park system. Another recent add is the

Deception Pass Bridge connects Fidalgo and Whidbey islands.

Ben Ure cabin, a unique lodging for two people on Ben Ure Island in Cornet Bay. It's reservable, and you'll need to paddle to get there.

Deception Pass also has extensive group-camping facilities: three separate camps accommodating sixty-four, thirty-two, and thirty-two campers, respectively. They can be reserved through the reservations number above.

Also on site is the Cornet Bay Environmental Learning Center, a rental facility for groups of up to 186, with a commercial kitchen, dining room, laundry, and sleeping cabins. Call (360) 902-8600 for rental details. A historical interpretive center, open year-round for tours, is located at the park's Bowman Bay area north of the main campground. Call (360) 675-2417 for information. Bike-in or paddle-in campers can reserve one of five sites specifically for non-motorized visitors; there is also one Cascadia Marine Trail site nearby.

Important notes: this is one of only eight state parks where reservations are accepted—and probably necessary—year-round. And beware those loud, loud jets from nearby Whidbey Naval Air Station.

About the name: The "Deception" came from Captain George Vancouver's discovery that he had mistaken Fidalgo Island, separated from Whidbey by the thin, turbulent channel here, for a peninsula of Whidbey Island while exploring the area. Vancouver's assistant, Joseph Whidbey, got his name on the larger island.

Getting there: From Interstate 5 at Mount Vernon, follow SR 20 about 18 miles west to Whidbey Island and Deception Pass Bridge, 9 miles northeast of Oak Harbor. From the Mukilteo–Clinton ferry proceed about 50 miles north on State Route 525 and SR 20.

8 Washington Park ★★★

SITES	RESERVATIONS	CONTACT
🏕️ 🚐	Local residents only	City of Anacortes (360) 293-1918
	OPEN	
73 sites, 46 water/electrical hookups, RVs to 40 feet	Year-round	

Washington Park is a great little secret, well kept by the City of Anacortes, which is lucky enough to own it and does a nice job running things. Visiting Washington Park is a lot like going to the San Juans without ever leaving shore. This beautiful, 220-acre park on Fidalgo Head, just beyond the Anacortes Ferry Terminal, is one of the loveliest waterfront getaways in the Northwest. Alas, the forested campground is comparatively cramped and pedestrian, lacking privacy in most sites. The last time we visited—in the interest of full disclosure, on a sunny August weekend—sites seemed to be occupied by an average of about 3.5 cars each. Rangers would be well served to crack down on the demo-derbyness of the place. But some decent sites are available, and if you're here in the offseason, any or all of them can be quite pleasant. Besides, you don't have to sit in the Winnie all day, and the rest of the park is an absolute gem. The day-use area near the campground has a pleasant saltwater beach, picnic area, and boat launch, but the highlight is a 2.3-mile loop road that skirts the shoreline all the way around the park. The narrow road can be driven one way, or better yet walked or cycled, to grand waterfront picnic spots with views of Rosario Strait, the San Juans, and all the pleasure-craft headed toward them. The park also has a laundry room, RV dump station, and hot showers. This is a wonderful place to catch your breath and get up early for that long wait in line for a ferry to the San Juans: The park is about a twenty-minute walk or five-minute bike ride from the ferry terminal.

Getting there: From Commercial Avenue (State Route 20) in downtown Anacortes, turn left (west) on 12th Street and proceed about 2 miles, staying left where the road to the Washington State Ferry terminal veers right.

9 Spencer Spit State Park ★ ★ ★ ★

SITES	RESERVATIONS	CONTACT
37 sites, no hookups, RVs to 20 feet	(888) 226-7688 or www.parks.wa.gov	Washington State Parks (360) 902-8844
	OPEN	Spencer Spit State Park (360) 378-2044
	Mid-March through October	

If exploring all or part of Lopez Island is high on your to-do list, Spencer Spit should be your base camp. Spencer, one of the very best campgrounds in the San Juans, doesn't have a lot of the drive-through, full-hookup amenities many modern campers are looking for. But its seven walk-in, beachfront spots make it a true gem for cyclists, tent campers, "car-top" boaters, and sea kayakers. The small (138-acre) park is a designated Cascadia Marine Trail campsite, and its sixteen moorage buoys make it a popular boat-in campground for mariners of all sorts. The rest of the campsites are in a pleasant, wooded upland area; about half accommodate RVs. Kids will have a blast on the park's trails and on its narrow, sandy spit, with saltwater on each side and a sizable lagoon in the center. The park also has two group camps, one for up to fifty people with ten walk-in sites and a large grassy common area; the other has three walk-in sites for up to twenty people. One of the sites has a cool Adirondack shelter with eight bunks. Call the reservation number above to reserve a group site.

A wealth of great Lopez Island day trips beckons. Watch for whales and sea lions across the island at Shark Reef Sanctuary, Otis Perkins Day Park, or Agate Beach Day Park, or hop the ferry to Friday Harbor. Special close-quarters alert: The park has an RV dump station, but unlike most state parks, this one has no hot showers!

Park history: Spencer Spit was a traditional clamming and crabbing site for Native Americans. It was homesteaded in the late 1800s and sold to the Spencer family, who lived here for fifty years. Washington State Parks acquired the site in 1967.

Getting there: From the Lopez Island ferry terminal, follow signs 5 miles southeast: Go left at Center Road, left at Cross Road, right at Port Stanley Road, and left at Bakerview Road, which leads into the park.

The sun slips below the San Juan Islands in North Puget Sound.

10 Odlin County Park ★★★◄

SITES	RESERVATIONS	CONTACT
🏕️ 🚐 30 sites, no hookups, RVs to 30 feet	Summers only; up to 90 days in advance; (360) 378-1842	San Juan County Parks (360) 378-8420
	OPEN Year-round	

This is a perfect first-night stopover for cyclists bound for a tour of Lopez, the favorite San Juan island of most two-wheeled tourists, thanks to its many miles of (relatively) flat roads. It's also an excellent overnight camp for sea kayakers. The camp is a short roll (just over a mile) from the ferry dock on Lopez, and only 3 miles from Lopez Village, so getting there even late in the evening doesn't pose too much of a challenge. For boaters, the eighty-acre campground has a boat launch and low-bank waterfront access, with nine sites right on the rare sandy beach (five for hikers/bikers/kayakers only). Reservations are recommended; be patient with the limited hours of the reservation line. Spencer Spit State Park (see above), a Lopez highlight, is a short ride or drive away. The campground has limited amenities: water and pit toilets. Not a lot of space for RVs here, although the more modest ones can be shoehorned in.

Getting there: From the Lopez Island ferry terminal, follow Ferry Road 1.3 miles south to the park, on the right.

11   San Juan County Park ★ ★ ★ ★

SITES	RESERVATIONS	CONTACT
⛺ 🚐	Summers only; up to 90 days in advance; (360) 378-1842	San Juan County Parks (360) 378-8420
20 sites, no hookups, RVs to 25 feet	**OPEN** Year-round; limited services November 1 through March 31	

One of the rare public campgrounds in the San Juan Islands, this twelve-acre camp near Smallpox Bay on the west side of San Juan Island has a boat ramp and good beach access, with lush green lawn in the camping/day-use area. Its rocky bluffs and gravel beaches overlook Haro Strait, with views of the Strait of Juan de Fuca and even Vancouver Island. It's a favorite of scuba divers, who find some of the richest (natural) underwater treasures in the continental United States just offshore here. Most of the campsites are in an upland area; site 18, a walk-in only, waterfront special with room for two (small) vehicles at its parking area, is likely to be the one you want but can't get. Watch for orcas and other sea creatures just off shore. Notes for whale watchers: An even better orca-watching viewpoint, nearby, is Lime Kiln State Park, 2.5 miles to the south. The whales are most often observed on incoming tides, which pushes fish up against the shore, making them easier prey. Watch for them in the four hours before high tide each day. In the summer, Dall's porpoises, humpback whales, pilot whales, white-sided dolphins, and other species have been observed in Haro Strait.

The park has a small picnic shelter, piped water, and flush toilets. Reservations are strongly recommended here. Summer prices in 2008 ranged from $7 for walk-in sites to $39 for premium, beachfront group sites.

Getting there: The campground is about 10 miles west of Friday Harbor on San Juan Island, via Beaverton Valley, Mitchell Bay, and West Side roads.

12   Moran State Park ★ ★ ★ ★ ★

SITES	RESERVATIONS	CONTACT
⛺ 🚐	(888) 226-7688 or www.parks.wa.gov	Washington State Parks (360) 902-8844
151 sites, no hookups, RVs to 45 feet	**OPEN** Year-round	Moran State Park (360) 376-2326

Umm, where's the water? That's the first question asked by many a first-time Moran visitor. Give 'em a half hour to look around, however, and few ever revisit the irony of San Juan Island's largest park lacking an easily accessible saltwater shoreline. There's so much more to Moran, the beach seems almost irrelevant. This sprawling 5200-acre park is one of the jewels of the state park system, with a rich mix of old-growth forests, fresh-water lakes, pleasant campsites (in three separate areas), and a 2400-foot mountaintop where the view is as gorgeous as any in the Northwest. Named for shipbuilder and former resident Robert Moran (who donated the park land and whose mansion now is the focus of nearby Rosario Resort), most of the park is wooded, mountainous terrain. Waterborne activities at Moran are on freshwater, not salt. Four small, picturesque lakes are found here, two ringed by campsites.

Campers pack the park's 151 campsites (fifteen are secluded walk-in sites; good for cyclists), which are spread through no less than five separate camping areas. The Southend camp, with nearly all sites on the lakeshore, is the most popular; Midway is another favorite with boaters who favor the nearby launch; Mountain Lake sites offer more privacy. Your best bet is to book well in advance through the state park's reservation system.

Everybody who gets in takes home a lasting memory. This is a huge, diverse park, with pleasant picnic grounds, two boat launches, bathhouses, swimming beaches, and moorage docks with rental boats. The park has an RV dump station and coin-op showers. Activities include fishing, kayaking, canoeing, or boating in Mountain or Cascade lake and hiking on the park's 30-mile trail system. One of those trails leads from the park's lowland camping areas to Moran's highlight—2400-foot Mount Constitution, the highest spot in the San Juans. At the summit (which also can be driven to during daylight hours), the view in all directions is spectacular. Climb up the stairway in the twelfth-century replica stone observation tower (built by the Civilian Conservation Corps in 1936) and you can see as far south as Mount Rainier and the Olympics, west to Vancouver Island, BC, north to Vancouver, BC, and east to the North Cascades.

Getting there: From the Orcas Island ferry landing, veer left and follow signs 14 miles northeast to the park.

13 Shaw Island County Park ✦ ✦ ✦ ✦

SITES	RESERVATIONS	CONTACT
🏕️ 🚐	Summers only; up to 90 days in advance; (360) 378-1842	San Juan County Parks (360) 378-8420
	OPEN	
11 sites, no hookups, RVs to 25 feet	Year-round, reduced services November 1 through March 31	

It's small, it's isolated, and it's decidedly low-tech. But if you're heading for the San Juans with just your bike or car and a tent, this is a great place to while away the time and get back in touch with your saltwater roots. Shaw Island itself is tiny and inhabited year-round by fewer than 200 people, so it's no surprise that the thirty-acre county park here mirrors that modesty. Campsites 1–6 are on a bluff above the water, the others in an upland area across Shaw Park Road. The tradeoff: You give up views and gain privacy from trees in the upper sites. The campground limits most sites to four people, but sites 10 and 11 are larger group sites for up to six people.

Shaw Island Park also serves as a popular boat launch site for canoeists and kayakers, who can paddle the short distance across Indian Cove to Canoe Island, home of a summer camp for teens. On shore, a short walk on a local road leads to another quiet beach on Squaw Bay, just to the west. The park is a popular boat-in destination for powerboaters

The day-use area at Bay View State Park offers a quiet respite.

and paddlers based in Friday Harbor, which is less than 4 nautical miles away.

This park also has a nice day-use area with a picnic shelter, a boat ramp, piped water, and pit toilets. If you come in the winter, bring plenty of water; there's none in the campground, nor anywhere else on Shaw Island. Summer prices in 2008 were $14 for wooded and $18 for waterfront sites. Summer reservations are a good idea.

Getting there: Follow Blind Bay Road away from the ferry landing. Turn left on Squaw Bay Road at the Shaw Island Community Center. Turn left on Indian Cove Road and look for the park entrance on your right. It's about 2 miles from the ferry landing.

14 Bay View State Park ✦ ✦ ✦

SITES	RESERVATIONS	CONTACT
🏕 🚐 🏠 76 sites, 30 full hookups, RVs to 60 feet, 4 cabins	(888) 226-7688 or www.parks.wa.gov	Washington State Parks (360) 902-8844
	OPEN Year-round	Bay View State Park (360) 757-0227

Bay View, a sleepy, relatively nondescript campground off State Route 20 in the Skagit Valley, is notable not so much for what's in it, but what's near it. Namely, the Padilla Bay National Estuarine Research Reserve—a long name for a fine bird-watching venue (particularly in winter) that's a relatively short drive from most Puget Sound–area homes. Many RV-equipped birders flock here in the winter, parking in Bay View's grassy, somewhat closely packed sites, all across the road from the saltwater day-use area, which has 1285 feet of shoreline. Padilla Bay in winter months is home to one of the state's larger population of migratory raptors and waterfowl, including bald eagles, great blue herons, various hawks, canvasbacks, harlequin ducks, black brant, and the occasional peregrine falcon. Harbor seals also occasionally are spotted in the bay. All are sometimes visible from viewing blinds or on a boardwalk at the Padilla Bay interpretive center (a short walk from the campground) or from a nicely maintained, 2.25-mile barrier-free trail along a dike at the south end of the bay, a short walk away. The interpretive center, (360) 428-1558, is open 10:00 AM to 5:00 PM, Wednesday through Sunday. The campground has an RV dump and coin-op showers.

Sites are split into three areas: 1–9, in the front section, are the only true "bay view" sites here (they're often booked well in advance in summer); sites 10–30 are utility spaces in a partially forested loop surrounding a large, open playfield. The remainder of sites have no hookups and largely consist of small back-in sites, with average to below-average privacy, in a wooded area.

This is one of many state parks to begin offering cabin camping in recent years. State park cabins are 12-by-12 feet and sleep four. They're equipped with heat and lights, single bunk beds, one double bed, a covered front porch, locking doors, a picnic table, a fire ring, and a grill, with restrooms and showers nearby.

Getting there: From Interstate 5 at Mount Vernon, take the SR 20 exit, turn west under the freeway, and proceed about 7 miles to Bay View–Edison Road. Turn right (north) and proceed about 4 miles to the park, where the campground is on the right (east) side of the road.

15 Larrabee State Park ★ ★ ★ ↑

SITES	RESERVATIONS	CONTACT
▲ 🏕🚐 85 sites, 26 full hookups, RVs to 60 feet	(888) 226-7688 or www.parks.wa.gov	Washington State Parks (360) 902-8844
	OPEN	Larrabee State Park (360) 676-2093
	Year-round	

Put this one on the must-visit list. Washington's oldest state park (established 1915) is also one of its finest, offering in one 2700-acre nutshell a tasty sampling of what makes north Puget Sound so soothing—and the Northwest itself so famous. Perched on a bluff between the smooth, stony cliffs of Chuckanut Mountain and the gently lapping shores of Puget Sound's Samish Bay, Larrabee is so well known as a primo day-use area for Bellinghamsters that it's often overlooked as a quality overnight getaway by everyone else. Campsites are adequate, but don't quite match the big-splash status of the rest of the park. Renovated in 1997, they're situated in tall (some old-growth) fir, madrona, and maple trees; they don't have water views. Unlike many of the RV sites, the tent sites offer decent privacy, and eight walk-in sites are favored by cyclists. All sites are pleasantly cool in the summer but can be dark and dreary in bad weather. And if you're a light (or even medium) sleeper, late-night Burlington Northern trains rumbling by a short distance away might be a problem.

That said, hikers and beachcombers will love the park's 9 miles of trails, including a popular hike to Fragrance Lake, high onto Chuckanut Mountain, offering sweeping views of the San Juan Islands. (Look for the trailhead opposite the main entryway on the east side of Chuckanut Drive.) The park also has an RV dump station, coin-op showers, and a boat launch popular with sea kayakers, swimmers, divers, and Frisbee-chasin' dogs.

Less than a half mile south on Chuckanut Drive is Clayton Beach, a fine DNR day-use area with ample parking, restrooms, and a gentle (kid-friendly, mountain-bike accessible) trail that leads about a half mile downhill to the sandy, Puget Sound waterfront. The trail is wet and muddy except in the summer. Sunsets from the gravelly beach here (which largely disappears at high tide) are simply spectacular.

Getting there: Larrabee is 7 miles south of Bellingham on Chuckanut Drive (State Route 11). From the south: Take Interstate 5 Exit 231, north of Mount Vernon; follow signs along Chuckanut Drive 14 miles to the park. Note: The south portions of narrow, winding Chuckanut Drive are not suitable for trailers or RVs, which should proceed to Exit 250 in Bellingham and follow signs to SR 11/Chuckanut Drive from the Fairhaven neighborhood.

16 Birch Bay State Park ★ ★ ★ ◀

SITES	RESERVATIONS	CONTACT
🏕️ 🚻🚐 147 sites, 20 water/electrical hookups, RVs to 60 feet	(888) 226-7688 or www.parks.wa.gov **OPEN** Year-round	Washington State Parks (360) 902-8844 Birch Bay State Park (360) 664-8112

If you can find an empty spot of sand amidst all the migratory Canadians, Birch Bay is a great place to while away summer afternoons, with gentle (OK, occasionally gusty) Strait of Georgia breezes keeping you company by day and a wealth of decent campsites greeting you at night. This camping area was in use for centuries by local Semiahmoo, Lummi, and Nooksack tribal members, who came here for the same reasons you might: miles of open beach. Clamming, sunbathing, general beachcombing, and kite-flying are the chief activities here, thanks to 8255 feet of saltwater shoreline. The park also has an RV dump station and coin-op showers. But there's much more to Birch Bay than just sand and gravel. The upland portion contains Terrell Creek Marsh, one of the last undisturbed salt/freshwater estuaries on north Puget Sound. A short nature trail loops through this rich wildlife habitat, where harlequin ducks and other rare, beautiful waterfowl often are spotted through the reeds. Campsites in this 194-acre park are standard state parks fare, spread in separate loops north and south of the park access road. Tip: The quieter northern loop, which contains all the utility sites, fills up first; it's tough to get into without a reservation during summer months. The park also has a primitive group site for up to forty people.

Local trivia: The bay was named by a botanist on the 1792 Captain George Vancouver expedition, who noted the many black birch trees in the area.

When the tide goes out in Birch Bay, it goes way out, offering miles of tidelands for campers at Birch Bay State Park to explore.

Getting there: Follow signs west from Interstate 5 Exit 270 (Grandview) about 8 miles to the park on Helwig Road, about 10 miles south of downtown Blaine, USA.

Other North Sound Campgrounds

The DNR camps at **Lily** and **Lizard Lakes** (nine total sites, no piped water) are hike-in campgrounds reached by a 3.5-mile trail from the Blanchard Hill Trailhead, Samish Lake Road south of Bellingham. A DNR camp off scenic State Route 9 is **Hutchinson Creek** (fourteen sites, no piped water), 2.5 miles east of Acme, off Mosquito Lake Road. Call DNR, (360) 856-3500, for directions and information.

In the Skagit Valley, **River Bend Park**, a public campground along the Skagit River in Mount Vernon, is an alternative to Bay View, but it's primarily an Interstate 5 motor home stopover, with twenty-five tent sites and ninety-five RV pull-throughs with hookups: 305 Stewart, Mount Vernon; (360) 428-4044. Another private campground, **Burlington KOA**, has twenty-four tent and seventy-six RV sites, many with hookups, along with the standard KOA amenities: 6397 North Green Road, Burlington; (360) 724-5511.

Other San Juan Islands Campgrounds

In the San Juans, a small number of private campgrounds compensate for the lack of available public campsites. On San Juan Island, the best campground is at **Lakedale Resort,** which has seventy-four lakefront campsites (seven with full hookups) and three small lakes for fishing and swimming, on Roche Harbor Road 4.5 miles from the ferry terminal. As the primary campground on the island, it's often overcrowded; get an advance reservation by calling (800) 617-CAMP. Rental boats and fishing poles are available here. The park is open May 15 to October 1. Campground reservations start on March 15. Other campgrounds include the **Pedal Inn,** 5 miles from the ferry terminal on False Bay Drive, where twenty-five biker/hiker sites can be reserved by calling (360) 378-3049; and **Snug Harbor Marina Resort,** on Mitchell Bay Road 8.5 miles from the terminal, which has seven campsites, a boat launch, and other services. Sites can be reserved by calling (360) 378-4762.

On Orcas Island, try **Doe Bay Village Resort,** (360) 376-2291, which offers fifty campsites (eight have hookups); primitive **Obstruction Pass** (see Boat-in North Sound/Islands Campgrounds, below); or **West Beach Resort** at Eastsound, (360) 376-2240, a private facility with sixty-eight campsites (eleven with full hookups and two with water-only hookups).

Boat-In North Sound/Islands Campgrounds

Private boaters will find an almost overwhelming array of quality public moorages with access to primitive beachfront or upland campsites, managed by Washington

---

BEST SUNSET CAMPGROUNDS

1. Fort Ebey State Park, Whidbey Island
We've seen some mind-blowing sunsets from the high, waterfront bluff adjacent to the camping loop at this central Whidbey Island state park. See p. 41.

2. Larrabee State Park, Northwest Washington
The sunset views across Samish Bay at Washington's oldest state park are fantastic. They're even better a mile up a short trail across the road, where a viewpoint opens up the sunset to the entire San Juan Islands chain. See p. 50.

3. Moran State Park, Orcas Island
The views from atop the lookout tower on Mount Constitution are always sterling, but never more so than at sunset. See p. 47.

4. Scenic Beach State Park, Hood Canal
Saltwater. The Olympic Mountains, close enough to touch. A red sky. Are we missing anything? See p. 66.

5. Pacific Beach State Park, Southwest Washington
Something about seeing that big red ball sizzle into the ocean warms the heart. See p. 99.

State Parks or the Department of Natural Resources (DNR). (Many of these also serve as Cascadia Marine Trail campsites.) Most have moorage floats or docks. Fees are charged during the summer, and fresh water is limited. Avid boaters say these parks offer some of the best boat camping (or boat-in camping) in the country. Boaters should note that most state marine parks have picnic tables, pit or composting toilets, and moorage floats for pleasure boaters, while most DNR-maintained sites are more primitive.

Popular boat-in spots include **state marine parks at Stuart Island** (northwest of San Juan Island; eighteen primitive sites on the north side of the island, with moorage in Reid and Prevost harbors); **Sucia Island** (sixty primitive sites and ample moorage floats on the north side of the island, 2.5 miles north of Orcas Island); **Patos Island** (seven sites and no piped water on the east side of the island, 4 miles northwest of Sucia Island); **Clark Island** (nine sites, moorage floats, and no piped water, northeast of Orcas Island); **Matia Island** (six sites on the island's northeast side, 2 miles north of Orcas Island); **Posey Island** (two primitive sites and not much else, just off San Juan Island's Roche Harbor); **Jones Island** (twenty-four primitive sites just off the southwest tip of Orcas Island); **Blind Island** (four sites and no piped water, north of Shaw Island); **Turn Island** (twelve primitive campsites and no piped water, a short float east from Friday Harbor); **James Island,** just east of Decatur Island on Rosario Strait (thirteen primitive sites and a moorage dock on the island's east shore); **Doe Island** (five sites, southeast of Orcas Island); **Saddlebag Island** (five sites, no piped water, east of Guemes Island and north of Anacortes); and **Skagit and Hope islands** (five primitive sites each; no piped water), both in Skagit Bay, off the northeast shores of Whidbey Island.

Of these, the Northern Boundary islands—Sucia, Patos, Matia, Clark, and Barnes—are the most scenic, best developed, and most heavily used. Sucia Island, with sixty campsites and moorage for some 700 boats, is a splendid spot but can look more like a small city than a wild refuge on summer weekends. Patos and Stuart islands also receive fairly heavy use. For information, call Washington State Parks, (360) 902-8844. An excellent guidebook to the marine parks, written with the mariner in mind, is *The San Juan Islands: Afoot & Afloat,* by Marge and Ted Mueller (The Mountaineers Books).

North Sound and San Juan Islands DNR sites include **Lummi Island** (four sites with no piped water, 1 mile south of Reil Harbor on the southeast tip of Lummi Island); **Obstruction Pass,** a 1-mile hike- or boat-in camp (nine sites on Orcas Island's east side near Olga, 1.5 miles off the Olga to Doe Bay Road, no piped water); **Point Doughty** (four sites with no piped water 3 miles northwest of Eastsound on the northwest side of Orcas); **Cypress Head** (ten sites, no piped water, moorage floats, on the east side of Cypress Island near Anacortes); **Pelican Beach** (four sites, group camp shelter, no piped water, moorage buoys, 4 miles north of Cypress Head on the east side of Cypress Island); **Strawberry Island** (four sites, no piped water, a half mile west of Cypress Island); and **Griffin Bay** (several sites on the southeast side of San Juan Island). For information, call the DNR's Northwest Region (Sedro-Woolley) office, (360) 856-3500.

Greater Seattle and Cascade Foothills

17 Wenberg State Park ★ ★ ★ ◀

SITES	RESERVATIONS	CONTACT
⛺ 🚐	(888) 226-7688 or www.parks.wa.gov	Washington State Parks (360) 902-8844
	OPEN	Wenberg State Park (360) 652-7417
75 sites, 30 full hookups, RVs to 50 feet	Year-round	

Lake Goodwin and a healthy crop of evergreen trees are the star attractions at Wenberg, a park that's most popular in the summer, when swimming in the lake and fishing for smallmouth bass and planted rainbow trout reach their respective peaks (the park also has a boat ramp and ample day-use parking). Given the abundance of power boats and Jet Skis on the lake in the summer, it's neither the quietest nor most scenic state park you'll ever find. But Wenberg, one of the few public camping venues within a day's drive of Seattle, is conveniently located and just far enough from town to make you feel as if you're actually camping. The park has an RV dump station and coin-op showers. Hookup sites are in the lower (southern) portion of the campground. Also on site is a large kitchen shelter for up to 150 people, a small dock on the lake, and a 0.5-mile hiking trail. Note: See important notice about this park's future on p. 25.

Getting there: From Interstate 5 about 12 miles north of Everett, take Exit 206 (Smokey Point) and drive west 2.4 miles to a stop sign. Turn right, and drive 2.7 miles. Turn left on East Lake Goodwin Road, and travel 1.6 miles. The park entrance is on the right.

18 Kayak Point County Park ★ ★ ★ ◀

SITES	RESERVATIONS	CONTACT
⛺ 🚐 ⛺	(360) 652-7992 or online at www.activenet10.active.com/snoco	Snohomish County Parks (360) 652-7992
	OPEN	
34 sites, 34 water/electrical hookups, RVs to 25 feet, 10 yurts	April to October for all campers; RVs only in winter	

ARCO's loss was a camper's gain. The oil giant purchased this plum slice of Puget Sound waterfront—the site of an early-century would-be, never-was town called Birmingham—in 1967, planning to plunk yet another refinery here. Didn't work out, thank heavens, and Snohomish County was wise enough to snatch up 670 acres of the land five years later. The point, one of the finer stretches of public saltwater beach north of Seattle, is a favorite summertime getaway for Everett-area families drawn to the beach area's fine picnic sites. The park also has become a popular windsurfing

A kingfisher agrees with the wind heading atop a sailboat mast in Puget Sound.

and, appropriately, sea kayaking venue. A 300-foot public pier juts into Port Susan, offering decent bottom-fishing and crabbing in season.

Often overlooked is the small but very nice campground tucked into the trees and shrubs. The sites all are nicely manicured and include water and electrical hookups. Note: If you want to camp and don't want to mess with the gear, Kayak Point offers rental yurts (round, frame-tent structures with skylights, wood floors, and heat). Ten yurts are grouped in a "yurt village" here, and can be reserved for $45 a night at this writing. Local entertainment options—not that you want these; you're camping!—include the Tulalip Tribe's nearby casino/outlet mall conglomerate, about a twenty-minute drive away.

Local trivia: The park gets its name from a pair of Eskimo kayaks once displayed at a former, private resort here by the Alaska-exploring sons of early property owner/resort developer H. W. F. Kilian.

Getting there: From Interstate 5 at Marysville, take Exit 199 (Tulalip), cross under the freeway on Tulalip Way, and follow signs 13 miles west to the park on Marine Drive.

19   Flowing Lake County Park ✦ ✦ ✦

SITES	RESERVATIONS	CONTACT
🏕 🚐	Summers only; www.activenet10.active.com/snoco	Flowing Lake County Park (360) 568-2274
	OPEN	
40 sites, 32 water/electrical hookups, RVs to 25 feet	Mid-May to September for all campers; RVs only in winter	

Flowing Lake, a great retreat from the sweltering summer heat that seems to hang in the Snohomish River Valley, is way out there in the bowels of the Puget Sound's rural thickage; in fact, it's tough to find without precise directions. Tucked onto the shoulder of this small lake, in a space you'd expect two large Microsoft-executive homes to fill, is a tidy, picturesque county park, with a decent campground in a wooded area near the lakeshore. It's not exactly Wild Kingdom: homes surround the lake on all other sides. And the campground has the kind of semi-crowded, busy feel of a private resort, which is what this space used to be. But if you close your eyes and stick your feet in the lake, it almost feels like wilderness. Highlights are swimming (in the fenced-off area, away from the water-ski boats), fishing, and just lounging in the shade.

Getting there: From Interstate 5 at Everett, follow U.S. Highway 2 east to milepost 10. Turn left onto 100th Street Southeast (Westwick Road). Just past the French Creek Grange, the road bears sharply to the left (north) and becomes 171st Avenue Southeast. Continue on 171st Avenue Southeast to 48th Street Southeast; turn right onto 48th Street Southeast and proceed to the entrance at the end of the road.

20 Saltwater State Park ★ ★ ✦

SITES	RESERVATIONS	CONTACT
🏕️ 🚐	None	Washington State Parks (360) 902-8844
	OPEN	Saltwater State Park (253) 661-4956
50 sites, no hookups, RVs to 60 feet	Year-round	

Considering its location, in a suburban area bordering on urban (Des Moines), Saltwater is a surprisingly diverse campground getaway. The eighty-eight-acre park is most often used by picnickers, sunset watchers, and scuba divers, who visit the underwater park just off the 1445 feet of public shoreline. But the campground is adequate, and 2 miles of seldom-maintained, but well-trod, hiking trails lead into the wooded uplands, offering nice views of Maury and Vashon islands and the leeward Olympics. McSorely Creek, a salmon-spawning stream, runs through the camping and picnic areas. Unlike some Puget Sound parks, this one has long been public property. Original development here was conducted by the Civilian Conservation Corps in the mid-1930s. The park has an RV dump station and coin-op showers. The biggest drawback: Plane noise. The park lies in the flight path for nearby Sea-Tac Airport.

Getting there: From Des Moines, follow the signs on State Route 509 (Marine View Drive) about 2 miles south to the park.

21 Dash Point State Park ★ ★ ★

SITES	RESERVATIONS	CONTACT
🏕️ 🚐	(888) 226-7688 or www.parks.wa.gov	Washington State Parks (360) 902-8844
	OPEN	Dash Point State Park (253) 661-4955
141 sites, 27 water/electrical hookups, RVs to 40 feet	Year-round	

This Federal Way–area park's campsites are pleasant enough, nestled in an alder/broadleaf maple forest. But it's Dash Point's scenic waterfront day-use area, not to mention its rarity as a public camping venue close to Seattle, that makes it worthwhile to visit for out-of-town visitors or locals looking to get the early-season kinks out of the RV or tent. The day-use area, reached via an underpass below State Route 509, has three well-developed picnic areas, with shelters and a slew of tables. It also has a Puget Sound rarity—a sandy beach. The campsites are scattered in two wooded loops across SR 509, which bisects the park. Some of the sites are broad and level, making particularly nice tent spots. Utility sites are in Loop B, to your right as you enter. A group camp for up to 100 people can be reserved in advance. The park has an RV dump station (it was closed for construction when this guide went to press) and coin-op showers. It's also a popular mountain-bike venue, leading to clashes between cyclists and the state park system's "wilderness" ethic.

Getting there: From Interstate 5 Exit 143, near Federal Way, follow 320th Street West for about 4 miles to its end at a T intersection. Turn right on 47th Street and proceed to a T intersection. Turn left on SR 509/Dash Point Road and proceed about 2 miles to the park. The camping entrance is on the west side of the street.

Other Greater Seattle–Area Campgrounds

In Kent is **Seattle/Tacoma KOA** (5801 South 212th Street, Interstate 5 Exit 152; [253] 872-8652), which has more than 140 sites for tents and RVs. **Aqua Barn Ranch** (15227 Southeast Renton–Maple Valley Highway, Renton; [206] 255-4618) is one of the best local tent areas, with 240 sites, many of them grassy. **Lake Pleasant RV Park** (24025 Bothell–Everett Highway; take I-405 north to exit 26; [206] 487-1785 or [800] 742-0386) is the biggest campground (and one of the nicest) in the greater Seattle area, with 189 campsites. Yurt fans can find rentals at Snohomish County's new **River Meadows Park,** 20416 Jordan Road, near Arlington, as well as tent camping on the open meadows near the Stillaguamish River; (360) 435-3441.

To the east, not far from Lake Sammamish is popular **Trailer Inn RV Park** (15531 Southeast 37th Street, off Interstate 90 exit 11a, Issaquah; [425] 747-9181), with 102 pull-through RV sites. **Blue Sky RV Park** (9002 302nd Avenue Southeast, Issaquah; [425] 222-7910) has fifty-one RV sites. **Issaquah Village RV Park** (650 First Avenue Northeast; [425] 392-9233 or [800] 258-9233) has fifty-nine RV sites, no tents allowed. On the west side of Lake Sammamish (take Interstate 90 exit 13) is **Vasa Park Resort** (3550 West Lake Sammamish Road; [425] 746-3260), a small park with decent tent sites. A bit farther out, but worth the drive, is the more natural-feeling **Snoqualmie River Campground,** on the banks of the river at Fall City, which has thirty-one tent sites and ninety-two RV sites, with utilities for RVs to 60 feet; (425) 222-5545.

Peeling madrona trees are found on shore bluffs around Puget Sound.

South Sound and Key Peninsula

22 Kopachuck State Park ★ ★ ★ ◀

SITES	RESERVATIONS	CONTACT
	None	Washington State Parks (360) 902-8844
	OPEN	Kopachuck State Park (253) 265-3606
41 sites, no hookups, RVs to 35 feet	Year-round	

A fine forested/saltwater park on Key Peninsula that's a quick trip (well, assuming you're not tied up in Narrows Bridge traffic for nineteen hours) from Tacoma and Gig Harbor, Kopachuck's campsites are nicely spaced in a Douglas fir–forested upland area. Down at the Henderson Bay beach (a short walk away), scuba divers, sea kayakers, cold-water-swimming fools, and other water fans will have a heyday. Cutts Island, aka "Deadmans Island," is part of the park and makes a nice paddle a half mile from shore in good weather.

The waterfront picnic area offers grand views of the Olympics. All in all, it's a pleasant spot. The park has an RV dump station and coin-op showers. Also available are two group-camping facilities for a total of up to fifty-five campers. Note: See important notice about this park's future on p. 25.

Getting there: From Tacoma, drive 7 miles north on State Route 16 to the second Gig Harbor exit; follow signs 5 miles west to the park.

23 Penrose Point State Park ★ ★ ★ ★

SITES	RESERVATIONS	CONTACT
	(888) 226-7688 or www.parks.wa.gov	Washington State Parks (360) 902-8844
	OPEN	Penrose Point State Park (253) 884-2514
82 sites, no hookups, RVs to 35 feet	Year-round	

Campers looking to sample the saltwater wonders of the South Puget Sound/Key Peninsula area won't go wrong at Penrose Point, one of the most enjoyable saltwater parks in the state. The campground, tucked on a wooded bluff inside Carr Inlet's Mayo Cove, is an idyllic place, quiet and fairly secluded. All sites are at least partially shaded, and all within a short walk of the beach. The day-use area at the beach is well equipped and wonderful, with a group camp, picnic facilities, boat moorage, and a shallow swimming beach on more than 2 miles of shoreline.

Picnickers enjoy the sunshine at Joemma Beach State Park. (Photo by Janice Ohlsen)

At low tide, the beach becomes truly massive, and a long sand-spit offers good exploring opportunities for the kids. Several miles of hiking trails wind through the trees in the park's upland area, including Penrose Point itself, a thumb of land pointing northeast into Puget Sound. The park has an RV dump station and coin-op showers.

Getting there: From Tacoma, drive north on State Route 16 to State Route 302 (Key Peninsula Highway) near Purdy. Proceed south on Key Peninsula Highway for about 9 miles, through the towns of Key Center and Home. Turn left at Cornwall Road (second road after Home Bridge) and follow signs to the park, on 158th Avenue KPS.

24 Joemma Beach State Park ✦✦✦✦

SITES	RESERVATIONS	CONTACT
🏕️ 🚐	None	Washington State Parks (360) 902-8844
	OPEN	Joemma Beach State Park
21 sites, no hookups, RVs to 35 feet	Year-round	(253) 884-1944

You have Joe and Emma to thank. And after a day spent on the beach here, you probably will. Joemma Beach, one of Washington's newer state parks, is the former R. F. Kennedy Multiple-Use Area. In 1995, the park was renamed to honor Joe and Emma Smith, early settlers who lived here from 1917 to 1932.

The 122-acre park on Key Peninsula's west shore now has campsites with a still-newish feel to them, in two small loops. Also on the premises are barrier-free vault toilets, two walk-in hiker/biker sites, a couple short hiking trails, 1000 feet of gravelly beach, a pair of Cascadia Marine Trail waterfront campsites, a boat launch, and a very nice moorage dock for overnighting boaters. It's a good fishing and crabbing spot. And the park offers a picnic shelter for up to fifty people; call for reservations. Note: See important notice about this park's future on p. 25.

Getting there: From Tacoma, follow State Route 16 to State Route 302 (Key Peninsula Highway). Turn west and proceed about 5 miles to Key Peninsula Highway. Turn left (south) and drive about 15 miles to Whiteman Road. Turn right and drive 4 miles to Bay Road. Turn right and drive about a mile to the park entrance, staying on the asphalt road into the park.

25 Jarrell Cove State Park ★ ★ ★

SITES	RESERVATIONS	CONTACT
22 sites, no hookups, RVs to 35 feet	(888) 226-7688 or www.parks.wa.gov	Washington State Parks (360) 902-8844
	OPEN	Jarrell Cove State Park (253) 265-3606
	Year-round	

This one's out there a ways; so far, in fact, that you really have to want to visit the north end of Harstine Island to get here. For that reason alone, Jarrell Cove is a quiet, occasionally lonely place, one that's visited by boat almost as often as by auto. The campground is small, sufficient, but not spectacular, with most sites set in a grassy area above the entrance dock (convenient for those arriving by boat), or in a grassy area in the center of the park. The cove itself is the attraction here, with two docks and moorage piers, four-teen mooring buoys, a pumpout station, and other facilities. It's a great place to spend a week exploring the south Sound by boat. If you're so lucky, you can spend the day exploring other marine state parks nearby: Harstine Island, McMicken Island, Stretch Point, Eagle Island, and Hope Island state parks are all within easy reach.

The park has one coin-op shower and a group camp for up to sixty-four people. One site is barrier free. It, and four of the park's other sites, are reservable; the rest are first-come, first-served.

Getting there: From Shelton, fol-low State Route 3 about 8 miles north to Pickering Road. Turn right and proceed

Bald eagles often take up residence along Puget Sound in summer months.

4 miles to Harstine Island Bridge. On the island, turn left at the stop sign at North Island Drive and follow signs 4 miles to the park.

26 Millersylvania Memorial ✶✶✶✶ State Park

SITES	RESERVATIONS	CONTACT
🏕️ 🚐	(888) 226-7688 or www.parks.wa.gov	Washington State Parks (360) 902-8844
	OPEN	Millersylvania State Park (360) 753-1519
168 sites, 48 full hookups, RVs to 60 feet	Year-round	

Millersylvania, the best public camping venue within a short shot of Olympia, got its start as the 850-acre estate of Johann Mueller, an Austrian general (and bodyguard of Emperor Francis Joseph I) exiled to these parts in the late nineteenth century. Now it's a very big, very pretty, very diverse state park with a nice camping area, almost 8.6 miles of hiking and 7.6 miles of biking trails, coin-op showers, and swimming (and good trout fishing) in Deep Lake, with a boat ramp for non-motorized boats and 100 feet of dock making it all accessible. The park even has its own 1.5-mile fitness trail. Campers have their choice: An open, grassy area with full hookups, or tent/small RV sites offering much more privacy, nicely set in a stand of stately old-growth firs.

The completing touch is a series of historic Civilian Conservation Corps–era buildings, which the Corps built while headquartered here as it worked on other local public parks in the 1930s. Check out the impressive, stately kitchen shelters, set in a grove of beautiful old-growth Douglas firs, near the lakeshore. These are reservable by phoning the state parks reservation line, above, and are equipped with wood stoves, grills, sinks, and outlets.

This is a great family park, with a lot of flat territory for bicycling and convenient Interstate 5 access. Note that the park's RV dump station at this writing had closed; ask park rangers for other nearby facilities.

Getting there: From Interstate 5 south of Olympia, take Exit 95 and follow signs, driving east on Maytown Road, then north on Tilley Road.

27 Kanaskat–Palmer State Park ✶✶✶

SITES	RESERVATIONS	CONTACT
🏕️ 🚐 ⛺	Summers only; (888) 226-7688 or www.parks.wa.gov	Washington State Parks (360) 902-8844
	OPEN	Kanaskat–Palmer State Park (360) 886-0148
50 sites, 19 electrical hookups, RVs to 50 feet, 3 yurts	Year-round	

It may have a funny name, but it's hard to find, too. Kanaskat–Palmer, tucked into the Green River Gorge Recreation Area between Black Diamond and Enumclaw, is better

Early-morning anglers wait for a bite on the dock at Millersylvania Memorial State Park.

known as a winter steelheader's parking spot than a campground. But it switches gears just fine for summer, offering pleasant campsites that increasingly are glommed onto by kayakers, rafters (this stretch of Green River white water is swift, dangerous, and not for rookies), and nature lovers who come for the park's unparalleled access to the river—13,000 feet of river frontage in all. The park also has 3 miles of hiking trails, coin-op showers, an RV dump station, and an eighty-soul group camp equipped with a couple nifty Adirondack shelters. A nearby attraction is Flaming Geyser State Park, a day-use-only area just downstream.

Getting there: From Interstate 5 at Tacoma, follow State Route 410 east to Enumclaw. Turn left (northeast) on Farman Road and follow signs 9 miles to the park.

Other South Sound Campgrounds

The Capitol State Forest has a series of small, primitive campgrounds, all managed by the Department of Natural Resources. They are **North Creek** (five sites), **Sherman Valley** (seven sites), **Porter Creek** (fourteen sites), **Middle Waddell** (twenty-four sites), **Fall Creek** (eight sites), and **Margaret McKenny** (twenty-five sites). Note that the noisy dirt bikes and off-road vehicles that frequent this area are allowed in Middle Waddell, which may still be too close for comfort for many campers. Also, most of these campgrounds are used by hunters in the fall. Another DNR-managed campsite is **Mima Falls Trailhead** (five sites), off State Route 121 near Little Rock. All these campgrounds are free and are accessed either from U.S. Highway 12 or SR 121, both west of Interstate 5. Call the DNR at (360) 577-2025.

For boaters and kayakers, boat-in-only state marine parks in the south Sound are on **Squaxin Island, Cutts Island, McMicken Island, Hope Island, Eagle Island,** and **Stretch Point.** Call Washington State Parks, (360) 902-8844, for details.

Mount Rainier smiles upon a birthday party at Fay Bainbridge State Park.

West Sound and Kitsap Peninsula

28 Fay Bainbridge State Park ★ ★ ★

SITES	RESERVATIONS	CONTACT
	None	Washington State Parks (360) 902-8844
	OPEN	Fay Bainbridge State Park (206) 842-3931
36 sites, 26 water hookups, RVs to 30 feet	Year-round	

Bring your camera. Fay Bainbridge, one of the very best things about Puget Sound's most yuppified island, is the only place we know of where one can pitch camp and get a direct, cross-Sound gander at downtown Seattle. In fact, it's one of the few saltwater-front campgrounds in the entire Seattle area. But there's a tradeoff: This park is in more of a neighborhood setting than a wild place. Beachfront homes are visible on either end of the small, seventeen-acre park, and there's little privacy between them. The somewhat cramped sites also are fairly exposed to the very active day-use area near the smooth, sandy beach, cluttered by picnickers and driftwood. (RVers might find this a good one to try in the winter, when spaces are empty and there's more room to spread out the awning.)

Still, spaces can be tough to land in the summer, especially since the park only has thirty-six to begin with. The park also has coin-op showers, an RV dump station, a group camp, and good picnic facilities with covered kitchen shelters, a boat ramp, and mooring buoys.

Local trivia: There is not, and never was, a "Fay Bainbridge." The park's name combines that of the island and the original property owners, Mr. and Mrs. Temple S. Fay, who graciously sold the land to the state for $5000 in 1944. All in all, it's a grand day-use park, and will do in a pinch for overnighters who don't mind rubbing elbows with others. Note: See important notice about this park's future on p. 25.

Getting there: From the Bainbridge Island ferry terminal, drive about 5 miles west on State Route 305 to the Day Road turnoff/traffic light. Turn right (north) and proceed about 2 miles to a T intersection. Turn left on Sunrise Drive Northeast and continue about 2 miles to the park entrance, on the right.

29 Kitsap Memorial State Park ✦ ✦ ✦

SITES	RESERVATIONS	CONTACT
🏕 🚻 🏠	(888) 226-7688 or www.parks.wa.gov	Washington State Parks (360) 902-8844
	OPEN	Kitsap Memorial State Park (360) 779-3205
42 sites, 18 water/electrical hookups, RVs to 40 feet, 4 cabins	Year-round	

A Hood Canal alternative to the aptly named Scenic Beach State Park is Kitsap Memorial, halfway between Poulsbo and the Hood Canal Floating Bridge. The fifty-eight-acre park has 1800 feet of rocky saltwater shoreline and a good day-use site, with acres of open, grassy fields that attract softball players, kite fliers, and dog runners. A set of large, reservable kitchen shelters also makes this a high-traffic day-use area, especially on weekends. The "Log Hall" alone accommodates 192 people; combined with the rentable Log Pavilion, the capacity is more than 200, making this a popular spot for wedding receptions and other events. For reservations information, call the park number above.

The campsites are clustered in a somewhat dreary area of dense forest but recently were upgraded with water and electrical hookups at sites 1–18. Recent park enhancements include four cabins, one of which is a restored historic structure, the Hospitality House, which can be reserved in advance by calling (800) 360-4240.

The park has an RV dump station and coin-op showers. A fifty-six-person group camp also is available, and can be reserved at the state parks reservation number above. Three primitive sites are reserved for small groups of hikers and bikers.

Getting there: From Poulsbo, follow State Route 3 west for 3 miles to the park, on the left side of the highway near milepost 57.

30 Scenic Beach State Park ★ ★ ★ ★ ★

SITES	RESERVATIONS	CONTACT
 52 sites, no hookups, RVs to 60 feet	(888) 226-7688 or www.parks.wa.gov	Washington State Parks (360) 902-8844
	OPEN	Scenic Beach State Park (360) 830-5079
	Year-round	

Scenic Beach very well could be the nicest state park you've never heard of. We'll admit it's located in an odd, out-of-the-way place and doesn't offer the most modern amenities. Some RVers might well balk at this park's rare 5-star rating, given its lack of utility hookups. But Scenic Beach is one of the flat-out most beautiful tent campgrounds we've ever had the privilege to visit—and revisit, and revisit—over the years. The setting is sublime. Located on an eighty-eight-acre thumb of land—a former homestead—jutting into Hood Canal near the quaint town of Seabeck, the campsites (eighteen are pull-throughs) are nicely spread through large firs in a hilly, upland area. And the waterfront picnic area, set on a majestically wooded bluff overlooking the gravelly saltwater beach, is magnificent. Wild rhododendrons burst into bloom in May, and the view across Hood Canal into the Olympics is stunning; from this angle, you're looking right up east-slope Olympic valleys (namely the Duckabush and Dosewallips), and the mountains loom large. **Note: On our most recent visit here in 2011, maintenance and upkeep of this jewel of a park had slipped badly; we're hoping it recovers in time to maintain the five-star rating.**

Nearby, on elegantly landscaped grounds, is Emel House, the stately old homestead for this former resort property. The house can be reserved for weddings and other functions. It accommodates up to forty people indoors, and up to 150 if they spill

The picnic area at Scenic Beach State Park is lovingly kept.

out onto surrounding grounds. Call the park's contact number above for information or reservations. Also reservable (use the state park general reservation number above) is the park's group camp, which accommodates twenty to fifty campers. The main camping area has an RV dump station and coin-op showers. If it all gets to be old hat after a few days, troop down the road to the Seabeck Store and chew the fat around the potbellied stove with the local boys.

Getting there: From State Route 3 near Silverdale, take the Newberry Hill Road exit and drive 3 miles west to Seabeck Highway. Turn right and drive 6 miles, proceeding through Seabeck. Turn right on Scenic Beach Road (just after Seabeck Elementary School), continue about a mile to the park entrance at the end of the road.

31 Illahee State Park ★ ★ ◄

SITES	RESERVATIONS	CONTACT
🔺🚐	None	Washington State Parks (360) 902-8844
	OPEN	Illahee State Park (360) 478-6460
25 sites, 2 full hookup sites, RVs to 40 feet	Year-round	

An interesting park in an odd location, Illahee is a waterfront site tucked below one of Bremerton's suburban neighborhoods. The park is split in two, with a boat launch and small saltwater mooring dock in the lower, waterfront portion, and a picnic area and campground in the wooded upper sector—part of the "last stand of old-growth forest in Kitsap County," according to State Parks. One of the largest yew trees in the country is also found here. But the waterfront area is the primary draw. It's a popular shore-fishing, picnicking, and sun-worshipping spot. The fifty-six mooring buoys and 356 feet of moorage docks are protected by a breakwater and often draw anglers and scuba divers.

The small camping area is unspectacular but sufficient, set in a forest very high above the waterfront portion (quite a hike). A group camp houses up to forty people. Coin-op showers and an RV dump station are available. As a campground, it's nice enough. But something about traipsing through Bremerton's commercial and suburban sprawl to get wild doesn't exactly appeal to the natural camper in most of us.

Getting there: From State Route 303 in East Bremerton, follow Sylvan Way west to the park.

32 Manchester State Park ★ ★ ★

SITES	RESERVATIONS	CONTACT
🔺🚐	(888) 226-7688 or www.parks.wa.gov	Washington State Parks (360) 902-8844
	OPEN	Manchester State Park (360) 871-4065
53 sites, 15 water/electrical hookups, RVs to 60 feet	Year-round	

This 111-acre waterfront park in South Kitsap County—a short drive from Seattle via the Fauntleroy ferry—is a pleasant place with an intriguing history. It was built in the early 1900s as a U.S. Coast Artillery base to mine the waters of Rich Passage to protect Puget Sound Naval Shipyard in the event of war. The base was converted to a Navy fuel supply depot during World War II. Remnants of those operations remain, including a giant concrete shell of a 1901 torpedo warehouse that's now used as a picnic shelter. (This for those of you who thought none of that military spending ever comes home to roost!) A trail leads from the day-use area to the 3400 feet of shoreline—mostly rocky beach—and some lingering gun emplacements. You're liable to see scuba divers here in the summer months. And it's not a bad place to launch a kayak or other cartop watercraft. The camping area isn't quite as unique, unfortunately, with fifty sites split into two unremarkable wooded (fir and large maple) loops. Three hiker/biker sites also are available. The park has 2 miles of hiking trails, a horseshoe pit (there used to be two here; if you took the other one, please return it), an RV dump station, and coin-op showers.

Getting there: From Port Orchard, follow signs from Beach Drive; from the Southworth ferry terminal, follow State Route 160 and Colchester Drive to Manchester, proceed north on Beach Drive, and follow signs. From State Route 16, take the Sedgwick Road exit and follow signs to the park.

33 Blake Island State Park ✦ ✦ ✦

SITES	RESERVATIONS	CONTACT
	None	Washington State Parks (360) 902-8844
	OPEN	
48 primitive boat-in sites	Year-round	

Seattleites who want to treat visiting relatives to the shiny side of the Northwest's cultural past can take a boat trip to Tillicum Village on the east side of Blake Island, where an authentic Northwest Native American salmon dinner is served up nightly in the summer. But those who want them to see the nitty-gritty of its cultural present take them by boat or kayak to the island's backside, where a boat-in-only state park offers a wide choice of boat- and hike-in campsites, many very private and secluded. Some areas even have piped water, and most have picnic tables and fire rings. Pit toilets are distributed throughout. The four main camping areas here are separated by 15 miles of hiking trails. Cascadia Marine Trail sites are found on the west end of the island. Two picnic shelters, accommodating up to 100 people, can be reserved by calling (888) 226-7688.

Boaters usually come from Port Orchard or Bremerton; sea kayakers can make it here on a short paddle from Manchester State Park, 1.5 miles to the west. Once they get here, they can stroll the 5 miles of saltwater beach and argue for several hours about how those thirty blacktail deer got over here.

Historical note: The island is rich in history, beginning with its use as a campsite for the Suquamish tribe. It's believed that Chief Sealth, in fact, may have been born here. Later, the island was acquired by William Pitt Trimble, who named it after himself and built a spectacular estate and library, which he abruptly abandoned after his wife drowned in Elliott Bay in 1929. The estate burned long ago after years of plundering and vandalism. (See the interpretive sign at the site.)

Getting there: Blake Island, 3 miles west of Seattle and 1.5 miles east of Manchester, is accessible only by boat.

34 Belfair State Park ✦ ✦ ✦

SITES	RESERVATIONS	CONTACT
184 sites, 47 full hookups, RVs to 75 feet	(888) 226-7688 or www.parks.wa.gov	Washington State Parks (360) 902-8844
	OPEN	Belfair State Park (360) 275-0668
	Year-round	

Belfair, in a stunning, waterfront location, doesn't quite live up to its potential. It might yet; the park at this writing is part of a large-scale planning process for south Hood Canal parks. But in the meantime, it still makes a worthy getaway if you're selective about where you camp. Campsites in the park, located near the town of Belfair at the southern crook of Hood Canal, are found in three main areas: a set of camping loops in broad, open, flat lawn just off the beach, with forty-seven full hookup sites and imported shrubs and trees; and a third, more natural (though darker) "tree loop" just to the north, which has no utility sites, and an RV size restriction of 25 feet. The two main loops are open year-round; the tree loop is open summers only. None of the campsites rate very high on the privacy scale.

Some campsites at Belfair State Park line the shores of Hood Canal.

The beach has 3700 feet of saltwater shoreline on shallow, tepid Hood Canal, much of it at the site of a long-since-abandoned commercial oyster bed. Shellfish commerce has fled, but many oysters still remain, seemingly making this a hotspot for oyster pickers. Alas, in recent years, pollutants have closed the beach here to oyster gatherers and clam diggers. Big Mission and Little Mission creeks flow through the park; they contain chum salmon runs in the fall. Just inland from the beach, Belfair has another unique feature: a tidal "swimming pool" that fills with warm saltwater when the tide comes in. This is the best—and cleanest—place for a dip in the sixty-three-acre park. The park has coin-op showers, a kitchen shelter, and group camping for up to fifty people; call the park contact number above.

The campground often is full in the summer. Reservations are recommended here. Note that the RV dump station here has closed. The next closest aren't very close: they're at Kopachuck and Manchester state parks.

Historical note: Thousands of ancient arrow points have been found in this area. The site of the current park likely was a village or meeting site for the Twana, aka Skokomish, people, who lived throughout what is now the south Hood Canal region.

Getting there: From State Route 3 at the town of Belfair, follow signs 3 miles west on State Route 300.

35 Twanoh State Park ★ ★ ★ ↟

SITES	RESERVATIONS	CONTACT
	None	Washington State Parks (360) 902-8844
	OPEN	Twanoh State Park (360) 275-2222
47 sites, 22 full hookups, RVs to 35 feet	Year-round	

Twanoh State Park, best known for its day-use beach area (great saltwater swimming in summer) on the north side of State Route 106, has a nice, secluded camping area on the south side. The nicely manicured campsites are found among big trees, with smaller tent sites in one loop, RVs in the other. The scenery is pleasant, with cool shade along Twanoh Creek, which—like most Hood Canal streams—comes alive with chum salmon in the fall. The campground also has coin-op showers but no RV dump station. Several miles of trails follow the creek through the greenery on the hillside above (bring your bug dope). Also note the old stone buildings here; most were built by Civilian Conservation Corps crews in the 1930s. Some facilities here are barrier free. A group camp accommodates up to fifty campers. Reserve it by calling (888) 226-7688.

Local trivia: The trees in the campground are large, but by no means old-growth. This former private resort site was logged in the 1890s. Note the very old, very large cedar stumps in the area. This park's 3167 feet of beach become a popular smelt-dipping area in the winter.

Getting there: From Belfair, follow State Route 3 to SR 106 and proceed 8 miles west to the park, which straddles the highway.

A finger pier juts into Hood Canal at Twanoh State Park.

Other West Sound/Kitsap Peninsula Campgrounds

Winghaven Park on Vashon Island is a pleasant, twelve-acre, undeveloped beach-front campsite, part of the **Cascadia Marine Trail** system (the Cascadia Marine Trail is a water trail that includes campsites from Olympia to Vancouver, British Columbia; call Washington Water Trails Association, [206] 545-9161). It's three-quarters of a mile from the ferry terminal, below Vashon Highway Southwest. Other designated Cascadia campsites in the immediate area are found in **Fay Bainbridge** and **Fort Ward state parks,** on Bainbridge Island, and in **Lisabeula Park,** on the southwestern shore of Vashon Island on Colvos Passage.

Kayakers also should note several other Vashon public beaches accessible only from the water: Department of Natural Resources (DNR) **Beach 85** near Point Beals; DNR **Beach 83** on Maury Island near Portage; DNR **Beach 79,** northeast of Tahlequah; and DNR **Beaches 77** and **78,** two small beach patches on Colvos Passage on Vashon's west shore. Call the DNR south Sound office, (360) 825-1631.

Two state forests in this area offer free DNR campsites. The most easily accessible is **Green Mountain Horse Camp** (twelve sites, pumped water, 5 miles west of Bremerton, in Green Mountain State Forest). To the southwest are seven Tahuya State Forest camp-grounds: **Toonerville** (four sites, no piped water); **Aldrich Lake** (four sites); **Tahuya River Horse Camp** (eight sites); **Kammenga Canyon** (two sites); **Camp Spillman** (six sites); **Twin Lakes** (six sites); and **Howell Lake** (five sites). All are popular with riders of beasts, both gas- and hay-powered. Call the DNR south Sound office, (360) 825-1631, for directions and information.

2. OLYMPIC PENINSULA
AND THE PACIFIC COAST

It takes more than a bit of dry humor to set out, armed only with tents, sleeping bags, and bug dope, into a land that receives world-record sorts of rainfall: Like, 12 *feet* per year. But people have been doing it on the Olympic Peninsula for more than a century now—and they keep coming back with damp-but-happy faces.

Laughing at the rain—or possessing the inner steel to be able to pretend to—is part of the recipe for camping success on the Peninsula, which didn't exactly become one of the world's greatest tree-growing factories by virtue of its arid weather.

Over the years, in fact, we've come to suspect there should be two certified "Guaranteed to Keep You Dry" ratings for Gore-Tex, E-Vent, and other waterproof fabrics: One for those that'll keep you dry in October up in the Queets Basin, and another for those that'll keep you dry everywhere else on the planet, where it only rains downhill.

Not that it rains here all the time. Just a lot of it. Up to 140 inches a year, in fact, on the west side of the Peninsula, where legendary forests on the Hoh, Bogachiel, and Queets rivers turn all that humidity into grow juice, producing trees so big that that they'll make you nervous. And longtime visitors know full well that the leeward side of the mountain range, particularly its northern edges, lies in a wondrous "rain shadow" area where the precipitation is less than one-eighth of that in places just over the divide. Portions of the northeast Olympic Peninsula actually get less than half the amount of rain that typically hits Seattle.

In spite of all this weather—or perhaps because of it—it's a magical place, the Peninsula. Surrounded on three sides by water, it has long been an island unto itself. The jagged-edged Olympics rise from the center of it like 6000-foot castle walls, protecting for centuries the splendid alpine interior from loggers, hunters, miners, and other riffraff. Thanks to the rain, which created the world's only temperate rainforest here, oceans of forest surround (well, surrounded) these walls, stretching 50 miles or more in some places to the Pacific. And there, the sea meets land on some of the most unspoiled ocean beaches left in America, period.

Sound like a good place to camp? It really isn't. Trust us (and Yogi Berra): Nobody goes to the Olympics anymore. Too crowded. Please stay away.

By now, you've already figured out the obvious: When the weather clears (and in a different way, even when it doesn't) the place is gorgeous, too gorgeous. And it's so close to the bulk of people living within the shadow of the Space Needle that it should be illegal. Seriously, there really ought to be a law. (And by the time you read this, the fee-happy National Park Service probably will have come up with one.)

Your camping choices on the Peninsula are as diverse as the land itself, which seemed so frighteningly rugged for so long that no white settlers ever ventured into it until about 100 years ago. The northern area sets a saltwater table of campsites on Puget Sound and Strait of Juan de Fuca beaches that you'll want to keep coming back to. The east side combines the alpine wilderness highlands of Olympic National Park with the quiet saltwater shores of Hood Canal. The west side is a delicious concoction of massive trees and crashing waves. The southwest coast carries its own magic, from the "longest beach in the world" at Long Beach to the stately grandeur of the North Head Lighthouse, one good musket shot from the spot where Lewis and Clark finally stumbled into the Pacific two centuries ago.

Trudging in their long-vanished footsteps has become a life's pursuit for many of us. Even if it means getting a little wet around the edges.

Opposite: *The North Head Lighthouse graces a bluff above Cape Disappointment State Park.*

Fort Flagler State Park is a diverse outdoor playground.

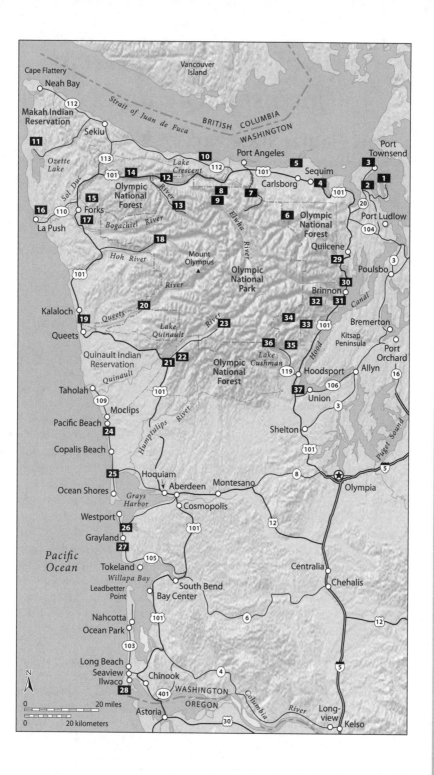

Strait of Juan de Fuca and Northside Olympics

1 Fort Flagler State Park ★ ★ ★ ★ ★

SITES	RESERVATIONS	CONTACT
🏕️ 🚐	(888) 226-7688 or www.parks.wa.gov	Washington State Parks (360) 902-8844
115 sites, 14 water/electrical hookups, RVs to 50 feet	**OPEN** March through October; year-round for day use	Fort Flagler State Park (360) 385-1259

If we had to pick one Washington campground to spend the entire rest of our camping days, it might well be Fort Flagler, one of the most scenic, diverse parks in the state, and arguably one of the finest in all the West. Flagler, another Puget Sound converted military post, is special not for any one thing, but for the so very many things it does so well.

Flagler is one of three 1890s forts surrounding Port Townsend, all of which can be seen from the shore of the park. The earliest fort, Old Fort Townsend, burned in 1895 and never was effectively rebuilt, although a state park still marks the site. But the other two, mighty Forts Worden and Flagler, lived long lives as keepers of the gates to Puget Sound. Big artillery guns at the two forts, coupled with similar firepower at Whidbey Island's Fort Casey, combined to form a "triangle of fire," guarding the door to the inner waters' thriving population centers. Today, replica guns shipped in from the Philippines (the original guns were scrapped after WWII) symbolically stand guard over one of the state's greater recreations treasures.

The campground itself isn't all that remarkable. Sites are clustered on a flat, tidal upland with very little privacy between sites, or in an upper camping area on a bluff above the water with more trees and less space for RVs. But the surrounding setting is spectacular, and the campground is the best base from which to explore this unique 784-acre park. Fort Flagler occupies the entire north end of Marrowstone Island and has a stunning stretch of beach, its own lighthouse, fascinating abandoned gun emplacements and other military artifacts, two boat launches, moorage floats, a fishing pier, an underwater park, a youth hostel, hiking trails, extensive group camps, and a host of other wonders. Because the park is so big and spread out, this is a good place to bring your bicycle.

The park has more than 19,000 feet of saltwater shoreline on Admiralty Inlet, Port Townsend Bay, and Kilisut Harbor, but the far northern beach is a standout day-use area. It's accessible either from the campground area or a narrow road that drops from the blufftop Environmental Learning Center to the picturesque Marrowstone Point Lighthouse. The entire stretch of fine-graveled beach in between—more than

A bald eagle takes flight on a shoreline.

a mile—is open for strolling, and the views across the water to Port Townsend, east to Whidbey Island, and northeast to Mount Baker are sublime. Seals and sea lions often are seen playing offshore here, and it's a favorite destination of sea kayakers, scuba divers, beachcombers, and salmon anglers. The large, open playfield just off the beach south of the camping area is a highly popular kite-flying venue. The park has an RV dump station, a group camp for up to 100 people, a hostel and other rental buildings, and coin-op showers.

Getting there: Follow signs from State Route 20 and proceed to the park at the north end of Marrowstone Island, 8 miles northeast of Hadlock, on Fort Flagler Road.

2 Old Fort Townsend State Park ★ ★ ★ ✦

SITES	RESERVATIONS	CONTACT
🏕 🚐	None	Washington State Parks (360) 902-8844
	OPEN	
40 sites, no hookups, RVs to 40 feet	April to mid-October	Old Fort Townsend State Park (360) 385-3595

There's not much "fort" left in the Port Townsend area's oldest fort, but Old Fort Townsend State Park, 4 miles south of town, remains a decent camping area and saltwater playground. The campsites aren't as close to the beach as they are at the other two nearby forts (Flagler and Worden), and they're 150 feet above the water. But this campground received major upgrades in summer 2002, beach-bluff access is easy, and the place doesn't fill up quite as fast. The park also has a group camp for up to eighty souls, a nice picnic area, and 6.5 miles of good hiking trails through its wooded uplands, most of which offer grand views of Admiralty Inlet and, in clear weather, Cascade Mountain peaks. It also has an RV dump station and coin-op showers.

Historical note: Unlike its sister forts, this one was built to protect residents from a potential foe that pre-dated world wars: area Native Americans. The first fort on the site was built in 1856–57 by the U.S. Army, which used logs plastered together with an inventive paste—made from ground clam shells. The fort never saw much action, although its troops were bolstered during the July 1859 "Pig War" dispute with England over San Juan Island. The fort later served as an enemy-munitions defusing station during World War II. We trust they didn't leave any shells lying around. Note: See important notice about this park's future on p. 25.

Getting there: Follow signs about 4 miles south from Port Townsend on State Route 20 to Old Fort Townsend Road.

3 Fort Worden State Park ✦ ✦ ✦ ✦

SITES	RESERVATIONS	CONTACT
🏕️ 🚐 80 sites, 50 full hookups, 30 water/electrical hookups, RVs to 50 feet	(360) 344-4431 or online at www.parks.wa.gov/fortworden.	Washington State Parks (360) 902-8844
	OPEN	Fort Worden State Park (360) 344-4400
	Year-round; upper campground closed late November through mid-February	

You don't need a tent, RV, or even sleeping bag to "camp" at Fort Worden, a 434-acre, well-preserved military fort whose old wood buildings—built around the turn of the twentieth century as non-commissioned and commissioned officers' housing—today offer a variety of overnight accommodations. The park's grounds seemingly always are active with some festival, retreat, or convention, and the entire property takes days to

Port Townsend residents pedal an artful creation to Fort Worden State Park.

explore. But the campground is nothing to sneeze at, either. While it's not as scenic as the one at Fort Flagler, the RV-equipped campground is one of the region's most extensive. It's actually two camps in one: The lower loop boasts fifty spacious, level (not at all private) full hookup sites on the bluffs of Point Wilson, with great views of the point's namesake lighthouse. The upper loop boasts thirty mostly level, very long campsites with water and electricity, and a dump station nearby. Both areas offer grand views across Admiralty Inlet to Whidbey Island on clear days. This isn't a great tent campground, but tenters are more comfortable on the upper loop. RVers love the entire place: It's a "rally site" for groups of ten to twenty-two self-contained RVs; call (360) 344-4435. Popularity comes with a price: campsites at Fort Worden usually are a bit more expensive than at other Washington State Parks.

The park's wealth of other attractions—abandoned gun emplacements, a Coast Artillery Museum, 11,000 feet of gravelly saltwater beaches, marked hiking and cycling trails, museum exhibits, and more—make this a great place to camp with children. Fishermen also tend to congregate here. Point Wilson, one of the best places on Puget Sound to fish from shore for migratory salmon, gave birth to the "Point Wilson Dart," a slim, heavy fishing lure that local salmon anglers developed to cast far offshore from the beach near the Point Wilson Lighthouse. The park has an RV dump station and coin-op showers. Camp spaces are booked solid during the summer; you'll need a reservation. It's not unusual for the lower camping loop to be full on weekends in the middle of winter. Note that Fort Worden, unlike other Washington State Parks, maintains its own reservation system, with a shorter (five-month) reservation window. You can now check site availability and make reservations online, at www.parks.wa.gov /fortworden; or by calling the number above.

Getting there: From State Route 20 at Port Townsend, follow signs to the park, about 1 mile north of downtown.

4 Sequim Bay State Park ★ ★ ★

SITES	RESERVATIONS	CONTACT
⛺ 🚙	(888) 226-7688 or www.parks.wa.gov	Washington State Parks (360) 902-8844
76 sites, 16 full hookups, RVs to 45 feet	**OPEN** Year-round	Sequim Bay State Park (360) 683-4235

Sequim Bay, tucked into thick trees just off U.S. Highway 101, is easy to miss by traveling campers bound for grander Olympic Peninsula stops. But it rarely avoids the attention of RVers, who know it's the only state park in this area. They often make it a single-night stopover on a US 101 loop around the Peninsula. Alas, the campsites at this ninty-acre park are only so-so, with the exception of a small handful of forested tent sites near 4900 feet of shoreline on the waters of Sequim Bay. The park did make some recent improvements, removing some sites in the hookup loop to make the others roomier. It made a difference. Also, the day-use area on the waterfront is very nice, offering boater services, moorage, and launching. The park has two kitchen shelters, horseshoe

Beachcombing is always good along Sequim Bay.

pits, a boat launch, an RV dump station, a picnic area, and a tunnel that connects to a baseball field and tennis courts. One thing you won't usually find: The rain that makes the Olympic Peninsula notorious. The Sequim area is in the "rain shadow" of prevailing southwesterly storms striking the Olympics and averages only about 17 inches of rain per year—about a tenth as much as the opposite side of the mountain range.

Getting there: The park is about 3 miles southeast of Sequim on US 101.

5 Dungeness Recreation Area ★ ★ ★ ◀

SITES	RESERVATIONS	CONTACT
🏕️ 🚐 66 sites, no hookups, RVs to any length	By mail beginning each January 2, for sites 34–66 only; (360) 683-5847 or www.clallam.net /CountyParks/html/parks_dungeness.htm	Dungeness Recreation Area (360) 683-5847 ccpdu@olypen.com
	OPEN	
	February through September	

Not far from the mouth of the Dungeness River—and adjacent to the scenic Dungeness National Wildlife Refuge—this blufftop campground is one of two underrated sites operated by Clallam County. Campsites, some of which offer good back-window views of the Strait of Juan de Fuca, are separated either by head-high shrubbery or short, thick trees, offering good privacy with ample sunlight. A short walk away is the main trailhead to the Wildlife Refuge, where you can walk the sandspit formed by the Dungeness River about 4.5 miles to its end. It's worth the walk: The spit, particularly its inner lagoon, is often alive with migratory waterfowl, and marine mammals are often seen offshore. At the spit's tip, the historic New Dungeness Lighthouse is sometimes open for tours. The park has an RV dump station and coin-op showers. Sites were $16–18 at this writing.

Getting there: From U.S. Highway 101 at Sequim, proceed about 4.5 miles west to Kitchen–Dick Road. Turn right (north) and follow signs about 3 miles to the park.

6 Deer Park ★ ★ ✦

SITES	RESERVATIONS		CONTACT
🏕	None		Olympic National Park (360) 565-3130
	OPEN		
14 sites	Mid-June to October		

The view is to die for, but everything else about Deer Park will make you pine for that nice tent space in your backyard. This national park campground, open summers only, is primitive, very remote, and miserably dusty in the dry season. But the view is worth the trip up Blue Mountain. At 5400 feet, this is one of the more lofty campgrounds in the state, and aerial views of the Strait of Juan de Fuca, Dungeness Valley, and most of northern Puget Sound are unique. The fourteen tent sites (there used to be eighteen; we're wondering if the National Park Service would like this camp to just go away altogether) are almost an afterthought. But tenters seeking solitude might find it pleasant in good weather. Deer Park, the former site of one of Washington's earliest ski lodges, is no place for RVs. Sites are too small, the 18-mile, mostly gravel road too rough (it's the kind of mountain road that makes nervous-Nelly passengers wish they were driving). Call the park to make sure the road is open before embarking. This camp also serves as a trailhead—for the Grand Ridge Trail, a 7.5-mile, one-way hike to Obstruction Point. It's the highest trail in Olympic National Park, reaching 6500 feet at its summit. Note: Bring your own water. There's no piped supply at Deer Park.

Getting there: From U.S. Highway 101 about 6 miles east of Port Angeles, follow Deer Park Road 18 miles to the campground at road's end.

7 Heart O' the Hills ★ ★ ★ ★

SITES	RESERVATIONS		CONTACT
🏕 🚐	None		Olympic National Park (360) 565-3130
	OPEN		Heart O' the Hills Ranger Station (360) 452-2713
105 sites, no hookups, RVs to 21 feet	Year-round, weather permitting		

Heart O' the Hills is one of the nicest campgrounds in Olympic National Park and one of the better camps in all of the north Olympics. The Port Angeles–area park, perched at Olympic's northern gateway, is set in tall, old-growth trees. Suitable for tents and/or smaller RVs, it's quiet, clean—and generally packed with RVs from Nebraska all summer. But you can usually stumble across a site midweek without too much trouble. Beware the predatory night-stalking raccoons, particularly Old Three Legs, one of our longtime friends. Just across the road is a major trailhead, with paths leading to Lake Angeles,

Heather Park, and on to Klahhane Ridge near the Hurricane Ridge day-use area, which is 17 miles above the campground via a steep, winding, but well-maintained road. Note: The park has an RV dump station and piped water year-round. Although the park is open year-round, the Park Service inexplicably shuts its gate, making it a walk-in only camp when it snows at 1800 feet in the northern Olympics.

Getting there: From U.S. Highway 101 at Port Angeles, follow signs 5 miles south on Hurricane Ridge Road.

8 Elwha ★ ★ ★

SITES	RESERVATIONS		CONTACT
	None		Olympic National Park (360) 565-3130
	OPEN		Elwha Ranger Station
40 sites, no hookups, RVs to 21 feet	Year-round		(360) 452-9191

West of Port Angeles, nestled between the two long-controversial—and now, praise be, short-lived—dams on the Lower Elwha River, is the often-overlooked Elwha area of Olympic National Park. The road following the river here is home to two fine, albeit non-spectacular, campgrounds. The first, Elwha, is about a half mile away from the river, with forty flat campsites set in fairly thick mixed coniferous and deciduous forest. A beefy kitchen shelter covers you in extremely bad weather, of which there is much in the winter (when the campground water is shut off). Not far up the road is the Whiskey Bend Trailhead, which provides access to Olympic National Park's famed Elwha River Trail. The trail roughly follows the route of the historic 1899 Press Expedition into the interior Olympics, which (believe it or not) were scarcely explored before then. The lower Elwha offers fair trout fishing in the summer.

Local trivia: A proposal to remove both dams on the Elwha and return the river to its former status as a major producer of chinook and other salmon species has been approved by Congress; it's now just a matter of time and money until the Elwha becomes a majestic, free-flowing stream once more.

Getting there: From Port Angeles, drive 9 miles west on U.S. Highway 101, to Elwha River Road, turn left (south), and proceed 3 miles to the campground, on the left.

9 Altaire ★ ★ ★

SITES	RESERVATIONS		CONTACT
	None		Olympic National Park (360) 565-3130
	OPEN		Elwha Ranger Station
30 sites, no hookups, RVs to 21 feet	Late May through September		(360) 452-9191

The second Olympic National Park campground on the Elwha River, Altaire, is the most popular, even though it's down in a bit of a hole and much darker than Elwha. Altaire, however, has waterfront—right on the banks of the cool, clear Elwha. Some sites actually put the river at your feet—assuming you can snare one in the summer at this popular park. A major trailhead just up the road (it leads to Olympic Hot Springs, Boulder Lake, Appleton Pass, and on to the Sol Duc drainage) makes this a much-sought-after overnight spot for hikers either embarking or disembarking. The Glines Canyon Dam, the upper of two dams on the lower Elwha River, is just up the road, and worth a look—at least for a while. It's scheduled to be demolished sometime in the 2010s. This shady, damp campground is somewhat primitive, and can be very chilly in less than hot weather. But it's a lovely setting.

Getting there: From Port Angeles, drive 9 miles west on U.S. Highway 101 turn left (south) on Elwha River Road, and proceed about 4 miles to the campground, on the right, just after a bridge over the river.

10 Salt Creek Recreation Area ✦ ✦ ✦ ✦ ✦

SITES	RESERVATIONS	CONTACT
🏕 🚐	By mail beginning each January 2; information at (360) 928-3441 or www.clallam.net /CountyParks/html/parks_saltcreek.htm	Salt Creek Recreation Area (360) 928-3441
92 sites, 39 water/electrical hookups, RVs to any length	**OPEN**	
	Year-round	

Every so often, we stumble upon one of those special outdoor places we love so much that we hesitate to ever write about it. This is one of them. Salt Creek, one of the state's best (and formerly overlooked) campgrounds, sits perched on a bluff above the Strait of Juan de Fuca. Like so many other prime waterfront campgrounds in Washington, this one takes advantage of the very qualities that made it public property in the first place—the kinds of sight lines needed for heavy artillery. Salt Creek, the jewel of Clallam County's park system, is the former home of Camp Hayden, a World War II–era 16-inch gun emplacement. Not much of the military base remains, but a diverse, relaxing getaway has arisen from its remains.

Salt Creek's campsites, all situated either on a steep bluff above Tongue Point or in a terraced, grassy field in the center of the park, are a wonderful escape any time of the year, with more than three-fourths of them offering a saltwater view. The grassy sites afford no privacy, but each offers a gorgeous view of the Strait of Juan de Fuca, where you can watch the parade of cargo and military ships, peer across to Victoria, or scan for orca whales, otters, and sea lions in the saltwater. Tenters will likely prefer the more-private, wooded sites 53–92, where views are tough to turn your eyes away from.

But there's plenty of active stuff to do here, as well. Striped Peak, which looms above the campground to the east, is ringed by hiking trails and old logging roads that make for fine daylong exploration by hikers or, especially, mountain bikers. Keep your eyes peeled off the road's shoulders for buried ruins of the park's military past; they're getting more and more difficult to find as the hillside's forest grows back into place after clear-cutting several decades ago on this DNR land.

There's not much sandy beach here, largely because of the strait's rocky, often

treacherous shoreline (the inviting, sandy beach at Crescent Bay to the west is part of a private RV resort). But Tongue Point Marine Reserve, on the west side of the park, is one of Washington's best tidal-pool viewing spots. It's a protected marine reserve that's a true delight at low tide, when a jagged rock formation seemingly rises from the deep to offer acres of exploring. Salt Creek has an RV dump station and coin-op showers; be prepared to wait in line for both in summer.

Needless to say, the 196-acre park has been thoroughly "discovered" since we began camping here, sans crowds, back in the 1970s. Since earlier editions of this guide, the park has grown up to meet modernity—for better or worse. It now has thirty-nine utility campsites, and has recently added a reservation system. Beginning every January 2, you can mail in reservation requests in advance for that calendar camping year. Forms can be downloaded from the Internet at the address above, or requested by calling the reservations number. The process might go online if it proves popular. Our advice: Pick a date, pick a site, and make a reservation. The word is finally out on Salt Creek, and yeah, we're probably somewhat to blame. So shoot us; we got you here, didn't we? (Tip: If you don't have a reservation, you still have a shot. Half the campground is first-come, first-served. The park reserves only sites 16–39, 51–68, and 71–73. Not surprisingly, those are many—but not all—of the nicest ones.)

Getting there: From Port Angeles, follow U.S. Highway 101 and State Route 112 about 13 miles west to Camp Hayden Road. Turn right (north) and drive about 4 miles to the campground, on the right.

11 Ozette ★★★

SITES	RESERVATIONS	CONTACT
	None	Olympic National Park (360) 565-3130
	OPEN	Ozette Ranger Station (360) 963-2725
15 sites, no hookups, RVs to 21 feet	Year-round; winter closures possible	

Remote Lake Ozette, Washington's largest natural lake, is a top destination in Olympic National Park, largely because of the wildly popular Cape Alava–Sand Point Trail that begins near its north shore. A small national park campground (far too small to handle the crowds, unfortunately) awaits here. The campground is popular not only with hikers, but canoeists and anglers who like to ply the waters and fish for trout, perch, kokanee, and other fish. Because it's inside the National Park, no license is required here. The campground is fairly rustic, with pit toilets and piped water, but no other creature comforts. Campers would be remiss in choosing not to follow the crowds down the nearby Cape Alava–Sand Point Trail, a classic Northwest beach hike that can be walked in an easy, 9.3-mile loop (actually, it's more of a triangle). Note: Between Memorial Day and Labor Day, you need an advance permit to camp overnight on the beach here. Call (360) 565-3130 for information.

Opposite: Beach walkers take to the sandy shores of the Strait of Juan de Fuca near Salt Creek Recreation Area.

Getting there: From Port Angeles, follow U.S. Highway 101 west to State Route 112. Proceed west to Hoko–Ozette Road. Turn left (south) and drive about 22 miles to the campground, near the Ozette Ranger Station.

12 Fairholm ★★★◀

SITES	RESERVATIONS	CONTACT
🏕 🚐	None	Olympic National Park (360) 565-3130
	OPEN	
88 sites, no hookups, RVs to 21 feet	April through mid-September	

Fairholm, on the far western shore of deep, majestic Lake Crescent, is the most easily accessible public campground in this area. Nestled in the firs just off the lake, the park's eighty-eight shady sites are fairly private, and all are within a short stroll of the shoreline. The only caveat: You can hear traffic on U.S. Highway 101 from those on the east side of the camp. The campground has a boat launch, an RV dump station, a nice play area and swimming beach (brrrrr!), and good campfire programs in the summer. It's also a popular spot for hikers. Olympic's Spruce Railroad Trail, a nice 4-mile, one-way Lake Crescent shoreline walk and one of the few trails in the Olympics open to mountain bikes, is a short distance up North Shore Road from here; it makes a good daylong cycle trip from the campground. Great trails in the Sol Duc River drainage are a 30-minute drive to the east. And the popular Marymere Falls–Mount Storm King Trail is a short distance back toward Port Angeles, as is Lake Crescent Lodge.

Getting there: From Port Angeles, follow US 101 southwest about 25 miles, skirting the east shore of Lake Crescent, to North Shore Road. Turn right and proceed about a half mile to the campground, on the right.

13 Sol Duc ★★★◀

SITES	RESERVATIONS	CONTACT
🏕 🚐	None	Olympic National Park (360) 565-3130
	OPEN	Sol Duc Ranger Station
82 sites, no hookups, RVs to 21 feet	Year-round; primitive winter camping	(360) 928-3380

This is the place to stay for people day-hiking in the Sol Duc Valley, one of the primo summertime destinations in Olympic National Park. The nearby Sol Duc Trailhead is the take-off point to beautiful Sol Duc Falls and beyond to Deer Lake, Seven Lakes Basin, High Divide, and a connecting trail to the Hoh River drainage to the south. The shady campground is typical National Park Service fare, adequate but not spectacular, with sites set in a mixed forest that's often visited by the valley's blacktail deer and other critters. It has an RV dump station and is suitable for RVs and tents. It's popular with patrons of nearby Sol Duc Hot Springs. A trail leads from the camping area to the Hot Springs, which charges a daily fee to soak in the warm waters of the springs, or cool water piped in from the crisp, clear Sol Duc River. Another worthwhile local attraction is the Salmon Cascades, where migratory salmon sometimes can be seen jumping a white-water obstacle when they're running upstream. Not to be missed when fish are present.

Note: The campground has no running water in winter.

Getting there: From Port Angeles, drive west on U.S. Highway 101 to Lake Crescent. A short distance beyond the lake, turn left (south) on Sol Duc River Road. Proceed 13 miles south to the campground.

Lake Crescent is one of the deepest and coldest bodies of water in Washington.

14 Klahowya ★ ★ ◀

SITES	RESERVATIONS	CONTACT
	None	Olympic National Forest Pacific Ranger District Forks office (360) 374-6522
	OPEN	
55 sites, some electrical hookups, RVs to 30 feet	May through September; limited winter services	

Spectacular, no. Convenient, yes. This Olympic National Forest camp is one of only a few situated right along U.S. Highway 101. That makes it a busy place in the summer. It sits on the south shore of the beautiful, clear Sol Duc River. But the noisy highway is nearby. (Be thankful there aren't as many jake-braked logging trucks over here as there once were.) The, camp—like most in this area, set in the mossy temperate Olympic rain forest—has both flush and pit toilets and piped water. Two walk-in sites provide more privacy for tenters without a lot of gear. A boat ramp makes it a driftboat-angler's favorite; the Sol Duc is a blue-ribbon steelhead and salmon stream. The very short Pioneer's Path interpretive trail begins in the camp, and you can take in an interpretive program at the campground amphitheater in the summer. Another interesting local landmark, the Kloshe Nanitch Lookout, is a short drive away. Consult a Forest Service map.

RVer's note: Electric hookups are available for a fee when the camp host or a Forest Service employee is present.

Note for shutterbugs and avid researchers: This campground does not, as another guidebook asserts, "feature great views of Lake Crescent and Mount Olympus"—unless perhaps you were to lift off from it in a helicopter.

Getting there: From Port Angeles, follow US 101 about 34 miles southwest (about 10 miles west of Lake Crescent) to the campground, near US 101's milepost 212.

BEST OCEANFRONT CAMPS

1. Kalaloch, Olympic National Park
The premiere saltwater campground in Washington State, with many sites right on a short bluff above the beach. Hint: Its adjacent camping area, South Beach, is even closer to the beach, but offers fewer services. See p. 92.

2. Cape Disappointment State Park, Southwest Washington
No disappointment here for fans of the ocean—a big, flat, beautiful one that's a short walk away from campsites and rental yurts. See p. 103.

3. Pacific Beach State Park, Southwest Washington
Preferred by RVers, it's as close to the ocean as you'll get without getting salt between your toes. See p. 99.

4. Ocean City State Park, Ocean Shores
The ocean's not within view, but certainly within earshot at this Ocean Shores area camp that's also a good place for tents. See p. 100.

5. Mora, Olympic National Park
It's a hike to the beach from here, but what a beach it is—Rialto Beach near LaPush, one of the more scenic along Washington's coast. See p. 89.

Other Northside Olympic Campgrounds

Along the strait, a half mile north of State Route 112 (about 20 miles west of Port Angeles), is **Lyre River**, a free, semi-primitive DNR campground. It's near milepost 46; (360) 374-6131. In the beautiful Dungeness River drainage of the Olympic Mountains southwest of Sequim is one Forest Service campground with ten (tent-only) sites: **Dungeness Forks**, on Forest Service Road 2880 at the confluence of the Dungeness and Gray Wolf rivers; Hood Canal Ranger District, Quilcene office, (360) 765-2200. In the Elwha River Valley, one of Olympic National Park's better-kept secrets is **Olympic Hot Springs**, a natural spring at an old hotel site reached by driving to the end of Elwha Road, then hiking 2.5 miles. A backcountry campground, **Boulder Creek**, is located nearby; (360) 565-3130.

At Lake Ozette, **Erickson's Bay**, a small, primitive campground on the west side of the lake, is accessible by foot or boat only. A swampy trail leads about 2.2 miles west to the ocean. On the northwest shore of Lake Ozette; no fee, no reservations; (360) 565-3130.

No public campgrounds are found at Sekiu or on the Makah Reservation at Neah Bay, but private spots are available. Mostly gravel lots for anglers' RVs, they're not really suitable for tents, but RVers might favor amenities such as full hookups. Some have good views of the strait or the harbor at Neah Bay. The list includes Neah Bay's **Tyee RV Park**, (360) 645-2223; Sekiu's **Van Riper's Resort**, (360) 963-2334; and **Olson's Resort**, (360) 963-2311. In the Clallam Bay area, try **Sam's Trailer and RV Park**; (360) 963-2402.

A somewhat pricey private camping option on Lake Crescent is **Log Cabin Resort**, which has thirty-six sites (full hookups; unlimited RV length) within a short distance of the lake's shore, 3 miles north of US 101 on East Beach Road; (360) 928-3325.

Westside Olympics and the Coast

15 Klahanie ✦✦✦

SITES	RESERVATIONS	CONTACT
🏕️ 🚐	None	Olympic National Forest
	OPEN	Pacific Ranger District Forks office
20 sites, no hookups, RVs to 24 feet	May to early September	(360) 374-6522

Klahanie, a small camp on the South Fork Calawah River, is a shady spot in a forest of hemlock, broadleaf maple, and some notable big, old spruce that are worth a visit here all on their own (do yourself a leg-stretching favor if you're driving U.S. Highway 101). The camp, not far from Forks, is pretty rustic, with pit toilets and hand-pumped water, but no garbage service. (We can envision a vampire scene unfolding here in one of the Twilight books set in nearby Forks.)

Sites are better geared to tents than RVs, but it makes a worthy overnight stop in a pinch on US 101 trips. A short day-hiking trail along the river begins in the campground. And remember, since this is on National Forest, not National Parks land, it's OK to walk your dog here. This camp has been closed on and off in recent years; call first to make sure it's open. When it is, it's cheap; at this writing, camp fees were only $5, making this a regional bargain.

Getting there: From US 101 about 1 mile north of Forks, turn east on Forest Road 29 and proceed about 5 miles to the campground.

16 Mora ✦✦✦✦

SITES	RESERVATIONS	CONTACT
🏕️ 🚐	None	Olympic National Park
	OPEN	(360) 565-3130
94 sites, no hookups, RVs to 21 feet	Year-round	

Two of the Olympic Peninsula's most gorgeous clear-water streams, the Sol Duc and Bogachiel, merge near the town of Forks, masquerading as the Quillayute River for the final miles to the ocean. Just downstream from the confluence is Mora, an Olympic National Park campground that's a longtime favorite, especially of Pacific Ocean beachcombers. The camping area itself here is not remarkable. Spaces are in a heavily wooded, almost dark, forest. But the campground's proximity to Rialto Beach makes it truly special. On a peninsula well stocked with fabulous sandy beaches, Rialto is a standout—one of those very few picture-perfect Washington scenes you can almost

A visitor checks out an old-growth Douglas fir on the Olympic Peninsula.

drive right up to. A series of sea stacks lurks in the mist to the north, and the unusually steep-sloped beach makes for frothing, always picturesque surf. The beach is almost always windy but great for strolling, with miles of unobstructed sand beckoning to the north. Rialto also is a major beach-hiking trailhead for coastal backpackers. Most day-use visitors walk 1.5 miles up the beach to Hole-in-the-Wall, a nifty surf-carved tunnel beneath the jutting headlands. The Rialto day-use area is a short walk from the campground on an old access road. Mora has an RV dump station and a group camp for fifteen to forty campers. The group camp can be reserved after March 1.

Getting there: From Forks, drive 2 miles north on U.S. Highway 101, turn west on La Push Highway (State Route 110) and follow signs for 12 miles, keeping right at the Y where La Push Road departs to the left.

17 Bogachiel State Park ✷ ✷

SITES	RESERVATIONS	CONTACT
⚠ 🏕️🚐	None	Washington State Parks (360) 902-8844
	OPEN	Bogachiel State Park (360) 374-6356
42 sites, 6 full hookups, RVs to 40 feet	Year-round	

Bogachiel State Park is more popular for its location—halfway up the Olympic Peninsula on U.S. Highway 101—than for what it contains. But what it contains is plenty good enough for most, particularly all you multiple-days-without-showers US 101 vaga-bonds. It's a simple place with forty-two sites situated in two camping loops, most of which are too close to the highway (like, yards) for our taste. A log mill across the road provides more noise when operating. But unlike most peninsula parks managed by the National Park Service or Forest Service, Bogachiel *does* have hot showers (the only ones on this whole stretch of US 101!)—the best investment of a couple quarters you'll make out here all summer. The park also has an RV dump station, a picnic area, and a boat launch on the lovely Bogachiel River, a noted winter steelhead fishery. A group camp with a covered shelter can house sixteen to twenty people. Call the park office to reserve. Note: See important notice about this park's future on p. 25.

Getting there: The park is on US 101, 6 miles south of Forks.

18 Hoh ✷ ✷ ✷ ✷

SITES	RESERVATIONS	CONTACT
⚠ 🏕️🚐	None	Olympic National Park (360) 565-3130
	OPEN	Hoh Ranger Station (360) 374-6925
88 sites, no hookups, RVs to 21 feet	Year-round	

The majestic old-growth forest of the Hoh River Valley is a national—indeed, world-wide—treasure, and the Hoh Rain Forest is where the great bulk of all those folks with sore necks (from craning) spend the night. As a result, it's one of Olympic National Park's most popular campgrounds, and landing a site here in midsummer can be quite the feat. Campsites are spread through wooded loops near the Hoh River and a short walk from the valley's famous rain forest trails, such as the Hoh River Trail, which winds 17 miles up the river to Glacier Meadows on the slopes of Mount Olympus, the park's tallest peak at 7965 feet. Any portion of the first 13 miles of trail, mostly flat, is great for day hiking. Shorter walks through the massive trees, fed by up to 140 inches of rain every year, also start nearby. The Hall of Mosses Trail (easy, 0.75-mile loop), which be-gins and ends near the visitor center, is spectacular in its own right. A good nature-trail primer for the area. (Note to hikers and photographers: The ethereal atmosphere and deep green hues of the rain forest emerge best on cloudy or rainy days. Put on some waterproof boots and go for it!) Nearby are two barrier-free trails, the Spruce Nature Trail (easy, 1.25-mile loop) and a separate paved, 0.25-mile nature loop.

Wildlife note: Black bears are not uncommon here, so don't leave food out. And Roosevelt elk are frequent campground visitors. One recent spring, in fact, the campground was shut down when a protective mother cow made a nursery of one of the camping loops. Watch for those big white rumps! Hoh Rain Forest has an RV dump station.

Getting there: From U.S. Highway 101 14 miles south of Forks or 21 miles north of Kalaloch, turn east on Hoh Rain Forest Road and proceed 18 miles to the campground.

19   Kalaloch ✦✦✦✦✦

SITES	RESERVATIONS	CONTACT
🏕 🚐	Up to 6 months in advance for camping late June through Labor Day; www.recreation.gov	Olympic National Park (360) 565-3130
	OPEN	Kalaloch Ranger Station (360) 962-2283
170 sites, no hookups, RVs to 21 feet	Year-round	

No two ways about it: This is one of the premier Therm-a-Rest plunking spots on the North American continent. Situated on a breezy bluff above one of the state's most gorgeous sandy Pacific Ocean beaches, Kalaloch (you know you're officially local when you pronounce it correctly, CLAY-lock) might be the best campground in the state. It's certainly one of the more difficult to get into during summer months. And it's one of very few where you can actually see the ocean (feel it, even) from some campsites.

On those rare days (even in the summer) when the fog lifts, sunsets from the beach at Kalaloch will carve their own spot in your soul. Not surprisingly, even though it's spacious, Kalaloch's 170 sites stay full for much of the summer. In the past, that forced prospective campers to play a prolonged game of campsite roulette—arriving early in the day, parking in the day-use lot or a roadside campsite, then patrolling like greedy vultures for anyone who even *looks* like they're to abandon a choice, waterfront spot. But for better or worse, things have changed. In 2003, Kalaloch finally entered the twenty-first century and began accepting campsite reservations. The service has since migrated online and has proven very popular among the organized types who don't like driving 3.5 hours from Seattle, only to be shut out of a campsite. Conversely, it's a major bummer for spur-of-the-moment road-trippers. No more lurking and bribing waterfront site owners with fresh fruit, meats, stove fuel, cash, or other bartering goods! Oh well. We'll leave it at this: The foolish man builds his Kalaloch hopes upon getting lucky. The wise man goes online and books. If you want a beach-bluff spot here in August, better get cracking the previous February.

The hassle, reservation or no, makes it just that much sweeter when you score that spot right on the bluff, overlooking the ocean. There's really no campground like it on the planet. Well, at least not on the Washington coast, where it's difficult to impossible to get this close to the pristine saltwater beach and still enjoy the creature comforts of camping.

Facilities are comparatively so-so: Kalaloch has an RV dump station (it costs $5), heated restrooms, and piped water, but the closest public showers are 10 miles south,

A Washington classic: The windswept campsites of Kalaloch Campground.

at Rain Forest Resort on Lake Quinault (worth the drive; the world's largest Sitka spruce is right across the road), or north in Bogachiel State Park, almost an hour up U.S. Highway 101. Although most of the sites here were originally designed for 1950s-sized cars, tents, and small trailers, some have been redesigned to accommodate larger rigs, and we're constantly amazed by the size of some of the diesel push-and-shovers that shoehorn in here. But the park, to its credit, has now reserved a handful of the prime, beachfront sites (where the bluff is ever-crumbling away) for tenters only. Another great recent improvement is a machine in the day-use parking lot allowing you to pay camp fees with credit or debit cards.

The fun doesn't end in the campground proper. About 3 miles to the south is the South Beach overflow area, open summers only. This somewhat primitive, flat gravel lot began as a sloppy-seconds campground with no running water, tables, fire pits, or facilities of any kind. But now that a restroom has been built there, it's become the campground of choice for many, particularly RV owners who can set up just about anywhere. Reason: It's almost right on the beach, with only an 8-foot bank and a pile of driftwood separating the dinner table from the pounding Pacific surf. Spectacular. Other local attractions include the short hikes down to other local beaches with more interesting topography. Beach 5 and Ruby Beach, in particular, are not to be missed.

Getting there: The campground is on US 101, 35 miles south of Forks and 73 miles north of Aberdeen (5 miles north of the US 101 bridge over the Queets River).

An angler wades into the cold waters of the Queets River.

20 Queets ★ ★ ◀

SITES	RESERVATIONS	CONTACT
🏕️ 🚐	None	Olympic National Park (360) 565-3130
	OPEN	
20 sites, no hookups	Year-round	

This quiet, remote campground on the surging banks of the Queets, one of the Olympic Peninsula's most powerful rivers, isn't easy to get to. Most times of the year, the Queets River Road, which winds 14 miles east from U.S. Highway 101 along the river's south shore, is a bump-atorium, with some potholes large enough to swallow a Volkswagen whole. And the road often washes out; call before you go. But it's worth the trip for those able to make it around or through them. The primitive campground is at the end of the Queets River Road, which doubles as a trailhead for the Queets River Trail, set in a deep forest of moss-draped Douglas fir, western red cedar, and broadleaf maple. Subtract points for the fact the forest is so thick that it always seems dark and damp in here. Picnic tables literally get covered by moss. But deer and elk are plentiful. There's no running water, flush toilets, or showers here. The summers-only Queets Ranger Station is nearby.

Getting there: From US 101, about 13 miles south of Kalaloch or 20 miles north of Lake Quinault, turn east on (gravel, often rough) Queets River Road and proceed 14 miles to the campground, to the left at the end of the road.

21 Willaby ★ ★ ★ ★

SITES	RESERVATIONS	CONTACT
🏕️ 🚐	None	Olympic National Forest Pacific Ranger District Quinault office
	OPEN	(360) 288-2525
31 sites, no hookups, RVs to 20 feet	Memorial Day through September	

Willaby, tucked into the giant trees on the south shore of Lake Quinault, a short walk from the venerable Lake Quinault Lodge, is one of our favorite Forest Service campgrounds. Sites in the fourteen-acre park are small but private, in thick, mossy, second-growth forest, with some along the lakeshore and many of the upper sites offering peekaboo lake views. It's really the closest thing to one of our previous favorite tent campgrounds across the lake on North Shore Road, July Creek, which the National Park Service inexplicably turned into a day-use-only area a number of years ago.

The beauty at Willaby stretches far upland: Winding through the campground is the 3-mile Lake Quinault Loop Trail, which connects your campsite to the lodge, about half a mile of shoreline, and some magnificent surviving old-growth forest just

up the hill. One segment of this trail, Big Tree Grove (also reached from a separate, South Shore Road trailhead), is a definite don't-miss. The campground, now concessioner-operated, has a boat launch and some moorage space, making it popular with boaters. Fishing for steelhead and other species is good in the river below, but you'll need a Quinault tribal guide.

Willaby has no showers, but they're available for a small fee just up the road at Rain Forest Resort. Note that the camp has two walk-in tent sites and ten of its total are listed as additional "overflow" sites for larger RVs.

Getting there: From U.S. Highway 101 at Lake Quinault, turn east on South Shore Road and proceed about 1.5 miles to the campground, on the left, just beyond the Quinault Rain Forest Nature Trail.

A visitor examines a world-record spruce tree near Lake Quinault.

22 Falls Creek ✦ ✦ ✦

SITES	RESERVATIONS	CONTACT
	None	Olympic National Forest Pacific Ranger District Quinault office (360) 288-2525
	OPEN	
31 sites, no hookups, RVs to 20 feet	Memorial Day through Labor Day	

Falls Creek is like a twin-brother camp to Willaby, located on the far side of Lake Quinault Lodge, where Falls Creek babbles into the lake. It offers similar good access to local rain forest trails and, like its companion, often serves as a launching pad for backpacking and day-hiking expeditions up the nearby Colonel Bob Trail in the Olympic National Forest or up the East Fork Quinault Trail at the head of the valley in Olympic National Park. The campground doesn't have quite the same pleasing aesthetic as Willaby, but it's a nice place, with some large firs and bigleaf maples looming over waterfront sites on Falls Creek and Lake Quinault. Low-impact tenters might take a liking to Falls Creek's ten walk-in sites. The camp also has a historic picnic shelter built by the Civilian Conservation Corps in the mid-1930s and still going strong.

Old-growth forest trails are easy to reach from Falls Creek Campground near Lake Quinault.

Local trivia: A short distance east is the world's largest Sitka spruce tree, 58 feet in circumference and up to 1000 years old—near the lakeshore at Rain Forest Village Resort. Worth the walk, and the look.

Getting there: From U.S. Highway 101 at Lake Quinault, turn east on South Shore Road and proceed about 2.5 miles to the campground, on the left.

23 Graves Creek ★ ★ �

SITES	RESERVATIONS	CONTACT
	None	Olympic National Park (360) 565-3130
	OPEN	Quinault Ranger Station
30 sites, no hookups, RVs to 21 feet	Year-round; limited winter services	(360) 288-2444

If the road is open (it washes out frequently; call first), it's worth the trek all the way to the end of South Shore Road to Graves Creek, near the trailhead of the East Fork Quinault and Graves Creek Trails. Well, for tent campers, anyway. The formerly free campground, in a mossy, mixed-forest area, often serves as a base camp for backpackers exploring farther up the valley. The primary destination is Enchanted Valley (26 miles round-trip), one of Olympic National Park's more notable backcountry destinations. But day hikers can trek the same trail to a grand river view from Pony Bridge (5 miles round-trip).

Getting there: From U.S. Highway 101 at Lake Quinault, turn east on South Shore Road and proceed 15 miles to the campground, at the end of the road.

BEST LEAVE-THE-GEAR-AT-HOME CAMPING

1. Camper's Cabins at Cama Beach State Park
Just bring your sleeping bag, cook kit, and groceries—and a stout windbreaker—to spend some quiet time at this waterfront Puget Sound getaway. See p.37.

2. Yurt Village, Grayland Beach or Cape Disappointment state parks
Both allow couples or families to enjoy the ocean beach and saltwater air without the hassle by camping in yurts, within a short walk of the ocean. See p. 102 and 103.

3. Officers' Quarters, Fort Flagler or Fort Worden state parks
You can think like a military officer (or re-create a scene from *An Officer and a Gentleman*) at former army-base buildings here, all within a short walk of prime saltwater beaches and other recreation opportunities. See p. 76 or 78.

4. North Head Lighthouse Keeper's Residence
The old homestead on a bluff above Cape Disappointment State Park is one of many historic structures rented to overnight guests. See p. 103.

5. Lakefront Cabins, Silver Lake Park, Whatcom County
This family favorite campground in Northwest Washington also offers lodging to the tent- or RV-less camper, ranging from tiny cabins to larger group facilities. See p. 123.

A Roosevelt elk keeps an eye on a hiker along the Hoh River Trail.

Other Westside Olympic Campgrounds

Don't overlook the string of very nice—and very free—state Department of Natural Resources campsites along the Hoh River. **Hoh Oxbow**, just south of the Hoh Rain Forest Road near U.S. Highway 101 milepost 176, has eight sites for tents and small trailers, but no running water. A small boat launch makes it a favorite angler's hangout, especially during winter steelhead season. **Cottonwood**, just off Oil City Road (turn west off US 101 near milepost 177, about 15 miles south of Forks) is similar, with nine sites. On Hoh Rain Forest Road are **Willoughby Creek** (3.5 miles east of US 101), with three small campsites and limited facilities; and **Minnie Peterson** (4.5 miles east of US 101), which has eight small riverside spots. Another primitive, but private, option is **South Fork Hoh**, reached by turning east off US 101 on Hoh Mainline Road (about 15.5 miles south of Forks) and proceeding 14 miles east. All five campgrounds are free and open year-round. The other free (and even more remote) DNR campgrounds in the area are **Coppermine Bottom** (nine sites), **Upper Clearwater** (nine sites), and **Yahoo Lake** (four sites). Contact the Washington Department of Natural Resources in Forks; (360) 374-6131.

A private campground in the Forks/La Push area is **Hoh River Resort**, near the river on US 101, which has twenty-three sites with hookups and other facilities; (360) 374-5566. A small camp serving as overflow for Willaby and Falls Creek at Lake Quinault is **Gatton Creek** (five tent; eight parking-lot RV sites), 3.5 miles east of US 101 on South Shore Road; call Pacific Ranger District, Quinault office, (360) 288-2525. Those who venture all the way to the end of North Shore Road (assuming it's not washed out) will come upon **North Fork**, a quiet but nondescript Olympic National Park campground with seven tent sites set near the North Fork Quinault Trailhead. It's free but primitive, with no running water; (360) 288-2525. An hour south of Lake Quinault is **Campbell Tree Grove**, a fourteen-acre Olympic National Forest campground on the upper Humptulips River, on Forest Road 2204, near the southern border of the Colonel Bob Wilderness. It's a free campground with eight tent sites and three small RV sites; (360) 288-2525.

Grays Harbor and Long Beach Peninsula

24 Pacific Beach State Park ★ ★ ★ ★

SITES	RESERVATIONS	CONTACT
64 sites, 32 electrical hookups, RVs to 45 feet	(888) 226-7688 or www.parks.wa.gov	Washington State Parks (360) 902-8844
	OPEN	Pacific Beach State Park (360) 276-4297
	Year-round	

Here's more proof that once in a while, things do improve in the historically financially strapped Washington State Parks system. Pacific Beach, formerly a cramped RV parking lot masquerading as a private resort campground, was renovated in 1995 by Washington State Parks. Campsites were reduced by half and spread out a bit, and the

Wide-open spaces are a hallmark of Washington's Pacific coast.

ten-acre park went on the state's reservation system. The result is a much nicer camp-ground that's still less than wild, given its location right in downtown Pacific Beach. Still, beachfront campsites are hard to find in these parts, and this park's 2300 feet of shoreline are home to the only campsites in any Washington State Park that offer a *true* Pacific Ocean view. Some sites are so close to the broad, sandy beach that it's really, really easy to forget you're in a residential area. Needless to say, it's a very popular RV spot. (Tenters, be advised: In this case, that 4-star rating above is offered up mostly for the RV crowd; you'll probably lament the park's lack of site privacy and the strong winds, which might conspire to dispatch your rainfly all the way to Humptulips should you fail to make triple knots. You might prefer Ocean City State Park, below.) The park is always popular, but particularly jammed during spring and fall razor-clam seasons. The beach is a noted kite-fly-atorium. Body surfers should pay heed to warnings of strong undertows here. The park has an RV dump station and coin-op showers.

Getting there: From Hoquiam, proceed 30 miles northwest (15 miles north of Ocean Shores) on State Route 109 to the campground, well-marked in the town of Pacific Beach.

25 Ocean City State Park ★ ★ ★ ★

SITES	RESERVATIONS	CONTACT
181 sites, 29 full hookups, RVs to 55 feet	(888) 226-7688 or www.parks.wa.gov	Washington State Parks (360) 902-8844
	OPEN	Ocean City State Park (360) 289-3553
	Year-round	

Let the rest of the world know if you find a way to keep sand out of the tent. It's never been done at Ocean City State Park, just north of Ocean Shores, one of the area's nicer oceanside campsites. The 131-acre park is rich in pine trees and thick shrubbery, which helps cut the persistent wind somewhat. Most of the campsites, split into three large loops, are quite private, making this the best spot in this area for tenters. Unlike other parks in the area, Ocean City has more than just the ocean competing for attention. You'll find good picnic facilities here, as well as a group camp for twenty to thirty tent campers, three primitive walk-in sites, and a swampy area popular with bird-watchers (the area is part of the Pacific Flyway zone for migratory waterfowl). The dunes here are also a great place to scope out lupines, buttercups, and other wildflowers in the spring. And, of course, the Pacific is always a short walk away. Not surprisingly, this is a popular place, especially during sporadic coast razor-clam seasons. Reservations are advised. The campground has an RV dump station and coin-op showers. The water system was recently upgraded here, but the restroom at the beach entrance was closed in 2008 due to fire damage.

Getting there: From Hoquiam, follow State Route 109 about 16 miles west to State Route 115. Turn left (south) and proceed 1.2 miles to the campground, on the right (about 1.5 miles north of Ocean Shores).

Campsites at Ocean City State Park are suitable for RVs and tents.

26 Twin Harbors State Park ✦ ✦ ✦

SITES	RESERVATIONS	CONTACT
🏕️ 🚐	(888) 226-7688 or www.parks.wa.gov	Washington State Parks (360) 902-8844
303 sites, 49 full hookups, RVs to 35 feet	**OPEN**	Twin Harbors State Park (360) 268-9717
	Year-round	

Twin Harbors, one of Washington's largest camping areas, unfortunately also can be one of its most crowded. Or at least feel like it. Even when it's not full, the campground here feels city-like, due to its large numbers of closely grouped campsites. And the campground is a significant walk from the beach. Another drawback: Twin Harbors is split in two by State Route 105, with half the sites on wooded lands east of the road, and the other half on the windy, more exposed sand dunes on the west side. The utility sites, like many others installed decades ago primarily for the benefit of visiting anglers during Westport's charter-salmon-fishing heyday, are crammed together, chock-a-block, on the east side. It makes you wonder whether the entire scheme should be rethought, and in fact, a comprehensive planning process is underway at this writing. The site, a military training ground in the 1930s, is a prime piece of near-oceanfront property, and it should be treated accordingly by the state.

Two trails lead to the ocean, and a nature trail winds through the sand-dune area between the campground and the beach, where wildflowers can be found in spring and early summer. This is an older park, and many of its facilities are showing their age. Some facilities, such as restrooms, have been upgraded, but there's still a ways to go. Tenters will prefer the westside loops (sites 192–299) for proximity to the beach, or sites 52–85 for more protection from the wind. Four primitive sites for hikers/bikers also are found on the east side of the park.

Although it's not as crowded as it was during Westport's salmon-fishing heydays of decades past, Twin Harbors is often booked during summer months, purely because of its proximity to the beach. Reservations are a good idea. Savvier campers, especially those in RVs, might find nearby Grayland Beach State Park a more pleasant, less cramped camping experience. Twin Harbors has an RV dump station and coin-op showers. Also available is a reservable group campsite for up to sixty people.

Getting there: Twin Harbors is 3 miles south of Westport on SR 105.

27 Grayland Beach State Park ✦✦✦✦✦

SITES	RESERVATIONS	CONTACT
63 sites, 60 full hookups, RVs to 40 feet, 16 yurts	(888) 226-7688 or www.parks.wa.gov	Washington State Parks (360) 902-8844
	OPEN	Grayland Beach State Park (360) 268-9717
	Year-round	

Grayland Beach is the most modern, clean, and comfortable campground in the Grays Harbor area, and one of the nicest camping spots on Washington's coast. Like most other beachfront campgrounds, this one is separated from a sprawling, 7449-foot ocean shoreline by a half mile of sand dunes and scrub grass. But the campsites are more spacious, the facilities more modern, and the entire place much quieter than nearby Twin Harbors, which is closer to the highway. The flat, nicely manicured sites, spread through six compact loops, are well suited to tents, but the plethora of long, level hookup sites makes this a favorite of RVers.

The relatively recent addition of sixteen camping yurts has made the park even more popular. The yurts, sixteen feet in diameter and ten feet high, have hardwood

Coastal razor-clam digging is a family tradition.

floors, electric heat and lights, screen windows, a skylight, and a locking door. They sleep up to six, and if you want to farm all the kids out into one, note that yurt sites also can accommodate an RV in the driveway (for an extra fee). The yurts are reservable year-round and make for a much more pleasant camping experience in winter than a tent would. Note that Grayland Beach has coin-op showers, but no RV dump station. It's a beautiful campground, and people know it: call well in advance for a reservation.

Getting there: Just south of the town of Grayland, follow signs on State Route 105 to the park (about 22 miles south of Aberdeen and 5 miles south of Westport).

28 Cape Disappointment ★ ★ ★ ★ ★ State Park

SITES	RESERVATIONS	CONTACT
⛺ 🚐 🏠 🛖	(888) 226-7688 or www.parks.wa.gov	Washington State Parks (360) 902-8844
240 sites, 83 water/electrical hookups, RVs to 45 feet, 3 cabins, 14 yurts	**OPEN** Year-round	Fort Canby State Park (360) 642-3078

It's big. It's historic. It's downright magnificent. Cape Disappointment (formerly Fort Canby) rarely lives down to its name—which, if you're curious, is the moniker given to this rocky prominence in 1788 by English sea captain John Meares, whose hopes of verifying the existence of the great Columbia River were dashed by his failure to negotiate the perilous river bar and enter the freshwater south of here.

Today, Cape Disappointment is home to one of the West's truly great campgrounds and one of Washington State's most scenic spots—a jewel in every sense, and a favorite of many generations of Northwest families. The park, sprawled out across 1882 acres at the southwestern tip of the state, is marked on the north and south by twin bookend lighthouses, North Head and Cape Disappointment. In between lies a massive campground, a sprawling picnic area, 42,600 feet of deliciously clean, flat ocean beach, miles of trails, and a rock jetty jutting into the roiling surf of the Columbia River bar (good bottom fishing for those who brave the waves). Like most coastal campgrounds, you can't see the beach from the campsites—it's a short walk away on many sandy trails. But the proud, beautiful North Head Lighthouse is (almost) always in view, even when the fog rolls in, and often is open for tours for a small fee.

The scenery is only part of the allure here. This wind-blasted land has a rich history. Lewis and Clark ended their long journey near here in 1805, plunking their sore feet into the icy Pacific. Their journey is well portrayed in the park's Lewis and Clark Interpretive Center, which details the explorers' journey to the Pacific, as well as the history of the two local lighthouses. (When it first blinked on in 1856, the Cape Disappointment lighthouse became the first in the state, and one of the first on the coast. North Head Lighthouse was added in 1898. Standing alone on a high bluff exposed to typically nasty winds, it's one of the most picturesque lights on the Pacific Coast.)

Lupine in bloom

The campground itself has an RV dump station, coin-op showers, and 240 sites spread in small, oceanfront loops through the sand dunes and in a grassy area farther upland, near swampy Lake O'Neil. They rate only about a "medium" on the privacy and modernization scales. But you can't beat the setting. Several loops offer sites close enough to the beach to constantly hear the roar and feel the salty breeze. Five primitive hike/bike sites also are available. Trails lead to the beach, old gun bunkers, local lakes, and elsewhere. Kids love cycling on the miles of roadway.

Cape Disappointment also was the first Washington State Park to feature yurts—frame-and-vinyl tent-like structures with wood floors, sleeping futons, and electric heat and lights. The structures open up camping—and Cape Disappointment—to folks who don't have all the gear. And we like how they're placed in regular camping loops here, not segregated off by themselves. The fourteen yurts, as well as three small cabins, can be reserved in advance. Also reservable are a variety of historic buildings, including the North Head Lighthouse Keeper's Residences. Reservations for all sites here are a must. This campground, the only major public camp on the Long Beach Peninsula, is typically full all summer, and it's one of only a handful in Washington to require reservations year-round.

Getting there: From downtown Ilwaco, follow signs on Robert Gray Drive 3.5 miles south to the park.

Other Grays Harbor/Long Beach Campgrounds

The Ocean Shores/Westport area has many private beachfront campgrounds. For current information, call the Ocean Shores Chamber of Commerce, (800) 76-BEACH or www.oceanshores.org; the Washington Coast Chamber of Commerce (Copalis area), (360) 289-4552 or (800) 286-4552, or www.washingtoncoastchamber.org; or the Westport–Grayland Chamber of Commerce, (360) 268-9422, (800) 345-6223 or www.westportgrayland-chamber.org. The Long Beach Peninsula is dotted by more than a dozen private campgrounds that serve as alternatives to Fort Canby State Park. Contact the Long Beach Peninsula Visitors Bureau, (800) 451-2542 or www.funbeach.com for current information. In the Satsop River drainage, **Schafer State Park** has thirty-two tent sites and ten RV sites with partial hookups; (360) 902-8844. Campers seeking to spread the long commute to the southwest coast over two days should consider an overnight stop at little-known **Rainbow Falls State Park** (forty-three sites and a large group camp; no hookups), 17 miles west of Chehalis on State Route 6; (360) 902-8844. Another stopover option for ocean-bound travelers is **Lake Sylvia State Park** (thirty-five sites with no hookups; two primitive walk-in sites; RVs to 35 feet). It's 1 mile north of the Lake Sylvia exit off State Route 12, near Montesano.

Eastside Olympics and Hood Canal

29 Falls View ★ ★ ★

SITES	RESERVATIONS	CONTACT
🔺 🏕️	None	Olympic National Forest Hood Canal Ranger District Quilcene office (360) 765-2200
	OPEN	
30 sites, no hookups, RVs to 35 feet	May through September	

Falls View is a pleasant Olympic National Forest camp just off U.S. Highway 101 near Quilcene. Tenters especially will appreciate the sites in a nice wooded area with just enough filtered sunshine and the rushing Big Quilcene River in a canyon below to lull you to sleep. A trail leads a short distance to the picturesque 100-foot falls; it's worth the walk. But RVs can squeeze in between the trees here, too. The right loop as you pull in has larger sites, including six pull-throughs, for rigs up to 35 feet. It's an especially lovely spot in May when wild rhododendrons are in bloom beneath the tall conifers. A popular local attraction, the 2835-foot Mount Walker Viewpoint, with sweeping views of Hood Canal, Mounts Baker and Rainier, and many Olympic mountain peaks, is 1.5 miles south of the campground on US 101, then 4 miles up a rough gravel road. Note: At this writing, Falls View has no piped water.

Getting there: Falls View is 3.5 miles south of Quilcene on US 101.

30 Seal Rock ★ ★ ★ ★

SITES	RESERVATIONS	CONTACT
🔺 🏕️	None	Olympic National Forest Hood Canal Ranger District Quilcene office (360) 765-2200
	OPEN	
41 sites, no hookups, RVs to 21 feet	Mid-April through September	

Here's a winner. This charming Forest Service camp on placid Hood Canal is one of our favorite overnight spots. It's close enough to the Seattle metro area to journey to after work and still reach by dark, but just far enough away to hide most of its charms from the inner-city camping hordes. Sadly, the Forest Service abandoned the reservation system here, which briefly made the park a safer bet for those arriving from the other side of Puget Sound. The campground is large, with sites very well spaced in several wooded upland loops. The choice spots are on the lower loop, where a dozen or more are located right above the rocky beach. And brace yourself for a rare treat: level, sand-filled tent pads! The waterfront here is a great place to gather shellfish or just sit in the shade of a madrona and scout for harbor seals and that elusive mammoth called

Mount Rainier, which sometimes pokes its head from the clouds far to the southeast. The campground, which has flush toilets, but no showers or an RV dump station, is fully barrier free, as is a very nicely built boardwalk nature trail on the beach bluff. Keep your eyes peeled for Trident submarines, which mosey over from the nearby Bangor base to make practice runs in ultra-deep Dabob Bay.

Getting there: The campground is on the shore of Hood Canal, about 2 miles north of Brinnon on U.S. Highway 101.

31 Dosewallips State Park ✦ ✦ ✦ ✦

SITES	RESERVATIONS	CONTACT
🏕 🚐	(888) 226-7688 or www.parks.wa.gov	Washington State Parks (360) 902-8844
	OPEN	Dosewallips State Park (360) 796-4415
140 sites, 40 full hookups, RVs to 60 feet	Year-round	

By all means, bring the kids. Dosewallips State Park is the 425-acre toy store of the Washington State Parks system. There's plenty to do here, from hiking and mountain biking to fishing and clamming on 5500 feet of Hood Canal shoreline—or just relaxing on the park's pleasant green lawns. Dosewallips, with waterfront on both sides of the Dosewallips River and a marshy estuary on Hood Canal itself (via a short trail to the other side of U.S. Highway 101), is a big, well-developed park and undoubtedly the most popular camp in Hood Canal country. The 140 sites are spread in a broad, grassy meadow area, a former homestead site, on the west side of US 101, and a beach area on the east side. There's little privacy between them, but the cushy grass feels mighty nice under the backs of tent campers. The second-growth forested upland area offers 4 miles of trails for hiking or cycling, and fishing from the river or Hood Canal is sometimes fruitful. Book early for summer. Dosewallips has an RV dump station and coin-op showers.

Local trivia: Check out the remnants of old spur (logging) railroad tracks on the park's southeast side. Wildlife lovers often spot elk here in the winter.

Getting there: The park is 1 mile south of Brinnon on US 101.

32 Collins ✦ ✦ ✦

SITES	RESERVATIONS	CONTACT
🏕 🚐	None	Olympic National Forest Hood Canal Ranger District Quilcene office (360) 765-2200
	OPEN	
16 sites, no hookups, RVs to 21 feet	Mid-May through September	

Insomniacs should love the east-slope Olympics. Just about anywhere you camp over here, a small-but-powerful white-water stream lies a short distance away—usually close enough to usher you off to slumberland with the roar of cold, clear water in your

Some campsites in Dosewallips State Park give the family room to spread out.

ears. Collins campground lies smack in the center of a river group that lines up, north to south: Dungeness, Big Quilcene, Dosewallips, Duckabush, Hamma Hamma, and Skokomish. Like most campgrounds on these wild mountain streams, this one is small and shady, but it's pretty and worth the drive. Collins, at 200 feet on the Duckabush River, has pit toilets, but you'll need to filter your own water from the stream. (Or, you can get fresh water 1.5 miles to the east, at a hand-pump well at Interrorem Cabin.) Like other National Forest camps in this area, there's no garbage service: You'll need to pack it out. Note that six of the campsites here are for tenters only.

Getting there: From U.S. Highway 101 2 miles south of Brinnon, turn west on Forest Road 2510 (Duckabush River Road) and proceed about 5 miles to the campground, on the left.

33 Hamma Hamma ★ ★ ★ ✦

SITES	RESERVATIONS	CONTACT
	None	Olympic National Forest Hood Canal Ranger District Quilcene office (360) 765-2200
	OPEN	
15 sites, no hookups, RVs to 22 feet	May through September	

Another small, pleasant Forest Service camp with many riverfront sites, Hamma Hamma, elevation 600 feet, lies on the banks of its namesake, one of the eastern Olympic Peninsula's most gorgeous rivers. It's the primary camping spot in the Hamma Hamma drainage. A short, barrier-free interpretive trail begins in the campground. Trout fishing in the river can be fun—even if not always productive—during the summer season. The campground has hand-pumped water (not potable) and pit toilets. (Potable water

The cool, gushing waters of Lena Creek

is available 2 miles west at Lena Creek Campground.) You'll need to pack out your own garbage. Since you asked about the name: It's likely an English bastardization of a Native word Hab'hab, the name of a Twana Indian village at the river mouth in Hood Canal. It's also the name of a reed that grows in the river.

Getting there: From U.S. Highway 101 14 miles north of Hoodsport, turn west on Hamma Hamma River Road (Forest Road 25) and proceed 6.5 miles to the campground, on the left.

34 Lena Creek ✦ ✦ ✦

SITES	RESERVATIONS	CONTACT
🏕️ 🚐	None	Olympic National Forest Hood Canal Ranger District Quilcene office (360) 765-2200
	OPEN	
13 sites, no hookups, RVs to 21 feet	May through September	

This pretty campground on the Hamma Hamma River is similar to Hamma Hamma (above), with one important distinction: It's within a short walk of the starting point of the Lena Lakes Trail, one of the most popular backpacking routes in the Olympics. That brings plenty of lug-soled campers to this quaint little riverfront camp at the confluence of Lena Creek and the Hamma Hamma. Lena Lake is 3.2 miles up the trail, and the more remote Upper Lena is about 3.5 miles—and 2800 vertical feet—beyond. Don't be surprised if you hear the clink of carabiners by firelight at Lena Creek. Lena Lake also is the primary climber's access route to the summit of The Brothers, the prominent twin-peaked, 6866-foot summit visible from much of the Puget Sound region. Lena Creek has well water (not potable) and pit toilets. You'll need to pack out your own garbage.

Getting there: From U.S. Highway 101 14 miles north of Hoodsport, turn west on Hamma Hamma River Road (Forest Road 25) and proceed 8 miles to the campground.

35 Big Creek ✦ ✦ ✦

SITES	RESERVATIONS	CONTACT
	None	Olympic National Forest Hood Canal Ranger District Quilcene office (360) 765-2200
	OPEN	
25 sites, no hookups, RVs to 30 feet	May through September	

An average Forest Service camp in an above-average place (near Lake Cushman), Big Creek usually serves as an alternative to private camps on Lake Cushman or Staircase, all located in more scenic spots near the lake. Still, it's a good location, particularly for those who plan multiple-day hikes in the area. Sites in the (second-growth) forested camp are quite private, a plus for tenters. And two creekside walk-in tent sites are a nice bonus for light travelers. Big Creek is situated amidst several popular hiking trails, Staircase Rapids, the North Fork Skokomish Trail, and Mount Ellinor, to name a few. The latter, accessible from two trailheads nearby, is a popular leeward Olympics day hike that brings the possibility of viewing mountain goats. Nature trails of 1.1 and 4.3 miles also begin in the campground itself. Big Creek has well water and vault toilets. You'll need to pack out your own garbage.

Getting there: From U.S. Highway 101 at Hoodsport, turn west on Lake Cushman Road (State Route 119) and proceed 9 miles to the campground, near the intersection of Lake Cushman Road and Forest Road 24.

36 Staircase ✦ ✦ ✦ ◀

SITES	RESERVATIONS	CONTACT
	None	Olympic National Park (360) 565-3130
	OPEN	Staircase Ranger Station (360) 877-5569
47 sites, no hookups, RVs to 21 feet	Early June through September	

Staircase, located mere yards from the trailhead of the magnificent Staircase Rapids Trail, along the beautiful North Fork Skokomish River, is a clear-cut winner for folks seeking solace on the Peninsula's eastern slopes. The national park campsites are scattered throughout a somewhat dark but peaceful area on the last "wild" stretch of the North Fork Skokomish before it reaches the headwaters of the Lake Cushman reservoir. It's a serene place with moss-draped trees, cool breezes—and hiking to die for. The Staircase Rapids Trail is a delightful 2-mile route that climbs both sides of the river. A log bridge a mile upstream that links the two side trails into one long loop sometimes

The "Staircase" of the North Fork Skokomish River is a short hike from Staircase Rapids Campground.

washes out; if that's the case when you visit, the two now-separate trails are both worth walking up and back, but the Rapids Trail on the near side of the river is more scenic. Both trails are easy enough for the whole family, and you'll pass through a wonderful patch of old-growth forest along the way. Note that the flush toilets once open here are now closed; it's pit toilets only.

Getting there: From U.S. Highway 101 at Hoodsport, turn west on Lake Cushman Road (State Route 119) and proceed 18 miles to the campground, at the end of the road.

37 Potlatch State Park ★ ★ ★

SITES	RESERVATIONS	CONTACT
🏕️ 🚐	None	Washington State Parks (360) 902-8844
	OPEN	Potlatch State Park (360) 877-5361
37 sites, 18 water/electrical hookups, RVs to 60 feet	Year-round	

Potlatch, on the site of an old gathering (or "potlatch") spot for the Skokomish and Twanoh tribes, has one of the more extensive day-use areas on Hood Canal, including a bathhouse, kitchen shelter, boat moorage floats, and a wealth of great picnic space. The 9500-foot expanse of shoreline is a popular scuba-diving, sea-kayaking, clam-digging, and oyster-picking spot. The camping area, located across U.S. Highway 101, is smaller, but sufficient, with thirty-seven spaces—many of which are large, pull-through sites. Potlatch has an RV dump station and coin-op showers.

Local trivia: Like many waterfront state parks, this one got its start as a private development, the Minerva Resort, which took over the prime real estate after an old sawmill burned down here.

Getting there: The park is on US 101, 3 miles south of Hoodsport and 12 miles north of Shelton.

Other Eastside Olympic/Hood Canal Campgrounds

Special notes: **Camp Cushman**, formerly Lake Cushman State Park, is a large (eighty-one-site; 500-acre) campground on ground leased by Tacoma Power that fell from public management to private during a Washington State Parks budget crunch. What a shame. It's still a decent campground—if you don't mind the constant summertime whine of Jet Skis. It's about 7 miles up Lake Cushman Road from U.S. Highway 101 at Hoodsport; (360) 877-6770. Also, **Elkhorn** (twenty sites), a Forest Service campground set in old-growth forest on Dosewallips Road (Forest Road 2610) and **Dosewallips** (thirty sites), an Olympic National Park campground farther up the same road, both remained inaccessible to vehicles when this guide was printed because of a 2002 washout on the access road near milepost 10. It's unclear when or if the road will reopen. Both can be camped by walking or cycling in; Elkhorn is about a mile beyond the washout, Dosewallips, which is near a major Olympic National Park trailhead, is about 5 miles from the washout. Call Hood Canal Ranger District, Quilcene office, (360) 765-2200, for road updates.

Other options: Five miles south of Quilcene, **Rainbow Group Camp** is a pretty spot with nine sites for up to fifty campers; Rainbow Canyon Trailhead and the popular viewpoint at Mount Walker are nearby; (360) 765-2200. On state-owned Olympic foothills between the Hamma Hamma and Skokomish River drainages, campers will find two free, summer-only DNR camps, **Lilliwaup** (six sites) and **Melbourne** (six sites, no piped water). Both are reached via Forest Road 24 (Jorsted Creek Road), which leaves US 101 about 2 miles south of Eldon; (360) 825-1631.

A remote Olympic National Forest site on the South Fork Skokomish, **Brown Creek**, has nineteen sites in old-growth forest, with access to hiking trails. Open year-round with no piped water; nearby **LeBar Horse Camp** has stock facilities, pit toilets, and potable water. Both are found 15 miles northwest of US 101 via the Skokomish Valley Road and Forest Roads 23, 2353, and 2340. In the remote Wynoochee Lake area, north of Montesano, is **Coho** (fifty-six sites, including ten walk-in tent sites), an Olympic National Forest campground with a boat launch and other amenities (beware Jet Ski noise!); (360)-765-2200.

3. NORTH CASCADES

Around the Judd household, it's so much a part of the family camping lore that long ago it became a standing joke.

Every few years or so, without fail, Dad would be shuffling through photos or flipping through slides when up would pop a dog-eared portrait of one of us kids sitting in a river, tripping over a log—or even, in the case of my older sister, doing something unseemly, such as drinking skanky meltwater directly from the spigot of one of those big, steel-sided Coleman coolers. At which point one of us would ask the inevitable: "Where was THAT?"

Dad, without so much as hesitating, would blurt: "Somewhere up above Winthrop."

Enough said.

The North Cascades, up above Winthrop, down below them, indeed, all around them, are like that: Due primarily to its relative lack of people and modernity, it is a place that holds the key to all manner of outdoor memories, most of them grand, all of them burned deep. The rugged, mountainous region below the Canadian border is perhaps the last, best untrammeled part of Washington. It's the sort of place where the overall feeling of "out there" is so striking that the moment continues to glow in memory long after the details of a particular visit are lost. Which is fine, because logistics are largely irrelevant. What you do remember about the North Cascades are all the important things: The unbelievable clarity of a liquid-glass mountain stream. The smell of your first plunge into a forest floor blanketed 3 feet deep with long, soft, pungent pine needles. The adrenaline surge upon hooking a trout longer than your forearm in a mountain stream narrower than a driveway.

Visitors who lug tents and trailers or drive RVs into the North Cascades get to sleep in some of the wildest, least strip-malled places left in the Northwest. Those who go a bit farther—down long, steep Forest Service roads that would make your mother, or anyone else on the passenger side, blanch, or up some of the thousands of miles of winding trails—can frolic in even greater wilderness, some of the most rugged left in the Lower 48.

That "rugged" cuts both ways. It's a boon to wildlife, as evidenced in recent years, when at least one and probably more packs of wild wolves have been observed reinhabiting their former range in the upper Methow Valley. But it can be disastrous for land-use managers, as violent storms occasionally wipe out roads that lead to great campgrounds. Regrettably, a number of North Cascades campgrounds have been lost in recent years, notably Buck Creek and Sulphur Creek along the beautiful Suiattle River, where flooding in 2006 left the access road washed out in three places. At this writing, no plans exist to reopen it. Likewise, the beautiful camping area in Rockport State Park has been closed indefinitely because of concern for falling trees. That, alas, is the price you pay for wild.

The North Cascades are one grand entity comprising many select pieces: The sprawling North Cascades National Park complex includes a national park, two national recreation areas, and two federal wildernesses. The curvy, potholed (but nonetheless charismatic) Mountain Loop Highway, which serves up wilderness—real wilderness—right in the backyards of millions of Puget Sound residents. Mount Baker, Mount Shuksan—and the unforgettable Heather Meadows area, one of the greatest places on planet Earth that you can drive to in a car. And, of course, Washington's own northern miracle, the North Cascades Highway, along with the stunningly beautiful Methow River Valley, which sips up clear water from some of the finest highlands imaginable up above Winthrop—then spits it out for a roller-coaster downhill river ride all the way to the Columbia River.

Unless you're blindsided by nasty weather—not unlikely, most of the year—it's tough to go wrong camping in the North Cascades. We can only hope that a few decades from now you can relax at home with your own grandkids, fishhook scars, tall tales, warm smiles, and faraway looks at the mere mention of the place—you know the place, what was that place?

Up above Winthrop. It's a pretty good place to pitch a tent. And an even better place to lock away in your soul.

Opposite: *Mount Shuksan in full summertime splendor*

Nooksack Falls is a worthy stop along the Mount Baker Highway.

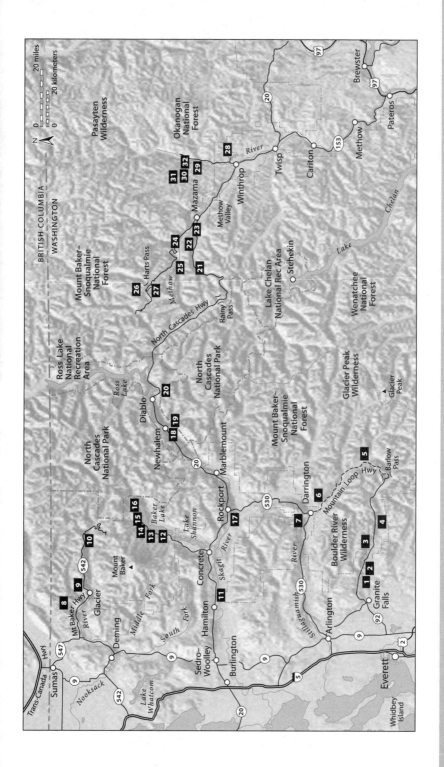

Mountain Loop Highway and Darrington

1 Turlo ★ ★ ★

SITES	RESERVATIONS	CONTACT
🏕️ 🚻🚐	(877) 444-6777 or www.recreation.gov	Mount Baker–Snoqualmie National Forest Darrington Ranger District (360) 436-1155
	OPEN	
19 sites, no hookups, RVs to 40 feet	Late May through September	

The first of a string of a dozen Forest Service camps on the beautiful Mountain Loop Highway—reopened for its full length between Granite Falls and Darrington in 2007, after serious storm damage in 2006—Turlo is on the south side of the road near the Verlot Public Service Center. Like most camps in this area, it's set on the crystal waters of the South Fork Stillaguamish River, with good access to a wealth of local hiking trails. The shady campground, set beneath thick firs and western red cedars, has pit toilets, and firewood usually can be purchased from the host. If you're after the choicest places to light up your firelog, set your eyes on sites 3, 12, 14, 15, 17, and 18. They're all on or near the river. If you're in a group with more than one rig, plan on heading up the road to Verlot; Turlo lacks extra-wide or multiple-family spots. The campground has three barrier-free sites (3, 4, and 5), and all sites have tent pads. Twelve sites are reservable; the others first-come, first-served.

Getting there: From Granite Falls, follow the Mountain Loop Highway 10.8 miles east to the campground, across the highway and a short distance west of the Verlot Public Service Center.

2 Verlot ★ ★ ★

SITES	RESERVATIONS	CONTACT
🏕️ 🚻🚐	(877) 444-6777 or www.recreation.gov	Mount Baker–Snoqualmie National Forest Darrington Ranger District (360) 436-1155
	OPEN	
25 sites, no hookups, RVs to 40 feet	Mid-May through September	

Verlot, just a short waddle up the road from Turlo, is a popular summer hangout for foot soldiers who've either just been, or soon will go, up the Lake 22 and Mount Pilchuck Trails—two of the most popular mountain day hikes within easy reach of the greater Puget Sound area. It's a pleasant campground, and if you want to blast off that trail dust, you'll have both nearby Benson Creek and the icy South Fork Stillaguamish, which gurgles nearby (decent trout and steelhead fishing in season). Half the sites in the easternmost of Verlot's two camping loops are on the river; several on the western loop are on either the river or Benson Creek, with two (sites 2 and 3) fronting on both. Campers in groups should note that Verlot has many tent sites with contiguous parking spaces; they're convenient for groups of campers with two or three cars. More than half the sites in the campground have tent pads. If you're torn between this camp and nearby Turlo, note that this one adds a slight touch of civilization: flush toilets. Verlot is also much sunnier, with a far thinner forest canopy. Half the sites here are reservable, and three (10, 11, and 25) are barrier free.

Getting there: From Granite Falls, follow the Mountain Loop Highway about 11 miles east to the campground, across the road and a short distance east of the Verlot Public Service Center.

3 Gold Basin ★ ★ ★ ◂

SITES	RESERVATIONS	CONTACT
92 sites, no hookups, RVs to 31 feet	(877) 444-6777 or www.recreation.gov	Mount Baker–Snoqualmie National Forest Darrington Ranger District (360) 436-1155
	OPEN	
	Mid-May through September	

Gold Basin is by far the most powerful camping magnet in the Mountain Loop corridor, largely because of its unusual size for a Forest Service camp in a relatively remote location. The sites are sprinkled in several loops near the South Fork Stillaguamish River, a

The Big Four Ice Caves, a popular Mountain Loop attraction, are worth photographing, but shouldn't be entered.

Red-crested mergansers cut their way through still water.

great water play and fishing venue. Although it lacks hookups, the campground also is by far the most RV friendly of all the public campgrounds in this area, with paved sites and more elbow room—not to mention coin-op showers! Expect crowds, and don't hesitate to take advantage of the reservation system, which allows about 60 percent of the sites to be booked well in advance. Gold Basin has both pit and flush toilets. A group camp at the west end of the complex can accommodate up to fifty people. Seventeen of the sites are barrier free, and sites 12–16 and 47–51 are walk-in sites for tents only (most of the walk-in sites are near the river and rank among the best in the campground). About half the sites here are equipped with tent pads. The kids will like the large, open playfield, suitable for Frisbee tossing and sister chasing. If you get bored with the campfire, take a stroll across the highway to Gold Basin Pond, a salmon-fry viewing area with a half-mile-long, barrier-free boardwalk.

Getting there: From Granite Falls, follow the Mountain Loop Highway 13.4 miles (2.4 miles east of the Verlot Public Service Center) to the campground, on the left (north) side of the highway.

4 Red Bridge ★★★↩

SITES	RESERVATIONS	CONTACT
15 sites, no hookups, RVs to 31 feet	(877) 444-6777 or www.recreation.gov	Mount Baker–Snoqualmie National Forest Darrington Ranger District (360) 436-1155
	OPEN	
	Late May through mid-September	

Another quite pretty but primitive South Fork Stillaguamish River camp, Red Bridge is situated near the river's confluence with Mahardy Creek. The prime sites, numbers

5–15, all front on the South Fork Stilly's broad river bar. The campground's elevation (about 1300 feet) often causes it to open a bit later and close earlier than other, lower-elevation camps on the Mountain Loop. It's another campground preferred by hikers; sites have good privacy, and all but one (number 13, of course!) are equipped with tent pads. Red Bridge has pit toilets and no piped water or showers. One site (number 4) is a double-sized, "family" spot. Ten of the fifteen sites here can be booked in advance.

Getting there: From Granite Falls, follow the Mountain Loop Highway about 18 miles east (7.1 miles east of Verlot Public Service Center) to the campground, on the right (south) side of the highway.

5 Bedal ★ ★ ◀

SITES	RESERVATIONS	CONTACT
21 sites, no hookups, RVs to 31 feet	(877) 444-6777 or www.recreation.gov	Mount Baker–Snoqualmie National Forest Darrington Ranger District (360) 436-1155
	OPEN	
	Late May to early September	

Explorers who venture beyond Barlow Pass onto the north–south (unpaved) section of the Mountain Loop Highway (properly known as Forest Service Road 20) will happen upon Bedal, an isolated, often chilly site at the confluence of the north and south forks of the scenic Sauk River. The campground is shady, quiet, and remote, set mostly in old-growth forest. Bring plenty of bug dope and a back-to-nature ethic: Bedal has pit toilets and no piped water or showers. It's very quiet here (aside from the pleasant river noise) and well situated for tenters. Sites are quite private; every one has its own tent pad, and more than half can be reserved in advance. Six sites are barrier free. A notable campground attraction: A large Adirondack shelter in site 18, built entirely of old-growth timber. North Fork Sauk Falls, a true gusher, is only a mile away and worth a visit.

Getting there: From Darrington, drive about 19 miles southeast on Forest Road 20 (Mountain Loop Highway). From Granite Falls, drive 31.5 miles east to Barlow Pass, then about 6.5 miles north on Forest Road 20.

6 Clear Creek ★ ★

SITES	RESERVATIONS	CONTACT
13 sites, no hookups, RVs to 25 feet	(877) 444-6777 or www.recreation.gov	Mount Baker–Snoqualmie National Forest Darrington Ranger District (360) 436-1155
	OPEN	
	Mid-May to September	

It really is. The creek, we mean. The clear waters of Clear Creek meet the equally glassy flow of the beautiful Sauk River near Clear Creek Campground, a rustic site near

Darrington, at the northern outlet of the Mountain Loop Highway. It's a pretty area in the summer, but facilities are painfully sparse—and, unfortunately, often unkempt, thanks to the day-tripping partiers who seem to trash the place occasionally. Clear Creek has pit toilets and no piped water or showers. (It also offers little privacy between sites—"a more open, communal" camping experience, sayeth the Forest Service.) All the sites have tent pads, two (12 and 13) are located close to the river, and two (8 and 9) are barrier free. The Forest Service is now collecting fees at this formerly free campground—a questionable move, in our opinion, until the place is spruced up. If you do wind up camping here, though, a wonderful diversion is within walking distance: The Old Sauk River Trail, a great, 6-mile day hike through the forest along the river. It begins a short distance to the south.

Getting there: From Darrington, drive about 3.5 miles south on Forest Road 20 (Mountain Loop Highway) to the campground, on the left (east) side of the highway.

7 Squire Creek County Park ★ ★ ★ ◀

SITES	RESERVATIONS	CONTACT
🏕 🚐	None	Snohomish County Parks (425) 388-6600 or
	OPEN	Squire Creek County Park
33 sites, no hookups, RVs to 25 feet	Year-round	(360) 436-1283

Hankering to explore the wilds of the Mountain Loop Highway or the nearby Glacier Peak Wilderness, but can't stomach the thought of parking your business end on a cold pit toilet seat? Get thee to Squire Creek, a Darrington-area park set in old-growth forest and promoting a "family" feel. This fifty-three-acre Snohomish County Park on the outskirts of Darrington offers nicely spaced campsites, two large picnic shelters, an RV dump station, and some nice local hiking trails. Many of the sites are pull-throughs—a bonus to RVers—and several are barrier free. The park is also close enough to Darrington (3 miles) to pick up supplies by foot or bicycle. Squire Creek, surprisingly enough, flows nearby, and you'll love the nearby views of White Horse Mountain, which looms over Darrington like a snowcapped guardian angel. Expect the campground to fill up on summer weekends—particularly in July, when the bluegrass festival is running at full steam. Fortunately, park managers say a reservations system is coming to Squire Creek in the near future. Call to see if it's active before you head for the park. Note to RVers: If you must have hookups and really want to stay in this area, consider Howard Miller Steelhead Park, about 19 miles north of Darrington in Rockport (see below).

Getting there: The campground is on the left (north) side of State Route 530, three miles west of Darrington; and 26 miles east of the SR 530/Interstate 5 junction near Arlington.

Other Mountain Loop Highway/Darrington Campgrounds

Two fine Forest Service campgrounds in the Darrington area, **Buck Creek** (twenty-six sites) and **Sulphur Creek** (twenty sites), remained inaccessible when this guide went

Whitehorse Mountain guards the north end of the Mountain Loop Highway near Darrington.

to press due to heavy flood damage on the Suiattle River Road (Forest Road 26). (**Update:** In spring 2011, the Forest Service announced plans to reopen Buck Creek by summer 2012, and Sulphur Creek the following year.) Be sure to call the Darrington Ranger District, (360) 436-1155, for updates before embarking.

Seven Forest Service group camps are nicely located near the South Fork Stillaguamish River, along the Mountain Loop Highway, with varying levels of services: **Wiley Creek** (tent/trailer facilities for up to 100 campers in two separate group sites, equipped with four shelters and a combination of tent/trailer spaces, 4 miles east of the Verlot Public Service Center); **Esswine** (facilities for twenty-five campers, 5.2 miles east of the Verlot Public Service Center); **Boardman Creek** (facilities for twenty to thirty campers near the South Fork Stillaguamish, 5.6 miles east of the Verlot Public Service Center); **Tulalip Millsite** (facilities for sixty campers, 8.2 miles east of the Verlot Public Service Center); **Marten Creek** (tent-camping facilities for twenty-five campers, 9.2 miles east of the Verlot Public Service Center); **Coal Creek Bar** (facilities for twenty-five campers near the South Fork Stillaguamish, 12 miles east of the Verlot Public Service Center); and **Beaver Creek** (facilities for twenty-five campers near the South Fork Stillaguamish), views of Big Four Mountain, 13 miles east of the Verlot Public Service Center. All six campgrounds must be reserved in advance, with fees at this writing between $60 and $75 per night; all have pit toilets and no piped water or showers. For reservations and information, contact the Mount Baker–Snoqualmie National Forest's Darrington Ranger District; (360) 436-1155.

This way, that way, or the other way.

The Department of Natural Resources oversees five small, free, primitive camp-grounds in the Mountain Loop corridor. Four are hike-in, summer-only sites from the Ashland Lake Trailhead, reached via Forest Service roads 4020 and 4021. They are **Beaver Plant Lake** (six sites, 2.1 miles from the trailhead); **Lower Ashland Lake** (six sites, 2.5 miles); **Upper Ashland Lake** (six sites, 3 miles); and **Twin Falls Lake** (five sites, 4.5 miles). Another remote DNR site, **William C. Dearinger** (twelve sites, no piped water) is located on the south bank of the Suiattle River, northeast of Darrington on SW-D-5400 Road. Contact the DNR's Sedro-Woolley office; (360) 856-3500.

Finally, while it's located a bit west of this area's target boundaries, another Snohomish County Park, **River Meadows**, is one to put on your long-range planning list. The 150-acre site on Jordan Road near Arlington offers tent and now RV camp-ing along the banks of the Stillaguamish. From State Route 530 near Arlington, turn right onto Arlington Heights Road, proceed 2 miles, bear right onto Jordan Road and continue about 3 miles to the park entrance on the right. Contact Snohomish County Parks, (425) 388-6600.

Mount Baker Highway and Baker Lake

8 Silver Lake Park ★ ★ ★ ★

SITES	RESERVATIONS	CONTACT
 89 sites, 53 water/electrical hookups, RVs to any length	(360) 599-2776	Whatcom County Parks (360) 733-2900 or www.co.whatcom.wa.us/parks/
	OPEN	
	Year-round; limited water in winter	Silver Lake Park (360) 599-2776

Not many out-of-towners are aware of 411-acre Silver Lake Park, a wonderful Whatcom County facility at the site of a former private resort and early 1900s homestead. The park, north of Maple Falls along the Mount Baker Highway, is set on a quiet, 180-acre mountain lake with a lot of green space. The campground includes a pleasant tent area and fifty-three RV sites, which can be reserved in bunches for group outings. Fishing, swimming, and canoeing on the calm lake are always fun, and rental pedal boats, fishing boats, and canoes are available. The lake holds rainbow and cutthroat trout, largemouth bass, bullheads, and sculpin.

Silver Lake Park is a popular fishing and boating venue.

Silver Lake Park also is home to a small museum; picturesque lakefront rental cabins; several large kitchen shelters; a day-use lodge with a dining room, which can be rented for meetings or retreats; and a horse camp (twenty-eight sites), across the highway and about a quarter-mile north. The Horse Camp, which has extensive stables and other horse facilities as well as RV hookups, is available (by reservation in summer) to non-horse campers, as well; many RVers prefer it because sites are more open to the sun than those in the heavily forested main campground.

Wherever you choose to park, kids will love the swimming beach and large playground in the main camp's day-use area—about a ten-minute walk from the camping loops. Note that Whatcom County residents get a price break as well as first dibs each year on reservations, which don't open up to others until April. The campground can feel pretty busy when it's full in the summer, but it's a downright peaceful place in the spring or fall, with only a highly vocal pack of local coyotes conspiring to keep you up at night.

Getting there: From Bellingham, drive about 25 miles east on Mount Baker Highway (State Route 542) to Maple Falls. Turn left (north) on Silver Lake Road and follow signs about 3 miles to the park entrance, on the right.

A small tarn awaits day hikers near Artist Point, at the end of the Mount Baker Highway.

9 Douglas Fir ★★★◀

SITES	RESERVATIONS	CONTACT
🏕 🚐	(877) 444-6777 or www.recreation.gov	Mount Baker–Snoqualmie National Forest
	OPEN	Mount Baker Ranger District (360) 856-5700
29 sites, no hookups, RVs to 26 feet	Mid-May through September	

Douglas Fir and Silver Fir, the Mount Baker Highway's two primary camping spots, are lovely firs, indeed. Douglas, the first encountered on the trek up the Mount Baker Highway (a designated National Scenic Byway), is a gorgeous, shady spot on the North Fork Nooksack, with thirty sites sprinkled among—you guessed it. The facilities are well-used, standard Forest Service issue: pit toilets, piped water. Three of the sites are barrier free; sites 2, 4, 5, 7, 9, and 12 are riverfront. More than half the sites here now have tent pads; those that do not are plenty flat and open enough for tenters. Look for your host in site 18. This isn't the most private campground in the world, with little underbrush to separate many of the sites. But the constant gurgling of the nearby North Fork Nooksack has lulled many a worn-out hiker, angler, photographer, and unabashed camper to sleep over the years. An added touch is a small riverfront picnic shelter with an outdoor kitchen (also reservable). All in all, a very nice spot. Note: Stop in at the (Forest Service) Glacier Public Service Center (summers only) near the campground. It's the best one-stop information source for trail and backcountry information in the region.

Getting there: From Bellingham, drive about 33 miles east on Mount Baker Highway (State Route 542) to the town of Glacier. Continue 2 miles east to the campground, on the left, near milepost 36.

10 Silver Fir ★★★★◀

SITES	RESERVATIONS	CONTACT
🏕 🚐	(877) 444-6777 or www.recreation.gov	Mount Baker–Snoqualmie National Forest
	OPEN	Mount Baker Ranger District (360) 856-5700
20 sites, no hookups, RVs to 31 feet	Mid-June to mid-September	

This is our favorite campground hideaway on the way to Mount Baker, and one of our favorites in all the lands of the sprawling Mount Baker–Snoqualmie National Forest. Silver Fir is tucked into a bend in the road, and a bend in the beautiful North Fork Nooksack River, just before both get steep and serious on their way up to a drop-dead gorgeous view at Artist Point, between Mounts Baker and Shuksan. The facilities are far from grand—pit toilets—but about half of the twenty spaces here are places you'll plunk your tent and not want to leave for a while. Fortunately, thirteen sites can be reserved, so you don't drive all the way up here and get shut out.

Particulars: Sites 2–4 are barrier free, and site 1 is a double site, a good choice for families or small groups with two rigs. Most sites are very private—a delight for tenters—and open onto the bouldered bank of the North Fork Nooksack, a stream to write home about. Although it's close to the Mount Baker Highway, the campground is intimate and extremely peaceful, especially in early fall, just before winter closing time. It's a great base from which to explore the wealth of hiking and outdoor recreation choices in the Nooksack drainage and the Artist Point/Heather Meadows area at the end of Mount Baker Highway. A winner.

Getting there: From Bellingham, drive about 33 miles east on Mount Baker Highway (State Route 542) to the town of Glacier. Proceed an additional 14 miles east to the campground, on the right just beyond the North Fork Nooksack River bridge.

11 Rasar State Park ★ ★ ★ ★

SITES	RESERVATIONS	CONTACT
🏕️ 🚐 49 sites, 20 water/electrical hookups, RVs to 40 feet	(877) 444-6777 or www.recreation.gov	Washington State Parks (360) 902-8844
	OPEN Year-round, weather permitting	Rasar State Park (360) 826-3942

Washington State Parks, budget-cut to the point of embarrassment throughout the '90s and early '00s by the recreational geniuses in the Washington State Legislature (write them, please), doesn't get a chance to open a new campground very often. Park officials took full advantage of the rare opportunity with Rasar, a sprawling, quiet, Skagit River park that opened in the late '90s to rave reviews from tenters and RVers seeking solace in the woods without venturing too far from the Puget Sound metro area. Campsites—flat, paved, and tidy—are nicely laid out in salal, huckleberry, and Oregon grape underbrush beneath hemlocks and firs. They come in the full range: Long pull-throughs with hookups for twenty RVs; eight small, private, walk-in sites for tenters; and three "primitive" sites for hikers and cyclists. The walk-ins include a pair of Adirondack shelters, each of which can sleep four people.

Facilities are as new as you'll find in a Washington State Park, and the nearby day-use area, complete with picnic and playground facilities, is a hit with kids and parents. The covered picnic shelter and stove can be reserved in advance at the number above, as can two group camp areas across the road from the main campground. Short trails lead from the day-use area across a sprawling hay field, where nice views of North Cascade peaks are seen to the east. About a half mile from the day-use area, trails open onto the slow-rolling Skagit River—often full to its banks and then some in the winter or spring snowmelt seasons. A flat sandbar here (large or small, depending on river flows) provides river access for anglers, sunbathers, or swimmers. (Note, however, that the current is extremely strong here; it's probably not a good place to take a dip anywhere beyond ankle deep.) In the winter, this would be a good place to watch eagles feeding on spawning chum salmon. All in all, it's quite a pleasant park, well worth a weekend trip or stopover

The mighty Skagit River flows near Rasar State Park along Highway 20.

on your State Route 20 vacation. And it is now on the state reservation system.

Getting there: From Burlington, drive 19 miles east on SR 20 to Lusk Road. Turn right (south) and proceed less than a mile to a stop sign at Cape Horn Road. Turn left and proceed about a mile to the park entrance.

12 Horseshoe Cove ★ ★ ★ ◀

SITES	RESERVATIONS	CONTACT
🏕 🚐	(877) 444-6777 or www.recreation.gov	Mount Baker–Snoqualmie National Forest Mount Baker Ranger District (360) 856-5700
	OPEN	
34 sites, no hookups, RVs to 34 feet	Mid-May through September; no services in winter	

Years ago, the people who run Puget Sound Energy (most of us locals grew up knowing it as Puget Power) forever changed the face of the lands south of Mount Baker by damming the Baker River, a northern tributary of the mighty Skagit, for hydropower purposes. The result—good, bad, or indifferent—is the Baker Lake National Recreation Area, a sprawling lowland region of mostly second-growth forest and, thanks to the twin concrete dams here, a pair of reservoirs, known as Lake Shannon (to the south) and Baker Lake (to the north). Baker Lake is prized for sport fishing (trout, kokanee, Dolly Varden, cutthroat trout); monster views of the south face of 10,778-foot Mount Baker; and campgrounds, half a dozen of which ring the lakeshore. The first encountered on a journey here is Horseshoe Cove, a tidy, shady, very pleasant spot in a mixed fir and alder forest just above the Upper Baker Dam. The sites (those in the higher number range are pull-throughs) are fairly closely packed but still offer decent privacy for tenters—arguably the best of any of the established Forest Service camps in the Baker Lake region. The campground has the usual Forest Service amenities (pit toilets, no showers)—but some bonuses, including for-sale firewood and, during our last visit, rental canoes available from the campground host. A swimming beach and boat launch are nearby—very convenient for boaters, canoeists, swimmers, and, regrettably, Jet Ski jockeys, who tend to congregate here in the summer. This is a popular spot; use the reservation system. Note: The campground also has three group sites for up to twenty-five people each; they must be reserved in advance. Sites 8, 10, and 11 and all three group sites are barrier free.

Getting there: From Interstate 5 at Burlington, follow North Cascades Highway (State Route 20) east 22.5 miles to Baker Lake Road (just west of Birdsview). Turn left (north) and proceed 14.8 miles to Forest Road 1118. Turn east (right) and proceed 2 miles to the campground.

BEST FALL COLOR CAMPS

1. Upper and Lower Bumping Lake, Gifford Pinchot National Forest
Few places in the Evergreen State are more glorious in October than Bumping Lake, where brilliant yellow larch, birch, and other trees stand out against clear, blue mountain skies in the scenic Gifford Pinchot National Forest. See p. 197.

2. Pearrygin Lake State Park, Winthrop
This spacious park near Winthrop sits in the center of fall-color central, the Methow Valley, but trees inside the park present their own fall spectacular. See p. 143.

3. Newhalem, North Cascades National Park
There's not much fall color in the camp itself. But walk or drive a short distance to the hillsides around the town of Newhalem and prepare to be wowed. See p. 134.

4. Johnny Creek, Icicle River
Johnny Creek is one of a half dozen campgrounds on the Icicle River near Leavenworth, where fall reds and yellows on the sparkling clear waters are a photographer's dream. See p. 162.

5. Hells Crossing, Chinook Pass Highway
We love the way the yellows and reds and oranges all fade into one delicious mélange along the waters of the American River. See p. 194.

13 Boulder Creek ★ ★ ◄

SITES	RESERVATIONS	CONTACT
🏕️ 🚐	(877) 444-6777 or www.recreation.gov	Mount Baker–Snoqualmie National Forest
	OPEN	Mount Baker Ranger District (360) 856-5700
8 sites, no hookups, RVs to 16 feet	Mid-May through September	

Boulder Creek, the smallest of the Forest Service camps around Baker Lake, isn't on the shoreline. It's about a mile west, set on the banks of Boulder Creek, just off Baker Lake Road. The campground is small and facilities limited (pit toilets, no piped water or showers). But it's not at all unpleasant, offering two large group sites (one, for up to twenty-five people, reservable), some peace and quiet (assuming you don't mind the sound of a gurgling, glacier-fed stream), and views of the mountain from some spaces.

Getting there: From Interstate 5 at Burlington, follow North Cascades Highway (State Route 20) east 22.5 miles to Baker Lake Road (just west of Birdsview). Turn left (north) and proceed 17.5 miles to the campground.

14 Panorama Point ★ ★ ★ ★

SITES	RESERVATIONS	CONTACT
🏕️ 🚐	(877) 444-6777 or www.recreation.gov	Mount Baker–Snoqualmie National Forest
	OPEN	Mount Baker Ranger District (360) 856-5700
16 sites, no hookups, RVs to 24 feet	Late May to early September	

If you have but one night to spend and are fortunate enough to grab an empty spot, Panorama Point is the place to stay at Baker Lake. One of the more picturesque Forest Service camps in the region, the aptly named park sits on a triangular point jutting into the heart of Baker Lake Reservoir, with some sites right on the lakeshore. Nine of the sites can be reserved; in midsummer, reservations are a good idea. A boat launch and swimming area are nearby. The campground, at about 800 feet in elevation, is densely forested and cool to the point of cold for much of the season. It's equipped with well water and pit toilets; no showers. Sites 10 and 13 are barrier free and equipped with tent pads; tent pads are also found at sites 12 and 15. This is a grand base camp for hiking in the area. Popular trails on the south slopes of Mount Baker, such as the Elbow Lake, Park Butte/Railroad Grade, and Mazama Park/Cathedral Pass trails, are a short drive away. Fishing, for kokanee salmon, rainbow and cutthroat trout, and Dolly Varden, often is productive in the lake. Canoeists can paddle across the deep, clear reservoir and embark on a charming hike on the East Bank Baker Lake Trail and can even add an overnight stop at Maple Grove Campground, on the lake's eastern shore. But beware the wakes thrown by Jet Skiers much of the summer. If you should run out of wieners, Baker Lake Resort, a (cluttered) private campground and store, is about a mile up the road.

Getting there: From Interstate 5 at Burlington, follow North Cascades Highway (State Route 20) east 22.5 miles to Baker Lake Road (just west of Birdsview). Turn left (north) and proceed 18.7 miles to the turnoff for the campground, on the right.

15 Park Creek ✦ ✦ ◀

SITES	RESERVATIONS	CONTACT
🏕️ 🚐	(877) 444-6777 or www.recreation.gov	Mount Baker–Snoqualmie National Forest
	OPEN	Mount Baker Ranger District (360) 856-5700
12 sites, no hookups, RVs to 22 feet	Late May through September	

Park Creek is where many of us have, at least once, roughed it (pit toilets, no piped water) after getting shut out of larger, better-developed campgrounds farther south on Baker Lake. But some people reserve sites at this small, heavily wooded camp on purpose now, because it's a short distance away from the lake and all its accompanying hubbub. Sites 1, 2, 3, and 5 are near Park Creek and pleasant enough in good weather. It's pretty dark in here, though; not a place you'd like to stay forever unless you're hiding from something or someone.

Getting there: From Interstate 5 at Burlington, follow North Cascades Highway (State Route 20) east 22.5 miles to Baker Lake Road (just west of Birdsview). Turn left (north) and drive 19.5 miles to Forest Road 1144. Turn left (west) and proceed a short distance to the campground.

16 Shannon Creek ✦ ✦

SITES	RESERVATIONS	CONTACT
🏕️ 🚐	(877) 444-6777 or www.recreation.gov	Mount Baker–Snoqualmie National Forest
	OPEN	Mount Baker Ranger District (360) 856-5700
20 sites, no hookups, RVs to 25 feet	Late May to mid-September	

It's a long ways out here, and not all that nicely developed, but Shannon Creek is another good alternative for Baker Lake revelers, particularly those pulling boat trailers. The rustic campground, on the west shore of the lake, is adjacent to a boat launch and swimming area. Although two sites (19 and 20) are walk-in camps for tenters, the campground overall is not a great place for tents, with gravelly surfaces and little privacy between sites. Campers in small RVs might find it suitable, however. The campground is equipped with pit toilets and piped water, but no showers.

Getting there: From Interstate 5 at Burlington, follow North Cascades Highway (State Route 20) east 22.5 miles to Baker Lake Road (just west of Birdsview). Turn left (north) and drive 22.8 miles to the campground entrance, on the right.

Opposite: Baker Lake Reservoir, on the mountain's south side, is home to a wide variety of campgrounds.

Other Mount Baker/Baker Lake Campgrounds

In the Mount Baker Highway corridor, **Excelsior Group Camp**, 6.5 miles east of Glacier on State Route 542, has pit toilets, no piped water, and two group sites accommodating fifty to seventy-five campers each; reservations: Mount Baker Ranger District, (360) 856-5700. Farther up the Nooksack drainage, **Hannegan** is a backcountry Forest Service campground that doubles as a major trailhead for treks into the western portion of North Cascades National Park. The camp is at the end of Forest Road 32; it has one pit toilet and no piped water. Call the Mount Baker Ranger District, (360) 856-5700, or Glacier Public Service Center (summers only), (360) 599-2714.

In the Baker Lake area, **Bayview Group Camps** north and south offer facilities for tent and RV camping for up to twenty-five campers each; they're reservable and have pit toilets, but no piped water. Call the Mount Baker Ranger District, (360) 856-5700, for information. Another option is **Grandy Lake Park**, a small Skagit County Park with rustic campsites on a lily-pad-covered lake set next to Baker Lake Road, a few miles north of State Route 20. The camp, open May to October, has about a dozen sites, mostly flat and graveled, set amidst a stand of alder and maple trees. A gravel boat launch with fishing access is found at the lakeshore. Contact Skagit County Parks, (360) 336-9414. Across the water, **Maple Grove**, about midway up Baker Lake on the east shore, is a paddle- or walk-in site along the newly expanded East Bank Baker Lake Trail. The campground, 4 miles from the southern East Bank Trailhead, has six wooded sites and no other facilities, but it's free. Call the Mount Baker Ranger District, (360) 856-5700. A prominent private campground in the area is **Kulshan**, operated by Puget Sound Energy. The camp has 116 sites, some with water and sewer hookups (no power). Call (360) 853-8341. Farther up the valley, the energy company also maintains **Baker Lake Resort**, which has a campground and cabins; (888) 711-3033.

North Cascades Highway and National Park

17 Howard Miller Steelhead Park ★ ★ ★

SITES	RESERVATIONS	CONTACT
🏕️ 🚐	(360) 853-8808	Howard Miller Steelhead Park (360) 853-8808
64 sites, 51 full or partial hookups, RVs to any length	**OPEN** Year-round	

Go figure. This is the only campground in the North Cascades—and probably one of very few in the state—that's more crowded in winter than summer. The lure won't be obvious by glancing at the frosty ground or frozen mud puddles. Peer down the banks of the Skagit River, however, and all becomes clear: spawning chum salmon, splashing near shore. And hundreds of bald eagles swooping after them. The Skagit, particularly the stretch between Rockport and Marblemount, is home to one of the largest wintering bald eagle populations in the Lower 48. Howard Miller Steelhead Park, a Skagit County campground and gathering spot near the riverbank, is as good a place as any to see them. The Forest Service operates a manned lookout site near here, and many bird clubs and other eagle fans congregate at the campground for float trips or delightfully simple, crisp days standing along the road with binoculars. Bird-watching activity, which begins in December, peaks around the first week of February, when Rockport hosts its annual Bald Eagle Festival. But the campground gets plenty of use by anglers, as well. The Skagit is a notable steelhead stream, and the park is named for an avid angler and former Skagit County commissioner who not only supported public fishing access on the river, but did something about it, acquiring these formerly private lands for the county. The campground is well-equipped for winter or any season, with RV hookups, flush toilets, showers, a covered picnic area, a playground, Adirondack shelters (each sleeping up to eight campers), an RV dump, and other niceties. Reservations can be made up to ten months in advance. Note: This is the only overnight campground in the immediate vicinity of the bald-eagle area with the recent closure of Rockport State Park to camping. State officials say the campground there, set in a beautiful old-growth forest, is too dangerous because of potential tree falls.

Getting there: From the State Route 20/State Route 530 junction at Rockport, turn south on SR 530 and proceed a short distance to the campground, on the right.

Opposite: *Bald eagles old and young can be seen on the Skagit and Nooksack rivers in the winter.*

18 Goodell Creek ★ ★ ◄

SITES	RESERVATIONS	CONTACT
🏕 🚐	None	North Cascades National Park Headquarters Sedro-Woolley (360) 854-7200
	OPEN	
21 sites, no hookups, RVs to 22 feet	Year-round; no services in winter	

This small, rustic site along the Upper Skagit River near the Seattle City Light village of Newhalem, elevation 500 feet, is the first North Cascades National Park campground encountered as you head east along the North Cascades Highway (for more on the National Park, see Colonial Creek, below). The facilities are sparse (pit toilets, gravel roads and sites), but it's a nice spot that also serves as a popular launch spot for Skagit River rafters. No piped water or other services are available here in the winter months, but there are no fees, either. Nearby is the small, rustic Goodell Creek Group Camp, available only by reservation; (877) 444-6677 or www.recreation.gov.

Getting there: Watch for signs near milepost 119 on the North Cascades Highway (State Route 20), just west of Newhalem.

19 Newhalem Creek ★ ★ ★ ★

SITES	RESERVATIONS	CONTACT
🏕 🚐	None	North Cascades National Park Headquarters Sedro-Woolley (360) 854-7200
	OPEN	
111 sites, no hookups, RVs to 40 feet	Mid-May to mid-October	

The town of Newhalem, a Seattle City Light administrative town turned tourist attraction, looks like an artificial Mayberry RFD dropped into the jaws of one of the most awesome river canyons in the North Cascades—the Upper Skagit. It's all a little disarming, at least until you get off the "downtown" streets and explore the patches of forest along the river. There you'll find Newhalem Creek, one of two major campgrounds in North Cascades National Park and thus a major summertime stopover. After touring Newhalem (it's less than a mile's walk away), the campground is a pleasant plunge back into the woods, with very tidy, nicely spaced sites (a boon for tenters, in particular) tucked beneath sweet-smelling fir trees. The North Cascades Visitor Center is within walking distance, making this a perfect first-day's stop on your tour of the North Cascades. The three loops are well spread out, each offering one barrier-free site. The campground has ample running water and an RV dump station, but, like every other national park we've ever visited, no showers—the only thing keeping this otherwise dandy campground from 5-star status! The campground also has two group sites accommodating twenty-four campers each. One is equipped with a large sheltered area. (To reserve a group site, call the reservation number above.)

Family camping planners, take note: A number of very scenic nature trails (such as the Trail of the Cedars, at the foot of Main Street in Newhalem, and the don't-miss

Newhalem Creek flows through the campground and town bearing its name.

spectacle of Ladder Creek Falls, hidden behind the nearby Gorge Powerhouse) begin near the campground. But with no lake nearby for fishing and boating, there's probably not as much to do here as at Colonial Creek, the other major National Park stopover just up State Route 20. Then again, there isn't as much hubbub here, either.

Getting there: Newhalem Creek is just west of the town of Newhalem. Follow signs from milepost 120 on SR 20.

The Rainy Lake viewpoint is an iconic and easy North Cascades stroll.

20 Colonial Creek ★ ★ ★ ★

SITES	RESERVATIONS	CONTACT
	None	North Cascades National Park Headquarters
	OPEN	Sedro-Woolley
142 sites, no hookups, RVs to 32 feet	Mid-May to mid-October	(360) 854-7200

How spectacular are the North Cascades for mountain fun lovers? It takes not just a national park, but a national park *complex* to contain and protect them. The North Cascade complex includes the national park, the Lake Chelan National Recreation Area, and the Ross Lake National Recreation Area. Each stands on its own as a premiere wild spot; together the complex comprises some of the most rugged, unpeopled terrain in the Lower 48. The North Cascades are wickedly rugged and savagely beautiful, with rocky, glaciated peaks interlaced with deep, lush valleys. Even the best efforts of industrialized man—Seattle City Light's hydropower project, which lights the Emerald City—have failed to steal the charm from these 684,000 acres of wild lands. In 1988, 93 percent of the complex was designated as the Stephen Mather Wilderness. Unlike most national parks, this one is mostly inaccessible to autos, with State Route 20, the North Cascades Highway, serving as the only transportation link through its core. Near the middle of a west-to-east trek on that scenic highway, most of the park's half-million annual visitors will encounter Colonial Creek Campground, the largest and most popular camping spot in the complex. (You can't miss it, actually; the campground straddles the highway.) Nestled near a creek mouth on the banks of frigid, aqua-blue Diablo

Lake, Colonial Creek, elevation 1200 feet, is a gorgeous spot with towering firs that provide solace and blank out most noise from the nearby highway. The campground's boat launch provides great small boat/canoe access to Diablo Lake (beware strong winds), not to mention a chance to test your true mettle by plunging into the icy cold waters for 3.5 seconds or until you turn blue, whichever comes first. A large wooden fishing platform is a recent campground addition. The sites rate about a medium on the privacy scale; some are barrier free.

Colonial Creek's natural charms aren't the only reason it's so popular. It's also centrally located, a big plus for hikers and Highway 20 day-trippers. In the campground is the trailhead to the Thunder Creek Trail, one of the longest hiking corridors in the park, with access to numerous side trails that climb steadily to the top or shoulders of rugged North Cascades peaks. Stop at the Newhalem Visitors Center, (206) 386-4495, for more trail information.

Getting there: Colonial Creek is at North Cascades Highway (SR 20) milepost 130, 10 miles east of Newhalem and 4 miles east of the Diablo Lake turnoff.

Other North Cascades Highway/National Park Campgrounds

On the west side of the North Cascades Highway, Cascade Road leaves State Route 20 at Marblemount and leads to three relatively remote campgrounds. **Cascade Island**, a DNR camp, has fifteen sites (no hookups), no fees, and is open year-round; (360) 856-3500. The next two campgrounds are National Forest camps, both rustic sites offering few services (vault toilets, but no piped water): **Marble Creek** (8 miles east of SR 20, twenty-three sites, no hookups, RVs to 31 feet, no piped water), is open from mid-May to late September. **Mineral Park** (16 miles east of SR 20, twenty-two primitive sites, no hookups, RVs to 15 feet, no piped water) is open from mid-May to mid-September. The latter is used mainly as a staging area for hikes into the Glacier Peak Wilderness. Note: Both of these campgrounds formerly were free—a status befitting their bare-bones public services. Now, they not only both charge fees but accept reservations through the Forest Service national reservation service; (877) 444-6777 or www.reserveusa.com. For more details, call Mount Baker Ranger District, (360) 856-5700.

Eagle-watchers or steelhead anglers who get shut out at Rockport's Howard Miller Steelhead Camp can try the private **Clark's Skagit River Resort**, (800) 273-2606, which has campsites with hookups, as well as rental cabins. North Cascades National Park visitors, particularly tenters, should check out **Gorge Lake**, a tiny, peaceful riverfront campground near the town of Diablo. It's a quieter alternative to the more bustling Colonial Creek. Call the national park, (360) 854-7200.

Hikers and boaters are in for a treat on **Ross Lake**, the behemoth body of water behind Ross Dam: a string of twenty national park campgrounds accessible only by boat or on foot. Hikers can begin the trek to these campgrounds by following all or part of the 31.5-mile East Bank Ross Lake Trail, reached by hiking the Panther Creek Trail (the trailhead is near Panther Creek Bridge, near milepost 138 on SR 20) about 3 miles to its junction with the East Bank Ross Lake Trail. The easier way out is via the marine route. Although the only boat launch on the lake is at Hozomeen Campground, accessible only through British Columbia, and the only way to get a kayak or canoe to the lake is to haul it a couple miles down a steep trail, there is another option. Visitors can rent kicker boats from Ross Lake Resort (206) 386-4437, and then go campground hopping. (The resort floats on the lake behind Ross Dam and is itself an adventure to reach.) The free campsites, most of which have mooring docks, are beautifully located on bluffs or in old-growth forest near the banks of the lake. They're open summers only. Because they're so hard to reach, sites usually are available. They're primitive, with pit toilets and no piped water. But it's hard to imagine a more peaceful setting anywhere in Washington State. They are **Green Point** (five sites; 1 mile from Ross Dam via boat); **Cougar Island** (two sites; 2 miles); **Roland Point** (one site; 4 miles); **Big Beaver** (seven sites; 4 miles); **McMillan** (three sites; 5.5 miles); **Spencer's Camp** (two sites; 6 miles); **May Creek** (one site; 6.5 miles); **Rainbow Point** (three sites; 7.5 miles); **Devils Junction** (one site; 10.5 miles); **Ten Mile Island** (three sites; 11 miles); **Dry Creek** (four sites; 11.5 miles); **Ponderosa** (two sites; 12 miles); **Lodgepole** (three sites; 12.5 miles); **Lightning Creek Horse Camp** (three sites, 13 miles); **Lightning Creek Boat Camp** (six sites; 13.5 miles); **Cat Island** (four sites; 14.5 miles); **Little Beaver** (five sites; 17 miles); **Boundary Bay** (three sites; 17.5 miles); **Silver Creek** (four sites; 21 miles). At the head of the lake, **Hozomeen** (122 sites; 23 miles) is accessible by auto, but only through British Columbia. Three other boat-in sites are found on nearby Diablo Lake. They are **Hidden Cove** (one site), **Thunder Point** (three sites), and **Buster Brown** (three sites). Call the national park, (360) 854-7200 for details.

Goldeneyes are common visitors to Northwest lakes and streams.

Methow Valley

21 Lone Fir ★ ★ ★ ◄

SITES	RESERVATIONS	CONTACT
🏕️ 🚐	None	Okanogan National Forest Methow Valley Ranger District (509) 996-4003
	OPEN	
27 sites, no hookups, RVs to 20 feet	June through September	

Lone Fir, a quiet, pretty, subalpine camp on Early Winters Creek, marks the progression into the dry-side Okanogan National Forest for North Cascades Highway travelers. The campground facilities are basic—pit toilets—and sites are too small for larger road-hog RVs. But it's a pleasant, quiet tent spot in a lovely alpine area, with nicely spaced sites offering peekaboo views of a series of stunning, craggy North Cascades peaks such as the Early Winters Spires. The campground also offers great access to hiking trails; Lone Fir Trail begins right in the campground and winds along and over Early Winters Creek, via four very stylish wood bridges. It's a great family walk. The popular Washington Pass Overlook on State Route 20 is about 6 miles west. Note: Lone Fir is at 3640 feet, so expect this to be a chilly stopover in the shoulder seasons. Note that this and other Forest Service camps in the area often stay open later in the season if SR 20 remains open, but the water is shut off when freezes set in.

Getting there: Lone Fir is near milepost 168 on SR 20. It's about 27 miles northwest of Winthrop.

22 Klipchuck ★ ★ ★ ★

SITES	RESERVATIONS	CONTACT
🏕️ 🚐	None	Okanogan National Forest Methow Valley Ranger District (509) 996-4003
	OPEN	
46 sites, no hookups, RVs to 34 feet	June through September	

Another scenic spot on crystal-clear Early Winters Creek, Klipchuck is the largest campsite in the upper Methow Valley, on the downhill side of North Cascades Highway. It's equally popular with dry-side forest fans and hikers, who can depart from here in any of a number of directions for short, medium, or long treks into the Okanogan National Forest. (A nice day-hiking trail follows the creek for 2 miles from the campground.) If you're not a hiker and just want to drink in the beauty of the dry-side North Cascades, you'd be hard pressed to find a better spot than this lovely campground nestled in a stand of majestic, sweet-smelling pines. Six of the nicely spaced, semi-private sites are for tents only. They're all quite nice. Trout fishing in the stream can be productive. Keep your eyes peeled for rattlesnakes in this area, however. The campground, which has pit toilets, is at 2920 feet. It can be downright hot in the summer, but wonderfully bright and crisp in the spring and fall. Note: This is a major departure point for backpackers and horse packers. The Driveway Butte Trailhead is adjacent to the campground.

Getting there: On State Route 20 about 19 miles northwest of Winthrop (near milepost 175), turn north on Forest Road 300 and go 1 mile to the campground.

23 Early Winters ✦ ✦ ◀

SITES	RESERVATIONS	CONTACT
🏕️ 🚐	None	Okanogan National Forest Methow Valley Ranger District (509) 996-4003
	OPEN	
12 sites, no hookups, RVs to 24 feet	June to October	

This is as close as you can camp to the, um, bustling downtown core of Mazama. Actually, it's getting closer to "bustle" status all the time, with the upper Methow Valley's popularity as a year-round recreation getaway for hikers, mountain bikers, and cross-country skiers. The drip-by-drip development—now apparently dripped dry— at a cross-country ski/mountain-bike mecca at the site of the oft-proposed, ultimately rejected Early Winters ski area has changed this area slowly, but not in a bad way. Even if it does, a sip of the old ways can still be enjoyed at Early Winters, an average Forest Service camp at 2160 feet, near the confluence of the Methow River and Early Winters Creek. Facilities are standard federal-government issue: pit toilets, and a lot of scenery. Bring your own toilet paper and camera. The campground also is fairly exposed to the sun, making it downright hot and dusty during the dog days of summer. And it's a bit too close to State Route 20 to pretend like you're away from it all. Still, it's cheap, as far as campgrounds go. The location is also quite good—straight across the valley

A typical tent site at Early Winters Campground.

from Goat Wall, smack in the middle of access points to the Methow Community Trail system, near roads leading to some of the area's great backcountry hiking and ski trails. It's a nice place to camp in late September, when the skies cool as fall begins early and in earnest, and the kids are all at school, where they belong. Note that this is where SR 20 closes on the east side for winter. If supplies run short, or even if they don't, make a trip to the Mazama General Store for duds and grub.

Getting there: Early Winters straddles SR 20 milepost 177, just north of the turnoff to the town of Mazama and a stone's throw from Wilson's Ranch.

24 Ballard ★ ★

SITES	RESERVATIONS	CONTACT
🏕 🚻🚐	None	Okanogan National Forest Methow Valley Ranger District (509) 996-4003
	OPEN	
7 sites, no hookups, RVs to 28 feet	June to October	

Methow Valley campers who *really* want to get out there (and, after all, isn't that why you came to the Methow in the first place?) can do so in the Lost River/Harts Pass area. Lost River Road, which begins near Mazama and turns into Forest Road 5400, leads to four National Forest camps on the upper Methow River, all within walking distance of grand trout streams and backcountry trailheads. Ballard is the first, but not the best, unless you like to pitch your tent atop fresh horse cookies (nearby Robinson Creek trailhead is a major horse-packing jump-off point to places such as Ferguson Lake). But it'll do in a pinch. Sites are fairly primitive. Ballard has pit toilets, no piped water, and no garbage service. Pack out what you bring in. Plus a little extra. The campground elevation is 2521 feet.

Getting there: From Mazama, about 15 miles west of Winthrop via State Route 20, follow Harts Pass/Lost River Road (County Road 1163) northwest for about 7 miles until the pavement ends and the road becomes Forest Road 5400. Continue about 2 miles to the campground.

25 River Bend ★ ★ ◄

SITES	RESERVATIONS	CONTACT
🏕 🚻🚐	None	Okanogan National Forest Methow Valley Ranger District (509) 996-4003
	OPEN	
5 sites, no hookups, RVs to 24 feet	June to October	

River Bend, the second of four National Forest camps on the upper Methow River via the Harts Pass Road, is another small camp favored by horse packers and hikers, most bound for destinations such as the West Fork Methow Trail (an angler's favorite) or nearby Driveway Butte (a steep, dusty, 8-mile round-trip hike with great views). It's also primitive, with pit toilets, no piped water, and no garbage service. Be prepared to rough it here. The elevation is 2600 feet.

Getting there: From Mazama, about 15 miles west of Winthrop via State Route 20, follow Harts Pass/Lost River Road (County Road 1163) northwest for about 7 miles, to where the pavement ends and the road becomes Forest Road 5400. Continue about 2.5 miles to Forest Road 540600. Turn west and proceed less than a half mile to the campground on the left. (Note: The road is rough and usually not suitable for RVs or trailers past Ballard Campground.)

26 Harts Pass ★ ★ ★ ◀

SITES	RESERVATIONS	CONTACT
	None	Okanogan National Forest Methow Valley Ranger District (509) 996-4003
	OPEN	
5 walk-in sites	Mid-July to late September	

Harts Pass is a thin-air special. Located on the way to the Slate Peak overlook, which at about 7200 feet is the highest place you can drive to in Washington, this campground is as high (6198 feet) as any auto-accessible camp we're aware of in the state. OK, so it's basically a tie with Meadows (below). In any case, bring your warm jammies, even in the summertime. The campground sits in wild, beautiful alpine country, just on the cusp of the remote, 500,000-acre Pasayten Wilderness in the northern Okanogan National Forest. The sites are a short walk from the parking area. The Pacific Crest Trail passes nearby, making this a popular staging area for hikers and backpackers. Note: Beware the horse flies, particularly in early summer! And keep your ears open at night for a howl here and there: In recent years, packs of wolves with pups have been observed in the upper Methow Valley, reinhabiting an area they long ago were driven away from. This campground and others in this area sometimes stay open later into the autumn during years when snows are slow to come to the Harts Pass area.

Getting there: From Mazama, about 15 miles west of Winthrop via State Route 20, follow Harts Pass-Lost River Road (County Road 1163) northwest for about 7 miles until the pavement ends and the road becomes Forest Road 5400. Continue just under 13 miles to the campground. (Note: The road is rough and not suitable for RVs or trailers past Ballard Campground.)

27 Meadows ★ ★ ★

SITES	RESERVATIONS	CONTACT
	None	Okanogan National Forest Methow Valley Ranger District (509) 996-4003
	OPEN	
14 sites	Mid-July to late September	

The highest of the high Methow Valley camps, Meadows is really out there; the oft-treacherous road access makes it a site that's used as often by starters, enders, or through-hikers on the Pacific Crest Trail as by car campers. But it's a magnificent base camp for roaming the true majestic heart of the North Cascades. The nice thing about hiking from the Meadows/Harts Pass area is that you start out high, so getting up above tree line is rarely a problem. The same warnings for other upper Methow campgrounds apply here: pit toilets, no piped water, and no garbage service. A lot of biting flies. But for most of us, the thin air here often seems to mask the hardships. The area is especially spectacular in early summer, when wildflowers burst onto the scene.

Getting there: From Mazama, about 15 miles west of Winthrop via State Route 20, follow Harts Pass/Lost River Road (County Road 1163) northwest for about 7 miles until the pavement ends and the road becomes Forest Road 5400. Continue about 13 miles to Forest Road 500. Turn south and continue about a mile to the campground. (Note: This road is rough and not suitable for RVs or trailers past Ballard Campground.)

28 Pearrygin Lake State Park ★ ★ ★ ★

SITES	RESERVATIONS	CONTACT
⛺ 🚐 🏠	(877) 444-6777 or www.recreation.gov	Washington State Parks (360) 902-8844
163 sites, 30 full hookups, RVs to 60 feet, 2 cabins	**OPEN** April through October	Pearrygin Lake State Park (509) 996-2370

Pearrygin Lake, an RVers favorite, is the primary camping venue near Winthrop, the mid-Methow Valley western-kitsch town that began its "civilized" life as a trading outpost for trappers and miners, then reverted largely into a mecca for polar-fleece-clad hikers, skiers, mountain bikers, anglers, and campers. The campground earns top honors not only because of its relatively high number of sites and amenities, but for a pleasant atmosphere that includes great picnic sites, a swimming beach and bathhouse, a busy boat launch, and a group camp suitable for forty-eight campers. The Methow Valley's summertime weather—dry, but not quite as hot as lower Central Washington climes—makes this 580-acre, lakefront park a summertime magnet for anglers (the lake produces hefty trout), boaters, and sun worshippers of all sorts. The heat is cut somewhat here by some nice old willows.

The campground, not surprisingly, is full most of the summer. Reservations are a good idea. Sites on the grass lawn are likely to be uncomfortably close together, particularly for tenters' tastes. But depending on your privacy quotient, the facilities might make up for that. Like most state parks (but unlike other Methow camping areas), Pearrygin Lake has piped water, flush toilets, coin-op showers, and an RV dump station. Kids will love the swimming beach, sprawling lawns, and play facilities. Adults will love the shade trees, boat launch, and dock. Wildflowers can be grand if you time your springtime trip right. Best of all, it's an easy mountain bike ride to downtown Winthrop for a bigger-than-your-head burrito at the Duck Brand Inn. Two camper's cabins also are available here; call for reservations.

Historical note: Most of the park is on acreage originally cleared and settled by Winthrop-area homesteaders in the 1890s. Much of it was vacated after Winthrop's mining "boom" fizzled by 1900. Plenty of mining reminders linger in this valley, however. Most of the remote backcountry roads in the Methow Valley began as mining horsepacking trails. Take the drive from Mazama to Harts Pass, or north on East Chewuch Road, to retrace those old hoofprints.

Getting there: From Winthrop, follow Bluff Street (it becomes East Chewuch Road) about 2 miles north to County Road 1631. Turn right (east) and proceed less than 2 miles to the park entrance, on the right.

29 Buck Lake ★ ★ ★

SITES	RESERVATIONS	CONTACT
🏕 🚐	None	Okanogan National Forest Methow Valley Ranger District (509) 996-4003
	OPEN	
9 sites, no hookups, RVs to 20 feet	June through September	

A small camp on a scenic lake northwest of Winthrop, Buck Lake is a favorite of mountain bikers, who kick up much summertime dust on county and Forest Service roads in this area. Like its Forest Service cousins in the Chewuch River drainage north of Winthrop, facilities at Buck Lake Campground are primitive—pit toilets and no piped water, showers, or garbage service. But it's definitely off the beaten path, and fishing can be productive in Buck Lake. The elevation is 3250 feet.

Getting there: From State Route 20 just west of Winthrop, follow County Road 1213 (it becomes West Chewuch Road) about 6.5 miles, until it becomes Forest Road 51. Proceed about 2.5 miles north on Forest Road 51 to Forest Road 5130 (Eightmile Creek Road). Turn left (northwest) and drive about a half mile to Forest Road 100. Turn left and go about 2 miles to the campground.

30 Flat ★ ★ ★

SITES	RESERVATIONS	CONTACT
🏕 🚐	None	Okanogan National Forest Methow Valley Ranger District (509) 996-4003
	OPEN	
12 sites, no hookups, RVs to 36 feet	June through September	

Flat, in a multiway tie for the shortest and possibly dumbest campground name in the state, is the first, and most heavily used, of four Forest Service sites along Eightmile Creek, a gorgeous, clear stream that's a tributary of the Chewuch River. Trout fishing in the creek can be very productive in the summer, and even if it's not, the cool creek waters feel ooh, so good on those gritty, sunburned, and Teva-scraped feet. Guaranteed. Flat is small and primitive, with tidy sites and few amenities (pit toilets; no piped water, showers, or garbage service). But it's in a lovely, pine-forested valley, and first-time visitors lulled to sleep by the creek often become repeat customers. The campground is at 2858 feet.

Getting there: From State Route 20 just west of Winthrop, follow County Road

The upper Methow Valley is a popular horseback destination.

1213 (it becomes West Chewuch Road) about 6.5 miles, until it becomes Forest Road 51. Proceed about 2.5 miles north on Forest Road 51 to Forest Road 5130 (Eightmile Creek Road). Turn left (northwest) on Forest Road 5130 and drive 2 miles to the campground.

31 Nice ★ ★ ★

SITES	RESERVATIONS	CONTACT
3 sites, no hookups, 1 RV site, maximum length 16 feet	None	Okanogan National Forest Methow Valley Ranger District (509) 996-4003
	OPEN	
	June through September	

Well, gee. It sort of is. Nice pretty much lives up to its name. It's a cozy little spot on Eightmile Creek, offering the same angling opportunities as other camps in this river drainage. But that's about it. The campground is really not much more than a roadside pullout, with three sites that seem to get their fair share of use in spite of the primitive amenities (pit toilets; no piped water, showers, or garbage service). The campground sits at 2728 feet, and is just up the road from Flat (see above). Although this camp has one site officially open to RVs, we don't think they make them small enough to fit in here anymore. And there's no turnaround space for trailers. Note: Even higher on Eightmile Creek (farther than most people are willing to go for the resulting payoff) are two additional Forest Service camps, Ruffed Grouse (four sites) and Honeymoon (five sites). Both are primitive, with no piped water or other services. Call the contact number listed above for information.

Getting there: From State Route 20 just west of Winthrop, follow County Road 1213 (it becomes West Chewuch Road) about 6.5 miles, until it becomes Forest Road 51. Proceed 2.5 miles north on Forest Road 51 to Forest Road 5130 (Eightmile Creek Road). Turn left (northwest) on Forest Road 5130 and drive 4 miles to the campground.

32 Falls Creek ✦ ✦ ✦ ✦

SITES	RESERVATIONS	CONTACT
	None	Okanogan National Forest Methow Valley Ranger District (509) 996-4003
	OPEN	
7 sites, no hookups, RVs to 18 feet	June through September	

It's the water. Dozens of beautiful, crystal-clear streams drain the rocky reaches of wilderness around and above the Methow Valley, often breaking into raucous white water or plunging over rock formations. It's one of the most alluring natural features of this valley, which has so many rocky peaks, stone faces, pine trees, and flowing streams, it seems more like high, dry Montana or Colorado country than Washington. This silvery grace is on fine display at Falls Creek Campground, near the confluence of Falls Creek and the Chewuch River, a major northern tributary of the Methow. The river and stream are gorgeous in their own right, but Chewuch Falls, a short walk from the campground on a barrier-free trail, is worth the trip alone. Falls Creek is small and somewhat remote, but charming, and a nice spot to pitch the tent or park a small RV. Note: This campground, at 2100 feet, is the most developed (and closest to Winthrop) of three Forest Service camps along the Chewuch. The others are Chewuch (sixteen tent/RV sites) and Camp 4 (five tent-only sites), both higher in the Chewuch Valley. These serve primarily as staging areas and horse camps for hikers headed into the Pasayten Wilderness. Call the contact number listed above for information.

Getting there: From State Route 20 just west of Winthrop, follow County Road 1213 (it becomes West Chewuch Road) about 6.5 miles, until it becomes Forest Road 51. Proceed just over 5 miles north on Forest Road 51 to the campground, on the right.

Other Methow Valley Campgrounds

Peace, solitude, white water, and pit toilets abound in the **Twisp River drainage,** midway down the Methow Valley west of the town of Twisp. A series of small, rustic Forest Service camps are found here, all with pit toilets; some with piped water; but none with showers, garbage, or other services. They're popular with anglers, hikers, horse packers, and backpackers headed up and over Sawtooth Ridge, through the Sawtooth Wilderness, to the Stehekin area of Lake Chelan in North Cascades National Park. Most of these rustic camps have primitive facilities, are open to tents or RVs to 22 feet from May through mid-October, weather permitting, and are accessed from the Twisp area via County Road 9114 and Forest Road 44. From east to west up the valley, they are **War Creek** (ten sites, 14.5 miles east of State Route 20); **Mystery** (four sites), **Poplar Flat** (sixteen sites, 20.5 miles east of SR 20); **South Creek** (four sites, no piped water, 22 miles); and **Road's End** (four sites, no piped water, 24.5 miles).

Other remote Twisp-area campgrounds are **Black Pine Lake** (twenty-three sites, reached via Twisp River Road, County Road 1090, and Forest Road 43), **Foggy Dew** (twelve sites, reached via State Route 153, Gold Creek Road, and Forest Road 4340), and **Twisp River Horse Camp** (twelve sites, reached via County Road 9114 and Forest Roads 44 and 4430, beyond War Creek). East of Twisp, just off SR 20, are **Loup Loup** (twenty-five sites) and **JR** (six sites). All of these campgrounds charge a nominal fee. For more information, call the Methow Valley Visitors Center, (509) 996-4000. Northeast of Winthrop and Twisp, a number of Forest Service campgrounds also are maintained by the Okanogan National Forest's Tonasket Ranger District. For a list, see the Okanogan Valley and Highlands section in the Northeast Washington chapter.

In summer, mountain bikers flock to the Methow Valley.

4. CENTRAL CASCADES

Never underestimate the importance of a very wide back door.

That might be the best moral to the story of camping in Washington's Central Cascades, a true rear exit for Puget Sound families seeking relief from summertime blazing heat—not to mention the thousands of meandering tourists clogging the aisles at Pike Place Market. The fact is that, over the years, many of us have come to take these close-in mountain lakes, valleys and peaks for granted. We hike them, ski them, and climb them. But sleep in them? Maybe another day. They are, after all, always going to be there. So they often seem to reside somewhere behind us when we make our mental maps for future campouts.

When it comes to getting away and camping out, many of us think first of Puget Sound or the Pacific Coast, spread right out in our front yards, always within touch and sight.

Intuitively, we know what's out back: Many miles of rock, alpine lakes, dirt roads, and indefatigable mosquitoes. We know it's big, wild, high, pleasant, and even (*gasp!*) occasionally uncrowded. But in camping terms, it's also foreign and a bit scary. So many of us insist on heading the other direction or, worse, repeatedly drive right through the Central Cascades without so much as stopping to pitch a tent and say hello. Even campers who make annual pilgrimages to the hot, dry, lake-studded lands of Eastern Washington often err by treating this region as a land to be passed through in the middle of a long drive to someplace else.

Trust us: He or she who takes heed of those brown "camping" signs along Interstate 90 and U.S. Highway 2 often will be richly rewarded.

The main east–west interstates in Washington are the top and bottom layers of a camper's sandwich of the gods, of sorts. The meaty filling, thousands of square miles of wild mountain lands, offers overnight experiences ranging from truly gnarly, hike-in wilderness to comfy splendor on the shores of manmade reservoirs.

Make no mistake: The Central Cascades are hardly bursting at the seams with luxurious campgrounds, or even convenient ones. For an area so vast, and so wild, it's surprising that the intrepid traveler is limited to what's there. Blame the topography: When it comes to camping, these mountains are a victim of their own wild nature. The Alpine Lakes Wilderness spreads across a huge chunk of this land, leaving it (thank heavens) off-limits to vehicle traffic, car camping, and just about everything else except silent walking. Even portions of this vast territory that are under no such human-conjured restrictions tend to throw up their own, natural barriers to large-scale Winnebago invasion. Winter weather is wicked here, with many feet of rain and tons of snow closing the region to all but the most determined small mammals in the off-season. As any Forest Service planner will tell you, washouts, forest fires, avalanches, and mud slides make it tough to keep existing Central Cascades campgrounds on the map from one season to the next. Adding more would be foolhardy, even if money were available to do so. Which it isn't. So campers should focus on what's already here. And this is not an unpleasant exercise.

Some of our favorite, quick escapes from Seattle are found in these hills: The close-to-home quiet pine forest of Lake Kachess; streamside campgrounds on the upper Cle Elum River; and the always-convenient, pull-in ease of Lake Easton State Park, all in the heart of the hills on Interstate 90. The diverse recreation lures of campgrounds on, around, and above Lake Wenatchee, off US 2. The quiet majesty and crystal-clear waters of the Icicle River drainage near Leavenworth. And those easy-to-find places near the major highways are just for starters. Determined campers who can live without a lot of amenities will find a wealth of gorgeous, if rough-around-the-edges, Forest Service camps on high, gravel roads throughout this area.

Contrary to popular myth, the Central Cascades aren't all sheer cliffs or clear-cut wastelands. And they're too close to home to ignore. This summer, resist the call of the saltwater and look to the rear. Spend some time in your high-altitude backyard. Find a favorite corner. Call it your own.

Opposite: *The cold, clear waters of the Icicle River are a summertime delight.*

Hikers take in the sunset on a ridgetop in the Cascade Mountains.

Stevens Pass Corridor and Lake Wenatchee

1 Wallace Falls State Park
2 Money Creek
3 Beckler River
4 Nason Creek
5 Lake Wenatchee State Park
6 Glacier View
7 Goose Creek

Leavenworth and Icicle Canyon

8 Tumwater
9 Eightmile
10 Bridge Creek
11 Johnny Creek
12 Ida Creek
13 Chatter Creek
14 Rock Island
15 Blackpine Creek Horse Camp

Snoqualmie Pass Corridor: North Bend to Easton

16 Middle Fork
17 Tinkham
18 Denny Creek
19 Crystal Springs
20 Kachess
21 Lake Easton State Park

Roslyn and Cle Elum River Valley

22 Wish Poosh
23 Cle Elum River
24 Red Mountain
25 Salmon La Sac
26 Owhi

Blewett Pass and Ellensburg

27 Beverly
28 Mineral Springs
29 Swauk

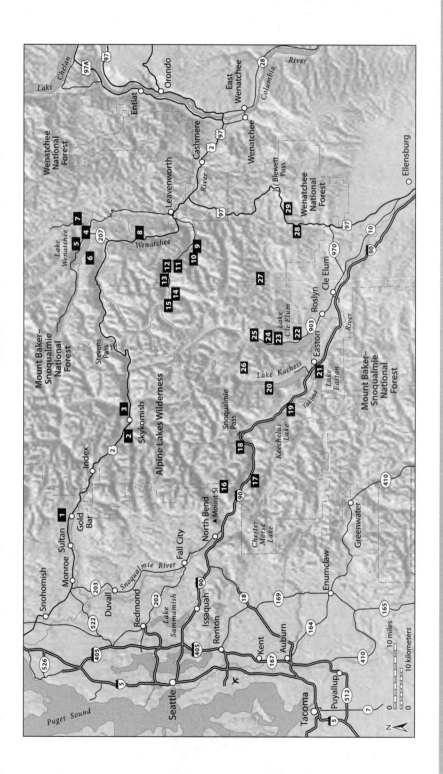

Stevens Pass Corridor and Lake Wenatchee

ı Wallace Falls State Park ✦ ✦ ◀

SITES	RESERVATIONS	CONTACT
🏕 🏠	None	Washington State Parks (360) 902-8844
	OPEN	Wallace Falls State Park
2 sites, 4 cabins	Year-round	(360) 793-0420

Let's face it: Very few people come to Wallace Falls to camp. It's the 7-mile round-trip hike to the scenic falls—one of the most spectacular in Washington's Cascade Range—that draws most visitors to this state park. Many, in fact, aren't even aware that the place has campsites. It almost doesn't. Four of its half dozen sites have been replaced by cabins. The two remaining walk-in sites are easy to miss, hiding in the trees near the trailhead. These tent sites, a short stroll from the car, are quite private and not unpleasant, with gravel floors, beneath tall alders and a few firs. A newer picnic shelter could provide a great emergency bivouac in bad weather. The hike is a definite don't-miss. The trail is steep in places, but well traveled. The falls, a 265-foot cascade of the South Fork Wallace River, can be viewed from below, or above, where a sweeping view of the Skykomish Valley is added incentive. Note: Unlike most state parks, this one has no coin-op showers.

Local trivia: The name Wallace is a misnomer. It was applied to the turn-of-the-century townsite of Wallace (now Startup) and is believed to be derived from the name of a Native couple, Joe and Sarah Kwayaylsh.

Getting there: From Interstate 5 at Everett, follow U.S. Highway 2 east 28 miles to Gold Bar. Turn left at the "Wallace Falls" sign at First Street, proceed 0.5 mile to May Creek Road, turn right and follow signs an additional 1.5 miles to the park entrance, on the left.

2 Money Creek ✦ ✦ ✦ ◀

SITES	RESERVATIONS	CONTACT
🏕 🚐	(877) 444-6777 or www.recreation.gov	Mount Baker–Snoqualmie National Forest Skykomish Ranger District
	OPEN	(360) 677-2414
23 sites, no hookups, RVs to 21 feet	Mid-May through September	

Railroads come to life at Money Creek. Too much to life for the liking of some, particularly those who don't appreciate being wakened from a sound sleep by a lumbering freight train. The Burlington–Northern line runs a stone's throw from this pretty

A shelter for soggy hikers in Wallace Falls State Park

campsite on the Skykomish. If evidence of railroads (present tense) makes you crazy, a grand place to examine railroads (past tense) is a short drive away. The Iron Goat Railroad Trail is an easy (and increasingly popular) hike along a former Stevens Pass railroad corridor. In fact, Money Creek is as good a place as any to make a base camp for exploring the entire upper Skykomish drainage along U.S. Highway 2. The camp sits at the confluence of Money Creek and the Skykomish, in a rare stand of old-growth firs that are drop-dead beautiful any time of the year. As an added bonus, both the east and west loops of the campground were renovated in 2002, with new pavement, pit toilets, tent pads, and other facilities. It's vastly improved from its former self. Strongly consider making a reservation before heading out here on weekends; more than half the sites are reservable. The camp's location right on US 2 makes it too visible to be ignored or missed by camping travelers. (If you have your choice, shoot for sites 6 or 7, riverfront in the west loop.) With the flood closure of Troublesome Creek and San Juan campgrounds, this campground gets heavy use in summer.

Getting there: The campground is 4 miles west of Skykomish on US 2, just before milepost 46.

3   Beckler River ★ ★ ★ ◄

SITES	RESERVATIONS	CONTACT
▲ 🚐 27 sites, no hookups, RVs to 21 feet	(877) 444-6777 or www.recreation.gov	Mount Baker–Snoqualmie National Forest Skykomish Ranger District (360) 677-2414
	OPEN	
	Memorial Day to Labor Day	

It's a bit rough around the edges, probably due to the occasional riotous flooding of the Beckler River, upon which (and alas, in which, during some winters) many of its campsites sit. But something about Beckler River keeps beckoning us back. Maybe it's the rushing white water, right at your feet as you sit at a campfire and soak up the good life. Or the fact that it's just far enough from civilization to feel wild, but close enough to run into Skykomish for fresh—well, reasonably fresh—marshmallows. It's a pretty site in second-growth forest, with typical Forest Service amenities—piped water, pit toilets, and picnic tables built to last. This is a good place to bring the mountain bikes; a lot of seldom-traveled Forest Service roads stretch out from here. Note: Seven of the sites here are for tents only; sites 4 and 12 are barrier free. The even numbered sites 4–14—all pull-throughs—are the most highly sought riverfront locales. The majority of sites here are reservable, and reservations generally are a good idea, given the scarcity of good campsites on the west side of U.S. Highway 2.

Getting there: From US 2 just east of Skykomish, turn north on Forest Road 65 and drive 1.5 miles to the campground.

4 Nason Creek ✦ ✦ ✦ ✦

SITES	RESERVATIONS	CONTACT
	None	Wenatchee National Forest Lake Wenatchee Ranger District (509) 763-3103
	OPEN	
73 sites, no hookups, RVs to any length	May through October	

By all rights, Nason Creek should have an inferiority complex. As Forest Service campgrounds go, this one is large and well equipped. But it's also right on the access road to

Some campsites in Nason Creek Campground rival those in adjacent Lake Wenatchee State Park.

Lake Wenatchee State Park, and many campers err in cruising right past it in the rush to land a campsite at the more popular lakeside campground. Nason Creek can't compete with the state park's reputation. But it's almost as close to the lake, and in many respects offers a nicer camping experience to the cramped, heavily shaded, somewhat claustrophobic sites at the state park. Many of the sites in this campground (it's bigger than it looks; note the three separate entrances off the access road) are creekfront and very spacious, making them even more popular among RVers than the oft-booked-up state park. But don't bet on finding open spaces here in the dead of summer, either. For good reason, the campground, elevation 1800 feet, is extremely popular with boaters, anglers, and other Lake Wenatchee vacationers. Unlike many Forest Service camps, this one has flush toilets and piped water. No showers, but you'll find them a short walk down the road at the state park.

Getting there: From U.S. Highway 2 at Cole's Corner (about 19 miles northeast of Leavenworth), turn north on State Route 207, following signs for Lake Wenatchee State Park. At about 3.5 miles, turn left on Cedar Brae Road and look for campground entrances on both sides of the road—and a third across the creek on the right.

5 Lake Wenatchee State Park ✦✦✦✦

SITES	RESERVATIONS	CONTACT
🏕 🚐 197 sites, no hookups, RVs to 60 feet	(888) 226-7688 or www.parks.wa.gov	Washington State Parks (360) 902-8844
	OPEN Year-round	Lake Wenatchee State Park (509) 763-3101

Long before the invention of the Winnebago—or the collapsible tent, for that matter—Native campers flocked to the shores of Lake Wenatchee to fish, relax, and meet the neighbors from the west side. That tradition continues today in the camping community at Lake Wenatchee State Park, a large gathering spot appropriately bringing together the best of eastern and western Washington. One of the few Washington State Parks in a true alpine-lake setting, Lake Wenatchee is a favorite of boaters, anglers, hikers, cyclists, and, in the winter, cross-country skiers and snowmobilers. Extending across both sides of the Wenatchee River's outlet from the lake, the park is actually two separate campgrounds: The south area comprises sites 1–100, tightly spaced, smallish sites in dense forest. Some people prefer this area because it's a close walk to a horse-rental facility and the park's sprawling beach swimming area. But RVers or privacy lovers will likely be more happy in the north area (entrance: 1 mile down the road beyond the south entrance at Cedar Brae Road), where sites 101–197 are more nicely spaced camp areas, many of them with pull-through access. Both camping areas have coin-op showers, flush toilets, and piped water. Most are a short walk from the Lake Wenatchee shoreline. In addition to the nearly 200 campsites, you'll find ten group campsites that accommodate up to eighty people, a boat launch, sixty picnic sites with three covered shelters, two RV dump stations, an amphitheater (yours truly has performed a book reading there, so the talent selection is clearly questionable!), 5 miles of trails for horses, and 7.5 miles of trails for humans. Boat and horse rentals also are available here in the summer.

Lake Wenatchee, elevation 1900 feet, is a great place to make base camp for exploration of the east side of the Glacier Peaks Wilderness. From this area, Forest Service roads follow the Little Wenatchee, White, and Chiwawa Rivers—all Wenatchee tributaries—and climb high into the beautiful east-slope Cascades. This is some of the most treasured alpine country in the state, and venturing into it—whether on foot, by car, or just by binoculars from the state park itself—is always a rewarding experience.

The park stays open all winter, when staff members groom 30 kilometers of trails for cross-country skiing, and more for snowmobiles. Winter camping is allowed in the south camping area, with one heated restroom left open.

Getting there: From Cole's Corner on U.S. Highway 2 (about 19 miles northeast of Leavenworth), turn north on State Route 207 and follow signs 3.5 miles to the south campground and day-use entrance, or 4.5 miles to the north entrance.

Cold, clear waters await swimmers in Lake Wenatchee.

6 Glacier View ★ ★ ★ ◂

SITES	RESERVATIONS	CONTACT
	None	Wenatchee National Forest
	OPEN	Lake Wenatchee Ranger District
16 sites, no hookups, RVs to 16 feet	May through September	(509) 763-3103

It can't match the facilities of nearby Lake Wenatchee State Park or the ease of access of Nason Creek, but Glacier View, a small, lovely Forest Service camp, has location on its side. Tucked into the southwest shore of the lake, this is primarily a tenter's haven (very small RVs or campers can get in here, but turnaround space is *very* limited). Most of the sites are walk-ins on the lakeshore, making this a very popular boater/angler camp during the summer (a gravel boat launch is on the premises). Some of our favorite sites are the walk-ins (numbered 1a, 1b, 1c, and 1d) on the west (left) side as you enter: Privacy is somewhat limited, but the payoff—fantastic lake and mountain views, and, in some cases, a gurgling stream waterfall right in your site—are well worth it. Take a few groups of your friends and take over the whole area. The campground has piped water and pit toilets. Note: The trailhead to popular Hidden Lake is located a short distance shy of the campground.

Getting there: From Cole's Corner on U.S. Highway 2 (about 19 miles northeast of Leavenworth), turn north on State Route 207 and proceed 3.5 miles to Cedar Brae Road. Turn left, proceed a half mile, veer left at the Lake Wenatchee State Park entrance, and continue about 5 curvy miles to the campground, which is about 1.5 miles beyond the end of the pavement.

7 Goose Creek ★ ★

SITES	RESERVATIONS	CONTACT
	None	Wenatchee National Forest
	OPEN	Lake Wenatchee Ranger District
29 sites, no hookups, RVs to 30 feet	May to mid-October	(509) 763-3103

Goose Creek, a typical Forest Service campground in typical east-slope Cascade forest, is a decent alternative to Lake Wenatchee State Park, which often is overcrowded. But it's not a great destination on its own. Noisy off-road vehicles bound for roads in the Entiat drainage often make this portion of the Wenatchee National Forest noisier than most campers would prefer. The elevation is 2900 feet, and the campground has pit toilets and piped water.

Getting there: From State Route 207 near Lake Wenatchee State Park, follow Forest Road 62 northeast for 4.5 miles, around Fish Lake, to Forest Road 6100. Turn right and drive 1 mile southeast to the campground.

Other Stevens Pass/Lake Wenatchee Campgrounds

Troublesome Creek (thirty sites;) and **San Juan** (nine sites; access via Forest Roads 65 and 63), two primitive but popular campgrounds on the west side of U.S. Highway 2, were severely damaged by flooding of the North Fork Skykomish River in 2006, and were closed when the original research for this guide was done. San Juan has since reopened after road repairs. Call the Skykomish Ranger District, (360) 677-2414, for details.

A popular westside Stevens Pass group campground is **Miller River** (seventeen back-in tent/RV sites for up to 100 campers), south of Skykomish via Old Cascade Highway and Forest Road 6410. It's open summers only; Mount Baker–Snoqualmie National Forest, Skykomish Ranger District, (360) 677-2414.

Lake Wenatchee-area campers seeking a more remote experience in the upper Wenatchee River drainage (northwest of Lake Wenatchee) can seek out three small, primitive Forest Service camps in the shadow of Glacier Peak, on the Little Wenatchee River. The campgrounds, all found on Forest Road 6500 (off Lake Wenatchee's North Shore Drive) are **Soda Springs** (five tent sites), **Lake Creek** (eight tent sites), and **Rainy Creek** (ten tent sites). The latter is the staging area for many Glacier Peak Wilderness expeditions, such as the popular Cady Creek/Little Wenatchee backpacking loop. All three campgrounds are open summers only and are free but primitive, with pit toilets and no piped water or other services; Wenatchee National Forest, Lake Wenatchee Ranger District, (509) 763-3103.

One river valley to the north of the Little Wenatchee lies the White River, another

BEST MOUNTAIN-VIEW CAMPING

1. Takhlakh Lake, Mount Adams
It takes a while to get there, and the water system has gone kaput. But you might not care once you see the view from your campsite. See p. 230.

2. Owhi Campground, Mount Baker–Snoqualmie National Forest
A remote camp with mostly walk-in, tent sites, Owhi offers sterling views of Three Queens Mountain and plenty of alpine splendor all around. See p. 175.

3. Deer Park, Olympic National Park
The campground is rustic, the access road a pain, but oh, the view—not only of the northern Olympic Mountains, but the Strait of Juan de Fuca, Mount Baker, and much, much more. See p. 81.

4. Panorama Point, Baker Lake
The name sort of gives it away. This lakefront campground on Baker Lake, like many others in this area, offers stunning views of the south face of Mount Baker. See p. 129.

5. Harts Pass, North Cascades
This alpine camp in the North Cascades is among the highest (6198 feet) in the state, and makes you feel more like a hiker than camper. The Pacific Crest Trail passes nearby. See p. 142.

Whatever you do, don't let it burn...

major Glacier Peak drainage. It's the site of three more small, primitive Forest Service campgrounds on Forest Road 6400 (White River Road). The first, **Napeequa Crossing** (five sites) serves as a popular staging area for expeditions into the Glacier Peak Wilderness (the popular Twin Lakes trailhead is nearby). The second, **Grasshopper Meadows** (five sites) is only about a mile from the third, **White River Falls** (five sites), which is set near the impressive falls of the same name. All three camps are primitive, free, and open summers only, with pit toilets but no piped water or other services; Wenatchee National Forest, Lake Wenatchee Ranger District, (509) 763-3103.

A similar string of campgrounds is found on the remote Chiwawa River Road (Forest Road 6200), northwest of Lake Wenatchee, along the eastern border of the spectacular Alpine Lakes Wilderness. From lower river to upper, they are **Grouse Creek Group Camp** (by reservation only), **Finner Creek** (three sites), **Riverbend** (six sites), **Rock Creek** (four sites), **Chiwawa Horse Camp** (twenty-one sites), **Schaefer Creek** (ten sites), **Atkinson Flats** (seven sites), **19 Mile** (four sites), **Alpine Meadows** (four sites), and **Phelps Creek** (seven sites) and **Phelps Creek Equestrian** (six sites), both near Trinity. All are primitive, with pit toilets and no piped water. Most require at least an $8 per night vehicle fee and/or a Northwest Forest Pass trailhead parking permit; Grouse Creek is $50 per group to reserve; Wenatchee National Forest, Lake Wenatchee Ranger Station, (509) 763-3103.

Four other small, free, primitive Forest Service camps are found in the upper Wenatchee drainage: **Theseus Creek** (three sites) on Road 6701, **Meadow Creek** (four sites) on Road 6300, **Deep Creek** (three sites) on Road 6100, and **Deer Camp** (three sites) on Road 6101; Wenatchee National Forest, Lake Wenatchee Ranger District, (509) 763-3103.

The Central Cascades' stunning Icicle Valley, top to bottom.

Leavenworth and Icicle Canyon

8 Tumwater ✦ ✦ ✦

SITES	RESERVATIONS		CONTACT
⛺ 🚐	Group campsite only; 877-444-6777		Wenatchee National Forest Leavenworth Ranger District (509) 548-6977
	OPEN		
84 sites, no hookups, RVs to 50 feet	May to mid-October		

Tumwater Canyon is a stunner, period. Motorists plunging down through the canyon, on the upper Wenatchee River along U.S. Highway 2, are treated to a jutting-rock and swirling, white-water spectacle as grand as any along a major highway in the United States. This gorgeous slice into the center of the Central Cascades surely was the main reason this route was designated a National Scenic Byway. The title is well deserved. In the upper reaches of this shady, cold-water bit of heaven is Tumwater, a large Forest Service campground 10 miles northwest of Leavenworth. It's not exactly as spectacular as the surrounding scenery, but it'll do as a decent overnight spot for weary US 2 travelers and hikers bound for the gorgeous Alpine Lakes Wilderness highlands above this river and in the Icicle Creek drainage. (The Hatchery Creek and Chiwaukum Creek trailheads both are nearby, leading into areas burned in the massive Hatchery Creek wildfire of 1994.) The campground is fairly average, with private, shrub-walled sites OK for tents and still large enough to accommodate medium-sized RVs. A group campsite is available for up to eighty-four campers. Bonus: Horseshoe pit! Campsite 41 is a group site for up to five vehicles.

Note: Bring that fleece sweater along. It's usually shady and quite cool in the shoulder seasons here at 2050 feet.

Getting there: Tumwater is 10 miles northwest of Leavenworth on US 2.

9 Eightmile ✦ ✦ ✦

SITES	RESERVATIONS		CONTACT
⛺ 🚐	Group campsite only; 877-444-6777		Wenatchee National Forest Leavenworth Ranger District (509) 548-6977
	OPEN		
45 sites, no hookups, RVs to 21 feet	Mid-April to late October		

The Icicle Canyon, one of the Central Cascades' loveliest collisions of high, ominous mountains and low, peaceful streams, is graced by seven Forest Service campgrounds, each and every one popular with the hordes of hikers, horse packers, backpackers, rock climbers, wildlife watchers, and others who flock here each summer. With more than 8000 feet separating the floor from the highest peak, Icicle Canyon is one of the deepest in Washington. Bordered on the north by Icicle Ridge and on the south by the Stuart Range, the Icicle drains much of the Alpine Lakes Wilderness, a truly Alps-like highland heaven. The first campground encountered is Eightmile, which fronts on Icicle and Eightmile Creeks. It has piped water and pit toilets and is tough to get into during much of the summer. Trailheads to Stuart/Colchuck and Eightmile Lakes, both popular backpacking destinations, are nearby. Several sites are double-sized, "family" sites. The elevation is 1800 feet.

Getting there: From U.S. Highway 2 at the west end of Leavenworth, drive about 7 miles southwest on Icicle Road (County Road 76). (The campground is named for Eightmile Road, which is found about a mile beyond.)

10 Bridge Creek ✦✦✦

SITES	RESERVATIONS	CONTACT
🏕️	Group campsite only; 877-444-6777	Wenatchee National Forest Leavenworth Ranger District (509) 548-6977
	OPEN	
6 sites	Mid-April through October	

A tiny camp about a mile up the road from Eightmile Creek (above), Bridge Creek is the domain of tenters only—a welcome relief, if you're a tenter. The campground, with all dirt roads and camping sites, can be dusty and hot in the summer, but all sites are peaceful places on the banks of Icicle Creek. Facilities are primitive, with hand-pumped water and pit toilets. The campground also has one group site; reservations required. The elevation is 1900 feet.

Getting there: From U.S. Highway 2 at the west end of Leavenworth, drive 9.4 miles southwest on Icicle Road (County Road 76).

11 Johnny Creek ✦✦✦✦

SITES	RESERVATIONS	CONTACT
🏕️🚐	None	Wenatchee National Forest Leavenworth Ranger District (509) 548-6977
	OPEN	
65 sites, no hookups, RVs to 50 feet	May through October	

Centrally located and always popular, this is the biggest, most diverse, and in many ways nicest campground in the Icicle Creek drainage. (Those whose rigs can't stomach much washboarding might also note that this is the last campground on this road before the pavement ends.) The camp, with sites along both Johnny and Icicle creeks, is set in pine forest and has hand-pumped water and pit toilets. Sites are split into upper and lower loops, and eight sites are walk-in, tent-only sites that afford nice privacy to the fabric-walled crowd. Some sites have nifty stone fireplaces with cooking surfaces and chimneys. Several sites are double-sized, "family" sites. Those in the upper loop, away from the river, have nice views of the upper Icicle Valley. In spite of the campground's

Campsites are basic, but the location is grand, at Johnny Creek Campground.

size, finding a site here on summer weekends can be tough. Be prepared to be flexible, and find some friends to sit around your campfire and lament the fact you didn't call far enough (about a year) in advance to get an overnight backcountry permit for the nearby Enchantment Lake Basin. The elevation is 2300 feet. Note that sites in the lower loop are a buck more than those across the road, in the upper loop.

Getting there: From U.S. Highway 2 at the west end of Leavenworth, drive 12.4 miles southwest on Icicle Road (County Road 76).

12 Ida Creek ★ ★ ★

SITES	RESERVATIONS	CONTACT
	None	Wenatchee National Forest Leavenworth Ranger District (509) 548-6977
	OPEN	
10 sites, no hookups, RVs to 30 feet	May through October	

This is the next stop on your itinerary if Johnny Creek is full. It has similar amenities—hand-pumped water and pit toilets. But it's quieter for tenters, and half the spaces here can accept a very small RV or trailer. A wealth of good day-hiking trails are within 2 miles of the campground. The elevation is 2500 feet.

Getting there: From U.S. Highway 2 at the west end of Leavenworth, drive 14.2 miles southwest on Icicle Road (County Road 76).

13 Chatter Creek ✦ ✦ ✦

SITES	RESERVATIONS	CONTACT
🏕️ 🚐 12 sites, no hookups, RVs to 22 feet	Group campsite only; 877-444-6777 **OPEN** May through October	Wenatchee National Forest Leavenworth Ranger District (509) 548-6977

If you're looking for one campground to put you smack-dab in the midst of everything Icicle Canyon has to offer, this is it. Chatter Creek's sites are small, making it best suited for tenters. And they come here in droves, using the camp as a bivouac spot for backpack trips on the Chatter Creek, Icicle Gorge, Jack Creek, and Trout Creek trails. The campground has pit toilets and hand-pumped water. The campground also has one large group site. The elevation is 2800 feet.

Access note: Icicle Road was damaged by flooding in 2008 below Ida Creek Campground, leaving it, Rock Island, and Blackpine Horse Camp inaccessible. Call to check on repairs before you go.

Getting there: From U.S. Highway 2 at the west end of Leavenworth, drive 16.1 miles southwest on Icicle Road (County Road 76).

Autumn leaves are reflected in an impoundment of the Icicle River near Leavenworth.

14 Rock Island ★ ★ ★ ◄

SITES	RESERVATIONS	CONTACT
🔺 🚐	None	Wenatchee National Forest Leavenworth Ranger District (509) 548-6977
	OPEN	
22 sites, no hookups, RVs to 21 feet	May through October	

A pretty spot in the upper Icicle Canyon, Rock Island offers twelve tent sites and ten tent/RV slots. The campground has hand-pumped water and pit toilets. A wealth of good day hikes and backpack routes are found nearby, as is that gorgeous river, which can't be beat on a hot day. The elevation is 2900 feet.

Access note: The Icicle Road was damaged by flooding in 2008 below Ida Creek Campground, leaving it, Rock Island, and Blackpine Horse Camp inaccessible. Call to check on repairs before you go.

Getting there: From U.S. Highway 2 at the west end of Leavenworth, drive 17.7 miles southwest on Icicle Road (County Road 76).

15 Blackpine Creek Horse Camp ★ ★ ★ ◄

SITES	RESERVATIONS	CONTACT
🔺 🚐	None	Wenatchee National Forest Leavenworth Ranger District (509) 548-6977
	OPEN	
10 sites, no hookups, RVs to 60 feet	Mid-May through October	

The end of the road in Icicle Canyon is a starting point for many Alpine Lakes Wilderness–bound hikers and horse packers: Blackpine Creek Horse Camp. The campground is at the site of the Icicle Creek trailhead, which leads to the popular French Creek drainage and connects to the French Ridge, Snowall Creek, and Meadow Creek trails to the south. The campground is not exclusively for the horse enthusiast, but the ten pull-through sites here are helpful if you're hauling a horse trailer. This is the only campground in the valley with horse-loading facilities. Tenters are thus left with the added challenge of setting up the tent without landing squarely atop a road apple or two. The campground has hand-pumped water, pit toilets, and, as usual, no showers, unless you're man or woman enough to shower under the pump while a buddy keeps it running. The elevation is 3000 feet.

Access note: The Icicle Road was damaged by flooding in 2008 below Ida Creek Campground, leaving it, Rock Island, and Blackpine Horse Camp inaccessible. Call to check on repairs before you go.

Getting there: From U.S. Highway 2 at the west end of Leavenworth, drive 19.2 miles southwest on Icicle Road (County Road 76).

Other Leavenworth/Icicle Canyon Campgrounds

For RVers who want to explore the Bavarian-kitsch village of Leavenworth but are not interested in roughing it at the multitude of no-hookup Forest Service camps in the

Standing dead trees remain from wildfires in the Icicle River Valley.

region, **Pine Village Resort/KOA** is an option. It offers all the extras: full hookups, cable TV, laundry facilities, hot showers—even a hot tub or two. It's on River Bend Drive, just east of town; (509) 548-7709. Another option for RVers in search of hookups is the large **Icicle River RV Resort**, 3 miles up Icicle Road; (509) 548-5420.

16 Middle Fork ★ ★ ★ ◂

SITES	RESERVATIONS	CONTACT
🏕️ 🚐	(877) 444-6777 or www.recreation.gov	Mount Baker–Snoqualmie National Forest North Bend Ranger District (425) 888-1421
39 sites, no hookups, RVs to 50 feet	**OPEN** Late May to mid-September	

Can you hear the band playing? We've struck it up because it's so rare that a new campground comes along in the Northwest, full accompaniment seems in order. Middle Fork, opened in 2006, is the first new camp to grace the venerable Mount Baker–Snoqualmie National Forest since the 1970s. And it's a small part of a larger story. This campground is part of a broad, ongoing effort by the feds and local activists in the Middle Fork Recreation Coalition to "take back" the Middle Fork Snoqualmie area, which in previous decades became a haven for random target-shooting, meth labs, garbage dumping, stolen car abandonment, and all manner of other unpleasantries. It's much improved today. New trails and trailheads in the area have introduced a new clientele, which tends to push the old one away. And Middle Fork campground is another cornerstone in reclaiming a grand recreation area, one literally in Seattle's backyard, that's been abused and/or underutilized for years, with many "unofficial" campsites spoiling and eroding area riverbanks.

The new campground is quite nice, situated in a second-growth forest along the Taylor River, a major Middle Fork tributary. Sites, arranged in one large loop in a former rock quarry, are pleasant, level, and quite private, with nice tent pads and room for small-to-medium RVs. Also on site are two group camps, a set of picnic shelters, three walk-in tent sites, and a short, looped nature trail. The entire campground is barrier free. A new 4-mile trail begins in the campground near sites 12 and 13 and follows the route of an old Civilian Conservation Corps roadway. A wealth of other hiking options is found in the immediate area, including trails to Goldmeyer Hot Springs and Snoqualmie Lake and other destinations in the beautiful Alpine Lakes Wilderness. Twenty sites here can be reserved in advance. Some of them offer great views of Mount Garfield.

Be advised that the last dozen or so miles of the access road are unpaved and can be quite rough. Keep going when you see signs saying ominous things such as "no turnaround beyond next bridge." The campground really is out there!

Getting there: From Interstate 90 near North Bend, take Exit 34, Edgewick Road. Drive north on 468th Avenue for about a half mile, then turn right on Southeast Middle Fork Road (Forest Road 56). Proceed about 12 miles to the campground, about a half mile beyond the Middle Fork Trailhead.

17 Tinkham ✦ ✦

SITES	RESERVATIONS	CONTACT
🏕 🚐	(877) 444-6777 or www.recreation.gov	Mount Baker–Snoqualmie National Forest North Bend Ranger District (425) 888-1421
	OPEN	
48 sites, no hookups, RVs to 35 feet	Late May to mid-September	

It's not exactly gorgeous, but as one of only two Interstate 90 campgrounds west of Snoqualmie Summit, it'll have to do. Tinkham, still hanging in there in spite of repeated flood damage through the years, offers sites set beneath shady (OK, flat-out dark), second-growth trees not far (not nearly far enough) from the roar of Interstate 90 and the South Fork Snoqualmie River. But it is centrally located, amidst a half dozen popular (too popular!) day-hiking trails. The campground has pit toilets and hand-pumped water. Sites 20–23 are barrier free. The truth: It's not a place we'd go to spend a relaxing weekend. But it makes do as a decent overnight stopover, with the added bonus of twenty-eight reservable sites. Bonus points to anyone who can figure out what happened to campsite 12.

Getting there: From Interstate 90 about 8 miles east of North Bend, take Exit 42, Tinkham, turn right (south) under the freeway, and follow signs about 1.5 miles east on Tinkham Road 55.

18 Denny Creek ✦ ✦ ✦ ✦

SITES	RESERVATIONS	CONTACT
🏕 🚐	(877) 444-6777 or www.recreation.gov	Mount Baker–Snoqualmie National Forest North Bend Ranger District (425) 888-1421
	OPEN	
33 sites, 11 electrical hookups, RVs to 35 feet	Mid-June through September	

Campers seeking a quick night's sleep on the west side of Snoqualmie Pass will find Denny Creek their best, most amenity-packed option. Located between Lodge Creek and the South Fork Snoqualmie River in a steep drainage below Interstate 90, the campground's thirty-three sites are set amidst shady trees along the gurgling stream, which tends to help drown out the annoying freeway noise. The campground, named for prominent Seattle settler David Denny, has hand-pumped water and, unlike many Forest Service camps, flush toilets (recently upgraded to barrier-free status). More pluses: All the sites have tent pads, ten front on the river, and a majority are reservable. A group site for thirty-five to forty campers is available.

The campground is located near several very popular day hikes, including the family-friendly Franklin Falls Trail and the spectacular Denny Creek Trail. The latter path leads to Keekwulee and Snowshoe falls, then on to Hemlock Pass and ultimately Melakwa Lake (4.5 miles) in the Alpine Lakes Wilderness. The paved frontage road

Denny Creek Campground was upgraded not long ago with more modern facilities.

leading northeast from the campground—the old Snoqualmie Pass highway—takes mountain bikers to Snoqualmie Summit, where the Pacific Crest Trail and the Iron Horse State Park cross-state trail can be accessed easily.

Note: The road to the campground is often flood-damaged in the winter. Call before heading here in the spring.

Getting there: From Interstate 90 about 13 miles east of North Bend, take Exit 47. Drive north under the freeway, turn right at the T intersection. Drive 0.25 mile, and then turn left on Denny Creek Road 58. Proceed 2 miles to the campground entrance on the left.

19 Crystal Springs ✦ ✦ ◀

SITES	RESERVATIONS	CONTACT
🏕️ 🚻	None	Wenatchee National Forest Cle Elum Ranger District (509) 852-1100
	OPEN	
24 sites, no hookups, RVs to 21 feet	Mid-May to mid-September	

Hidden in a forested cove behind the Keechelus Dam, which has made a big ol' lake out of what once was the high headwaters of the Yakima River, Crystal Springs is probably better known for its wintertime use—as a major Sno-Park trail-head for cross-country skiers and snowmobilers—than for summertime escapes.

But... surprise! All that snow melts away in May to reveal a quaint little campground, with decent sites for tents and very small RVs, including two double sites for small groups. Its proximity to noisy Interstate 90 is a big drawback, but this is a prime location for recreation. Hikers and mountain bikers can set out from here across the Keechelus Dam and connect with the Iron Horse State Park cross-state trail to the south, and Snoqualmie Summit and the 2-mile-long Snoqualmie Tunnel (dress warmly and pack a good flashlight) to the west. Another good cycling side trip is Lake Kachess, the next major reservoir north (see below). The campground has pit toilets, but no piped water. The elevation is 2400 feet—about 600 feet below, and east of, Snoqualmie Summit.

Getting there: The campground is just off Interstate 90 Exit 62, 10 miles east of Snoqualmie Summit, 20 miles west of Cle Elum.

20 Kachess ★ ★ ★ ★

SITES	RESERVATIONS	CONTACT
🏕️ 🚐	(877) 444-6777 or www.recreation.gov	Wenatchee National Forest Cle Elum Ranger District (509) 852-1100
	OPEN	
120 sites, no hookups, RVs to 32 feet	Late May through September	

You're in luck. Kachess, one of the largest Forest Service campgrounds in the state, also is one of the niftiest in the Central Cascades, with a wealth of nicely spaced campsites in second-growth pine forest along the banks of Kachess Reservoir northeast of Easton. This is an active place in the summer, with a wealth of opportunities

A sunny spot along the Lake Kachess Reservoir

to keep the whole family busy. The vast, cold reservoir has a swimming area and boat launch, and rentals are available in summer. The campground, which has pit toilets and piped water, also features thirty double-size family sites, a group camp for fifty people, a pleasant, barrier-free nature trail, a picnic area with grand views of the lake, and a host of other features. It's also a good base for heading out on some of the local Alpine Lakes Wilderness trails (the Rachel Lake trailhead is nearby). The lone drawback: All that boat and watersport activity can make it a bit noisy here, especially in early summer, when the reservoir is full. If you're seeking solitude, try camping here in late August or September, after the reservoir is drawn down far enough to drive the boaters off and turn the swimming beach into a big mudflat. For peak summer weeks, use the reservation system; forty-two sites can be reserved in advance.

Getting there: From Interstate 90 eastbound, take Exit 62 (Crystal Springs), cross over the freeway, and follow signs about 5 miles north to the campground.

21 Lake Easton State Park ✶ ✶ ✶ ⁂

SITES	RESERVATIONS		CONTACT
🏕️ 🚐	(888) 226-7688 or www.parks.wa.gov		Washington State Parks (360) 902-8844
	OPEN		Lake Easton State Park (509) 656-2586
140 sites, 45 hookups, RVs to 60 feet	Late April to mid-October for camping; year-round for day use		

It looks an awful lot like a pretty, natural alpine lake. Well, it isn't. But so what? You're the only one in the crowd who knows better, and nobody else will figure it out. Lake Easton actually is a reservoir, part of the same upper Yakima River water-storage system that created nearby Kachess Reservoir to the north. But the 516-acre state park on its northern shores is a lovely place, with campsites spread through loops wooded with stately firs on bluffs above the lakeshore. The park also has a walk-in group campsite for up to fifty people (call for reservations). The waterfront picnic/swimming area is particularly nice, and the lake becomes a decent rainbow trout fishery late in the summer, when the water warms. A boat ramp and 20-foot dock complete the water-sports picture. Don't forget the mountain bikes: Plenty of local backroads beckon, and connections to the Iron Horse State Park cross-state trail can be made easily (see Crystal Springs, above). The main drawback: freeway noise. The campground is quite close to Interstate 90, and the roar of trucks seems to bounce off the valley walls here—all night long. The park stays open in winter for day use, primarily by cross-country skiers and snowmobilers. You'll need a state Sno-Park permit to access the 37 miles of ski trails that begin here. Most of them are beginner/intermediate and quite pleasant.

Getting there: From Interstate 90 eastbound, take Exit 70 (15 miles east of Snoqualmie Pass; about a mile west of Easton) and follow signs a short distance to the park.

Roslyn and Cle Elum River Valley

22 Wish Poosh ★ ★ ★ ◄

SITES	RESERVATIONS		CONTACT
 🏕️ 🏞️🚐 34 sites, no hookups, RVs to 21 feet	None		Wenatchee National Forest Cle Elum Ranger District (509) 852-1100
	OPEN		
	Mid-May through September		

A lot of people hike many, many miles, carrying many, many pounds on their backs to rub shoulders and boot-soles with the Alpine Lakes Wilderness, one of the most spectacular alpine areas in the Lower 48. Others do it the easy way—by car, up the Cle Elum and Teanaway River valleys. The Cle Elum River Valley, which juts north toward—and ultimately into—the Alpine Lakes Wilderness from its start near the *Northern Exposure* TV series backdrop of Roslyn, offers some of the most "wild"-feeling camping in the state, and it's easy to reach from the Seattle area. The price you pay for that luxury is the lack thereof; most campgrounds in the Cle Elum River Valley are fairly spartan Forest Service camps, high on pine trees, clear water, blue skies, and wildflowers, and low on amenities. But two of these camps, Wish Poosh, the first encountered along State Route 903 (Salmon La Sac Road), and Salmon La Sac (see below), are comfortable enough to let you have it both ways. Wish Poosh is on the shores of Lake Cle Elum, actually a large reservoir on the lower river. It's extremely popular with boaters, who can launch here and ply the wide, flat waters. Note: The lake recedes farther and farther away from the campground as summer progresses! The camping area is quite nice, with four double-wide "family" sites, large enough to accommodate two RVs or two cars with tents. Perfect for families camping together. About half the sites are designated for tents, twenty-two for trailers and RVs. The campground has pit toilets and piped water.

Getting there: From Interstate 90, take Exit 80, follow signs about 4 miles to downtown Roslyn, then follow SR 903 (Salmon La Sac Road) 6.5 miles north to the campground, on the left.

23 Cle Elum River ★★★

SITES	RESERVATIONS	CONTACT
23 sites, no hookups, RVs to 30 feet	Group site only; (877) 444-6777 or www.recreation.gov	Wenatchee National Forest Cle Elum Ranger District (509) 852-1100
	OPEN	
	Mid-May through September	

Cle Elum River, the next in line (after Wish Poosh) on a drive up the Cle Elum River Valley, is the alternate campsite on Lake Cle Elum, a reservoir on the lower river. It's a standard Forest Service camp, with only two sites designated as tent sites, although tenters would be fine with most of them. The campground, at 2200 feet near the head of the lake (it turns to a large meadow in late summer and fall), has pit toilets and hand-pumped water. The gravel roads give it a rustic feel. Note that the large group camp (up to 100 people; reservations required) to the immediate right inside the entrance has been developed (at the expense of some individual sites) to replace the former group site at Salmon La Sac, farther up State Route 903.

Getting there: From Interstate 90, take Exit 80, follow signs about 4 miles to Roslyn, then follow SR 903 (Salmon La Sac Road) 11.5 miles north to the campground, on the left.

24 Red Mountain ★★◀

SITES	RESERVATIONS	CONTACT
10 sites	None	Wenatchee National Forest Cle Elum Ranger District (509) 852-1100
	OPEN	
	Mid-May through October; winter with no fees or services	

Tired of being surrounded by behemoth Winnebagos? They'd be hard pressed to follow you here. Red Mountain, a mile north of Cle Elum River Campground (see above), is classic, old-time Forest Service–style camping: fire pits, an occasional picnic table, and not much else (the campground has no piped water, not to mention showers). But it does allow you to pitch a tent within spitting distance of the gurgling, ultra-clear Cle Elum River, which will lull you to sleep in a heartbeat. We've seen this campground become home to far more than ten groups of overnight campers; tenters tend to spread out north and south of here along the river, practicing allowable "dispersed camping." It's not fancy, but for most tenters, it'll do. Note: Unlike other campgrounds on this stretch, Red Mountain isn't gated at the end of September. You can continue to camp here—for free—through the fall, until snows block access. Bring your own water, toilet paper, and garbage bags.

Getting there: From Interstate 90, take Exit 80, follow signs about 4 miles to Roslyn, then follow State Route 903 (Salmon La Sac Road) 13 miles north to the campground, on the left.

25 Salmon La Sac ★ ★ ★ ★

SITES	RESERVATIONS	CONTACT
🏕 🚐 60 sites, no hookups, RVs to 21 feet	(888) 444-6677 or www.recreation.gov	Wenatchee National Forest Cle Elum Ranger District (509) 852-1100
	OPEN Late May to mid-September	

It's not quite paradise. But you can hike there from here. Salmon La Sac, the largest and most popular campground in the Cle Elum River Valley, is one of the very nicest tent-plunking or RV-parking spots in the Central Cascades. Spread out on a plateau above the crisp, clear river, the campground accommodates both tenters and small-scale RVers, making this a prime summertime destination for hikers, anglers, mountain bikers, nature lovers, and unapologetically lazy campers. The campground took a major hit during the massive regional flooding of November 2006, when the river rose up and took about a third of this former 100-site campground with it. But it has since reopened and remains a great destination, albeit smaller.

The campground lies at the end of the pavement on Salmon La Sac Road, but many of the greater natural wonders in this area are found farther up the valley, which turns into a winding, gravel road above the campground. Salmon La Sac campers can cycle or drive up this road to stunning upper-river alpine meadows, chock full of wildflowers in spring and majestic colors in autumn. The road also leads to a string of trailheads leading to beloved Alpine Lakes Wilderness destinations: French Creek to Paddy Go Easy Pass (6 miles round-trip), Jolly Mountain (12.5 miles round-trip), and the Deception Pass Loop (15 miles), to name just a few. But you don't need to venture far to find great hiking from Salmon La Sac. Trailheads right near the campground put you on the path to Waptus Lake (16 miles round-trip) near Mount David, one of the more spectacular overnight destinations in the Alpine Lakes Wilderness (permits required; call the ranger station number listed). Day hikers can hoof it 5 miles to Cooper Lake, where you'll find a gorgeous walk-in campground (Owhi; see below), plus another trailhead for hikers bound for Pete Lake (15 miles round-trip).

If all that sounds a bit ambitious, you can stay "home" at your campsite and fish; the Cle Elum River offers a chance to hook into a rainbow, although fishing has been fairly slow here in recent years—it's usually more productive downstream in Lake Cle Elum Reservoir, or upstream at (hike-in) Hyas Lake. Salmon La Sac is a large, active campground, equipped with piped water, flush toilets, and Cayuse Horse Camp (thirteen sites, three horsies each). Some sites are barrier free. The main drawback is that many sites are bone-dry and quite dusty in the summer. But the campground makes up for that with some truly gorgeous, riverfront sites, many equipped with niceties such as campfire benches and stone cooking stoves, complete with chimneys. The elevation here is 2400 feet.

Getting there: From Interstate 90, take Exit 80, follow signs about 4 miles to Roslyn, then follow State Route 903 (Salmon La Sac Road) 15.5 miles north to the campground, across the bridge on the left.

The Cle Elum River near Salmon La Sac is a beautiful, and often destructive, force.

26 Owhi ★ ★ ★ ◂

SITES	RESERVATIONS	CONTACT
	None	Wenatchee National Forest Cle Elum Ranger District (509) 852-1100
	OPEN	
22 sites	Mid-June to October; winters with no fees or services	

It's not easy to find, but for tent campers, Owhi is a true hidden gem, worthy of the journey. The campground sits on the wooded shore of Cooper Lake, an absolutely stunning, clear-water lake near the edge of the Alpine Lakes Wilderness. The sites are all walk-ins, some quite private, others in a group setting. From some campsites, and especially from canoes in the middle of the lake, the view of the snow-clad Three Queens peak is spectacular. It's a great spot for tenters with canoes or small boats (no motors, internal combustion or electric); fishing in the lake can be productive after waters warm in midsummer. This is also a grand spot for further exploration on local trails. One trail from the campground leads 5 miles to Pete Lake, and beyond to

Anglers fish for trout in Cooper Lake, near Owhi Campground.

Spectacle Lakes, both popular backpacking destinations (permits required; call the Cle Elum Ranger District for details). The campground has pit toilets but no piped water or showers. The elevation is 2800 feet.

Getting there: From Interstate 90, take Exit 80, follow signs about 4 miles to Roslyn, then drive 21 miles northwest to the campground via State Route 903 (Salmon La Sac Road) and Forest Service Road 46.

Other Cle Elum River Valley Campgrounds

Beyond Salmon La Sac, the road up the Cle Elum River turns to (steep, rough) gravel, and campsites get downright rustic—although you'd be surprised at the size of RVs that somehow make it up here. The road eventually opens into a wide, green valley near the Cle Elum River's headwaters. Campers take advantage of all this space, popping up tents in many "unofficial" campsites, such as **Scatter Creek** at the south end of Tucquala Lake (this kind of camping is allowed in the National Forest). The Forest Service lists only one official, established camp on the upper Cle Elum: **Fish Lake** (three sites), at the north end of the same marshy valley, about 29 miles north of Roslyn. Camping is free but primitive, with pit toilets but no picnic tables, piped water, or other services; call Wenatchee National Forest, Cle Elum Ranger District, (509) 674-4411. Note: The access road, Forest Road 4330, can be treacherous; trailers and RVs aren't recommended. In addition, Scatter Creek crosses the road in a concrete basin in the upper valley. To reach Fish Lake and the end of the road, you must drive across it, which can be a risky proposition during spring melt-off. Also, day hikers can walk an easy 4 miles from the trailhead at the end of Road 4330 to Hyas Lake, which has a number of nice, albeit primitive, lakeshore campsites.

Blewett Pass and Ellensburg

27 Beverly ★ ★ ★

SITES	RESERVATIONS	CONTACT
⛺ 🚐	None	Wenatchee National Forest Cle Elum Ranger District (509) 852-1100
	OPEN	
16 sites, no hookups, RVs to 21 feet	June through October	

To many Washingtonians, the Teanaway River Valley northeast of Cle Elum is as close as you can come to Montana without ever leaving the Evergreen State. This dry, scenic, east-slope forest is filled with secret little "dispersed" camping spots, the locations of which occupants guard fiercely. But you can camp in established sites here as well. One such place is Beverly, a remote camp on the North Fork Teanaway River. It's out there, peaceful and primitive (pit toilets, no piped water or showers). The campground is popular with stream anglers and, especially, hikers. A nearby trail, Esmerelda Basin, is one of the most popular in the Alpine Lakes Wilderness. Another, the Beverly–Turnpike Trail, is often used by Stuart Range mountain and rock climbers. It's also the primary western access to the Ingalls Creek Trail, a popular backpack route along the southern edge of the Stuart Range, between the North Fork Teanaway and the Blewett Pass area to the east. The campground elevation is 3100 feet.

Getting there: From Cle Elum, follow County Road 970 about 8 miles northeast to Teanaway River Road. Turn left (northwest) and drive to the end of the paved road, about 13 miles. Bear right and continue north on Forest Road 9737 to the campground, about 4 miles.

28 Mineral Springs ★ ★

SITES	RESERVATIONS	CONTACT
⛺ 🚐	Group site only; (877) 444-6777 or www.recreation.gov	Wenatchee National Forest Cle Elum Ranger District (509) 852-1100
	OPEN	
7 sites, no hookups, RVs to 21 feet	Mid-May to late September; winters with no fees or services	

One of a handful of Forest Service camps along winding, occasionally washed-out U.S. Highway 97 (the Blewett Pass Highway), tiny, cramped Mineral Springs offers a handful of tent/small RV sites at the confluence of Medicine and Swauk creeks. It's close enough to the highway to feel the big trucks roll by. You'll probably want to camp here only if you can't get into Swauk, another 3.5 miles up US 97. Mineral Springs gets plenty of use in the fall, when hunters take over, and in winter, when snowmobilers and cross-country skiers move in. A group site for up to fifty campers is available by reservation only. The elevation is 2700 feet.

Getting there: From Interstate 90 near Cle Elum, follow County Road 970 about 12 miles northeast to the junction with US 97. Continue straight on US 97, proceeding another 6.3 miles north to the campground, on the left (west) side of the highway.

29 Swauk ★ ★ ★ ◀

SITES	RESERVATIONS	CONTACT
◮ 🚐	None	Wenatchee National Forest Cle Elum Ranger District (509) 852-1100
	OPEN	
22 sites, no hookups, RVs to 21 feet	Mid-April to late September	

Swauk, set along the gushing waters of Swauk Creek, near U.S. Highway 97, is many campers' favorite spot along Blewett Pass—a mountain pass that connects Interstate 90 near Cle Elum with U.S. Highway 2 near Leavenworth. The camp is in a pretty location: A mixed pine and fir forest, with some truly cozy sites, such as our favorite, number 18, down on the end. A nice picnic shelter is found in the day-use area. The main drawback is highway noise. Still, it's a nice spot, and the camp is a popular summer stopover for hikers, and winter haunt for snowmobilers, snowshoers, and cross-country skiers visiting the Swauk Sno-Park for adventures around Swauk and Blewett passes. The old Blewett Pass Highway intersects US 97 about 1.5 miles south of the campground. The campground has pit toilets but no piped water or showers. The elevation is 3200 feet.

Getting there: From Interstate 90 near Cle Elum, follow County Road 970 about 12 miles northeast to the junction with US 97. Continue straight on US 97, proceeding another 9.8 miles north to the campground, on the right (east) side of the highway.

Other Blewett Pass/Ellensburg Campgrounds

A slate of remote, backcountry campgrounds operated by the Cle Elum Ranger District offer alternatives to the more popular campsites listed above. Most of these are horse camps in the high, dry alpine areas of the Wenatchee National Forest, but they also make suitable camps for backcountry camping enthusiasts. They are **Ken Wilcox Campground** at Haney Meadows (nineteen sites), a campground/horse camp at 5500 feet, 8 miles off U.S. Highway 97 on Road 9712; **Red Top** (three sites), near the end of Road 9702, 28 miles northeast of Cle Elum; **Rider's Camp**, a dispersed camp area for groups, 25 miles west of Ellensburg on Road 3100; **Quartz Mountain** (three sites), 33 miles west of Ellensburg on Road 3100; **Manastash Camp** (fourteen sites), 26 miles west of Ellensburg on Road 3104; **Tamarack Spring** (three sites), 25 miles south of Cle Elum on Road 3120; **Taneum** (thirteen walk-in sites), 18 miles south of Cle Elum on Taneum Road 33; **Icewater Creek** (thirteen sites), 18 miles south of Cle Elum on Taneum Road 33; **Taneum Junction** (group site for seventy-five people/fifteen vehicles), 20 miles south of Cle Elum on Taneum Road 33; **Lion Rock Spring** (three sites), 23 miles north of Ellensburg on Road 35; and **South Fork Meadow** (three sites),

A sign points the way for hikers in Swauk Campground.

25 miles south of Cle Elum on Road 3300 Spur 119. All are primitive, with pit toilets, but no piped water or other services. Some of these campgrounds are free. Call the Wenatchee National Forest, Cle Elum Ranger District, (509) 852-1100.

Another remote, free campground in the area is **Indian Horse Camp** (ten tent sites), 19 miles northeast of Cle Elum on Middle Fork Teanaway Road. Call the Department of Natural Resources in Ellensburg, (509) 925-8510.

Finally, if you're stuck in windy Ellensburg visiting the kid in college, your best bet is the **Ellensburg KOA,** 32 Thorp Highway South., (509) 925-9319.

5. SOUTH CASCADES

You might want to seriously consider packing a few signal flares along with the s'mores fixings.

A person could get lost out here.

For many Washington campers, the South Cascades, a sprawling sea of deep, dark forests, ancient and contemporary volcanoes, silvery rivers—and indefatigable mosquitoes—are like that long-neglected storage room: You know there's stuff in there you want to see, but you have no idea how to even start wading through it.

Well, we know the feeling. Been there, done that, got high-centered on the Forest Service Road. We've spent more time than we care to admit kicking around in the deep woods of Mount Rainier National Park, the Gifford Pinchot and Wenatchee national forests, the Mount Adams Wilderness, and the Columbia River Gorge, looking for those rare slices of Cascade alpine heaven.

We have but one thing to report: Man, are they ever out there. In droves.

Just get a good map, and try not to confuse one bit of heaven with another. This portion of the state, from Mount Rainier south to the Bridge of the Gods and east to Goldendale, contains by far the highest concentration of campsites in Washington. The vast majority of them are small, somewhat remote National Forest sites, reached by driving 20 or more miles on forest roads, which more often than not are constructed of that fine, washboarded gravel. You know the type: roads you still feel in your large intestine a day later.

That should suggest something right off the bat: With some notable exceptions, these generally aren't the kinds of places you'll find your great aunt and uncle taking the Minnie Winnie for a couple weeks. Vast stretches of this undeveloped land are left to the rest of you infidels in tents and small RVs. You'll find yourself in luck. Many of the very best tent sites in the state, if not all of the West, are found in this area—on alpine lakes in the Goat Rocks Wilderness south of White Pass, on high-mountain streams near the Indian Heaven Wilderness, and on the rocky slopes of barely dormant volcanoes named Adams and St. Helens.

This is a big, diverse playground, and visitors will note that in most of it, the farther one travels east from the Cascade Crest, the more the activity of choice changes. Some campgrounds on the east side are fine camps in their own right, but their heavy use by dirt bikes or off-road vehicles could be a major turn-off for non-like-minded recreationists.

One thing is certain: You'll never get bored. They are a work in progress, these South Cascades. Think you've seen it all? Go back next week. Nature, in its own charming and destructive way, likely will have changed things around since the last visit. Truly knowing these lands is a lifelong project. And your life is getting shorter by the minute.

SPECIAL NOTE ON NACHES RANGER DISTRICT CAMPGROUNDS

The Naches Ranger District has turned many campgrounds in the Chinook Pass and White Pass areas over to a private concessionaire, Northwest Land Management, which now *requires* reservations at its campgrounds. Individual campground listings in the following pages include contact information, but here is an overview as there are some costs involved. Choose accordingly:

Concessionaire-operated camps in the **Chinook Pass area** include Lodgepole, Pleasant Valley, Little Naches, Sawmill Flat, Cottonwood, Hells Crossing, Soda Springs, Cougar Flat, Cedar Springs, and Lower and Upper Bumping Lake. These camps offer more services, but for a price. At this writing, campsites were $17–$19 per night—plus a reservation fee. Other campgrounds in the region still operated by the U.S. Forest Service generally offer fewer services, but at a reduced price of $7–$10 per night.

These include American Forks, Bumping Crossing, Crow Creek, Kaner Flat, and Halfway Flat. The latter camps do not accept reservations.

In the **White Pass area,** Northwest Land Management oversees Indian Creek, Hause Creek, Willows, and Windy Point. As with the above, these camps generally offer more services and cost $17–$19 plus a reservation fee (at this writing). The U.S. Forest Service still operates White Pass Lake, Dog Lake, and Clear Lake North and South, as well as many camps farther east along U.S. Highway 12. No reservations and generally fewer services, but only $5–$15 per night.

Opposite: *Mount Rainier gleams with alpenglow at dusk from Paradise Visitor Center.*

Mount Rainier National Park

1 Mowich Lake
2 Alder Lake/Rocky Point
3 Big Creek
4 Cougar Rock
5 Ohanapecosh
6 White River

Chinook Pass Corridor

7 The Dalles
8 Silver Springs
9 Corral Pass
10 Lodgepole
11 Pleasant Valley
12 Hells Crossing
13 Cedar Springs
14 Soda Springs
15 Cougar Flat
16 Bumping Crossing
17 Upper and Lower Bumping Lake
18 Little Naches
19 Kaner Flat
20 Crow Creek
21 Sawmill Flat
22 Halfway Flat
23 Cottonwood

Eastern White Pass Corridor

24 La Wis Wis
25 Summit Creek
26 Soda Springs
27 Walupt Lake
28 White Pass Lake (Leech Lake)
29 Dog Lake
30 Clear Lake North
31 Clear Lake South
32 Indian Creek
33 Peninsula
34 South Fork
35 Hause Creek
36 Willows
37 Windy Point

Mount St. Helens/West Slopes US 12

38 Lewis and Clark State Park
39 Ike Kinswa State Park
40 Mayfield Lake Park
41 Mossyrock Park
42 Taidnapam Park
43 Iron Creek
44 Tower Rock
45 North Fork
46 Seaquest State Park
47 Lower Falls Recreation Area

Southern Gifford Pinchot National Forest

48 Beaver
49 Panther Creek
50 Paradise Creek
51 Moss Creek
52 Oklahoma
53 Peterson Prairie
54 Goose Lake
55 Cultus Creek
56 Tillicum

Mount Adams

57 Morrison Creek
58 Blue Lake Creek
59 Adams Fork
60 Horseshoe Lake
61 Takhlakh Lake

Columbia River Gorge

62 Beacon Rock State Park
63 Columbia Hills State Park
64 Brooks Memorial State Park
65 Maryhill State Park

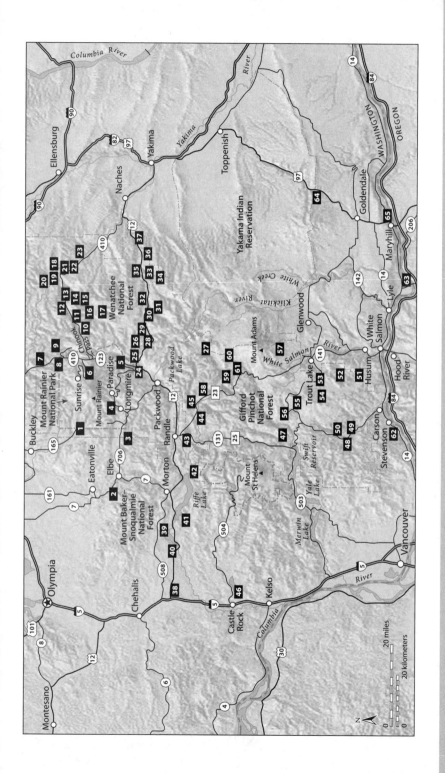

Mount Rainier National Park

I Mowich Lake ✦✦✦

SITES	RESERVATIONS	CONTACT
	None	Mount Rainier National Park
	OPEN	(360) 569-2211
30 sites	Late June through October	

Mowich Lake, Mount Rainier's most remote mountain camp for car campers (now that Ipsut Creek Campground on the Carbon River has likely been lost to auto access forever), is a walk-in campground in the northwest corner of the park, near some of Rainier's most scenic day-hiking trails. Campers who haul their stuff a short distance to the thirty loosely organized sites here are in for a treat—waterfront camping on a picturesque lake, with Rainier looming in the distance. From here, hikers can set out on the Spray Falls Trail, which leads to the falls, Spray Park, Seattle Park, the Carbon Glacier, and other, more distant destinations. Many are reached via the Wonderland Trail, which stretches 93 miles all the way around Mount Rainier.

The campground is fairly primitive, with chemical vault toilets and tables but no piped water or other services. Campfires are not allowed. Note that Mowich Lake Road does not open until early summer and usually remains rough and washboarded all summer. It also sometimes washes out. The campground elevation is 4929 feet. Note: Stays are limited to fourteen days at all Mount Rainier National Park campgrounds.

Getting there: From Puyallup, drive 13 miles east on State Route 410 to Buckley. Turn right (south) on State Route 165 and proceed through Carbonado. Just beyond the Carbon River Gorge Bridge, bear right onto Mowich Lake Road. Follow the road about 17 miles to its end. Note: The road is unpaved beyond its junction with the Carbon River Road.

2 Alder Lake/Rocky Point ✦✦✦✦

SITES	RESERVATIONS	CONTACT
	(888) 226-7688 or www.mytpu.org/	Alder Lake Park
	OPEN	(360) 569-2778 or
173 sites, 111 full or partial hookups	Year-round, except December 20 through January 1	(888) 502-8690 for lake levels

Alder Lake and Rocky Point, a subsidiary campground 4 miles to the east, are part of a sprawling Tacoma Power complex on Alder Lake, a 3000-acre Nisqually River reservoir behind 330-foot Alder Dam. They're both popular summertime destinations for boaters and water-skiers, although the lake turns to a large, stump-studded mudflat in late

Alder Lake is one of several nearby sites managed by Tacoma Power.

summer and autumn when the reservoir draws down. Campsites in three loops at the main Alder Lake area are pleasant, level, and tidy, set in a mixed forest that's not too shady during the cool season. Rocky Point is smaller, but equally well equipped, with twenty-five campsites, each with electrical/water hookups. A twenty-site group camp area also has full RV hookups. Fishing is good in season for bass, kokanee, and rainbow and cutthroat trout. Both camp areas have their own day-use/picnic area and boat launch; the Stacel Creek area at Alder Lake proper offers boat moorage. This campground's location makes it a good base camp for exploring Mount Rainier, as well.

Getting there: The main campground is at the junction of State Route 7 and School Road, near the Alder Parks Store (just west of the SR 7/ SR 706 junction at Elbe). Rocky Point Campground is 4 miles west on SR 7.

3 Big Creek ★ ★ ★

SITES	RESERVATIONS	CONTACT
🏕️ 🚐 29 sites, no hookups, RVs to 22 feet	(877) 444-6777 or www.recreation.gov	Gifford Pinchot National Forest Cowlitz Valley Ranger District (360) 497-1100
	OPEN	
	Late May to mid-September	

Big Creek, a small campground near the western entrance to Mount Rainier National Park, is a good alternative for those summer weekends when you just know the national park will be packed. Sites are nicely spaced and offer privacy that appeals to tent campers. Most RVers will find the campground's corners and narrow passages—between large hemlock, fir, and maple trees—difficult to negotiate, although the

A small waterfall greets day hikers along the Paradise River.

camp does have some pull-through sites. This is a good place to come tent camping with the in-laws (if there indeed is such a place): Four of the sites here are double-sized "family" spots, able to accommodate two vehicles. All the wonders of Mount Rainier's southwest side, including the Paradise day-use area, are a short drive away. The campground has pit toilets and piped water. The elevation is 1818 feet.

Getting there: Big Creek is 4 miles south of Ashford (about 23 miles north of Packwood) via State Route 706 and Forest Road 52.

4 Cougar Rock ★ ★ ★ ◀

SITES	RESERVATIONS	CONTACT
🏕️ 🚐	(877) 444-6777 or www.recreation.gov	Mount Rainier National Park (360) 569-2211
	OPEN	
173 sites, no hookups, RVs to 35 feet	Late-May to early October	

Cougar Rock, the main campground for southside (Paradise-area) visitors to Mount Rainier National Park, is now the only campground on the south side, after the rampaging floods of November 2006 wiped Sunshine Point, a former campground just inside the Nisqually Entrance, right off the map.

Even before this sole status, Cougar Rock was a victim of its own success. It's so scenic, and so popular in a park that's so overcrowded, you likely need a reservation to get in here between late June and Labor Day. Returning campers will be happy to note that the former mandatory reservation system in effect during peak summer months here and at Ohanpecosh Campground has now been ditched in favor of a more sensible voluntary reservations scheme.

Campers lucky enough to land a site here will find a small camping city, with great access to all of Rainier's summertime delights, including some of the best day-hiking in the state (weather permitting). Sites, set in small, subalpine trees, have medium privacy, and are suitable for both tents and RVs. Don't expect tent pads, though—this campground was laid out before the dawn of the Super Jumbo Colossal Costco tent. The campground has piped water, flush toilets, an RV dump station, an amphitheater, and other niceties. No showers, of course; the National Park Service doesn't want anyone to get too comfortable.

Group sites for twelve or more are available. The elevation is 3180 feet. Note: Stays are limited to fourteen days at all Mount Rainier National Park campgrounds.

Getting there: From Tacoma, drive south on State Route 7 to Elbe, and continue 12 miles east on State Route 706 to the Mount Rainier National Park Nisqually entrance. Proceed 6 miles to Longmire and another 2.3 miles to the campground entrance, on the left.

5 Ohanapecosh ★ ★ ★ ★ ◢

SITES	RESERVATIONS	CONTACT
⛺ 🚐	(877) 444-6777 or www.recreation.gov	Mount Rainier National Park (360) 569-2211
	OPEN	
188 sites, no hookups, RVs to 32 feet	Late May to mid-October	

Ohanapecosh is the premier camping area at Mount Rainier, and one of the finest in the state, thanks to its location along the beautiful Ohanapecosh River. The stream is crystal clear much of the year because it drains the eastern flanks of the mountain, where few glaciers are active enough to dispense glacial flour. Campsites are found on both sides of the river here, and they're all quite scenic, set in the forest at an elevation of 1914 feet.

This is a great place for families to camp and take day hikes right from their campsite. Trails leading from the campground up the river have it all: old-growth trees, an awesome river gorge spanned by a log bridge, a thundering waterfall, and access to the park's fabled Shadow of the Sentinels Trail, which leads between some massive, thousand-year-old western red cedars and Douglas firs. This river valley truly is one of the more beautiful, memorable spots in a state that's chock full of outdoor delights. A visitor center in the campground is a nice added touch, particularly for families. The campground is also strategically located: Stevens Canyon Road, the park's drive-through scenic showcase between here and the Paradise area on the south side of the mountain, begins just to the north. Or, proceed north on State Route 123 up the east side of the mountain to Chinook Pass and more jaw-dropping views along State Route 410.

The shady campground itself is wanting somewhat for privacy, but you probably won't mind in the plum sites along the river, where the rushing Ohanapecosh always seems to make everything seem all right. Not surprisingly, campsites are tough to come by here in the summertime. Reservations are no longer required here in summer, but still a good idea if you're camping between late June and Labor Day weekend.

Oh—Make sure you're on your best behavior at this camp: The staff here has earned a reputation for being, shall we say, a little excessively protective of the grounds. We've seen senior citizens shooed away for picnicking in the wrong place. And we personally received a major tongue-lashing here for committing the mortal sin of using a solar shower in the campground. You've been warned. Note: Stays are limited to fourteen days at all Mount Rainier National Park campgrounds. If Ohanapecosh is full, a good alternative is La Wis Wis, a Forest Service campground 7 miles to the south, near Packwood (see below).

Getting there: The campground is 5 miles north of the SR 123/U.S. Highway 12 junction near Packwood. During summer months, visitors from the Seattle area also can reach the campground via State Route 706 (Stevens Canyon Road) from the west, or SR 410 (Chinook Pass Highway) from the north.

6 White River ★ ★ ★

SITES	RESERVATIONS	CONTACT
	None	Mount Rainier National Park (360) 569-2211
	OPEN	
112 sites, no hookups, RVs to 20 feet	Late June to mid-September	

White River, an older campground in a pleasant locale near the river sharing its name, serves a dual purpose: It sucks in many of the hordes of tourists heading up to the spectacular Sunrise day-use area for hiking, picnicking, and photography, and it doubles as a trailhead for backpackers and climbers headed to some of the park's most spectacular backcountry sites. Needless to say, it all adds up to large crowds, which often push the limits of this campground. Take the RV size limit literally: Most campsites here are tiny, and many are cramped together, with only minimal, small-tree cover for privacy between sites. It's best enjoyed by tenters who don't mind being around many, many other tenters, particularly during the peak tourist season.

Fortunately, that's often the primary clientele: White River is the launching point for a trail to a viewpoint of the snout of the Emmons Glacier, then on up the White River to Glacier Basin, a popular backpack destination. (Note: The lower part of this route, along the river, was heavily damaged during the flooding of 2006; the trail was being reconstructed when this guide went to press.) The route extends beyond to Camp Schurman, a bivouac site for climbers headed up the Emmons Glacier route to the mountain's 14,411-foot summit. Another very popular trail to the Summerland/Panhandle Gap area

The Sunrise area is a prime attraction at Mount Rainier in the summer.

begins nearby, at Fryingpan Creek. The campground has an RV dump station. The elevation is 4400 feet. Note: Stays are limited to fourteen days at all Mount Rainier National Park campgrounds. If this campground is full, nearby Silver Springs (see below) is a great alternative, with far more spacious and livable campsites.

Getting there: From Enumclaw, drive 43 miles east on State Route 410 to the Mount Rainier National Park White River entrance. Proceed 5 miles west to the campground.

Chinook Pass Corridor

7 The Dalles ✦ ✦ ✦

SITES	RESERVATIONS	CONTACT
🏕 🚐	(877) 444-6777 or www.recreation.gov	Mount Baker–Snoqualmie National Forest White River Ranger District (360) 825-6585
	OPEN	
44 sites, no hookups, RVs to 21 feet	Memorial Day through Labor Day	

Like nearby Silver Springs (see below), The Dalles is a Forest Service camp outside the northern boundary of Mount Rainier National Park. The campground, situated in a stand of old-growth forest (which qualifies as rare anywhere in the Mount Baker–Snoqualmie National Forest), is quite pleasant, particularly on warm summer days, when the dense overhead canopy keeps the area cool. Sites on the west side are along the White River; eastside sites are set in the woods below State Route 410. A bonus for trip planners: More than half of the sites here can be reserved through the federal national reservation system, which allows online bookings. Saving a site in advance is a good idea in the summer. This park, as well as Silver Springs, gets plenty of overflow from Mount Rainier's overtaxed campgrounds (see Cougar Rock and Ohanapecosh, above). Crystal Mountain and the national park's spectacular Sunrise day-use area are short drives from The Dalles. The campground has pit toilets and piped water. The John Muir Nature Trail, a peaceful walk that's also barrier free, is nearby. Look for the giant Douglas fir along the way. The picnic area is a nice rest stop for road-weary summer Rainier visitors.

Getting there: The Dalles is 26 miles southeast of Enumclaw on SR 410 (7 miles north of Mount Rainier National Park).

8 Silver Springs ✦ ✦ ✦ ✦

SITES	RESERVATIONS	CONTACT
🏕 🚐	(877) 444-6777 or www.recreation.gov	Mount Baker–Snoqualmie National Forest White River Ranger District (360) 825-6585
	OPEN	
55 sites, no hookups, RVs to 30 feet	Mid-May to early October	

Silver Springs, one of four White River Ranger District campgrounds scattered in the forests north of Mount Rainier, is a good secret weapon for Mount Rainier–area explorers who don't want to fight the camping crowds within the national park itself. The campground is lovely, in a rare stand of old-growth forest along the White River. Sites, remodeled and repaved in recent years, are extremely spacious, offering great privacy

Opposite: Mount Rainier looms above Reflection Lake in the autumn.

for tenters and room to stretch out for RV or trailer owners. Some double-sized, family sites are an added feature for groups. A number of sites are barrier free. A natural spring is found in the midst of the campground, and the White River flows nearby.

Management practices here add a bit of flexibility to your itinerary: The majority of sites here can be reserved. Crystal Mountain and Sunrise both are short day trips from the campground, which has pit toilets and piped water. It's one of the better campgrounds you'll find in or around Mount Rainier National Park—with a fraction of the crowds.

Getting there: Silver Springs is 32 miles southeast of Enumclaw on State Route 410 (1 mile north of the Mount Rainier National Park boundary).

9 Corral Pass ★ ★

SITES	RESERVATIONS	CONTACT
🏕️	None	Mount Baker–Snoqualmie National Forest White River Ranger District (360) 825-6585
	OPEN	
20 sites	Mid-July through September	

Corral Pass, a high (5600-foot) camp in the Mount Baker–Snoqualmie National Forest northeast of Mount Rainier, often is used by hikers and horse packers as a base for exploring the nearby Norse Peak Wilderness. Day hiking can be fun right from this campground, providing you don't mind dodging a few horse pucks here and there. The campground itself is set in the forest and quite primitive, with pit toilets but no piped water or showers. It does have a horse-loading ramp, however—handy both for loading horses into trailers and piling Dad into the Mercury Navigator after a long trek into the mountains. A Northwest Forest Pass parking permit is required.

Getting there: From State Route 410, 31 miles southeast of Enumclaw, turn east on Forest Road 7174 and proceed 6 miles to the campground. (Note: The gravel road is rough and not suitable for trailers or RVs.)

10 Lodgepole ★ ★ ★

SITES	RESERVATIONS	CONTACT
🏕️🚐	Required; (877) 444-6777 or www.recreation.gov	Wenatchee National Forest Naches Ranger District (509) 653-1400
	OPEN	
33 sites, no hookups, RVs to 20 feet	May to late October	

Note the sweet smell of high, dry, mixed forest. State Route 410 explorers will note a marked difference as they follow the American River toward the east-slope Cascades. A string of Forest Service camps are found along the river, serving as great stopovers for long-distance travelers, or destinations for Seattle-area campers in need of a quick, dry-land wilderness fix. All these campgrounds border the 51,000-acre Norse Peak Wilderness, which stretches between the Chinook and Naches passes in the Wenatchee

The Naches Loop Trail is a great day trip for Chinook Pass–area campers.

National Forest. For the west-to-east traveler, the first campground on this stretch is Lodgepole, which has campsites scattered among pines, hand-pumped water, and pit toilets. Recent renovations to this camp make it much more pleasant, and for hikers, it's strategically located: The Norse Peak Wilderness lies due north, the 166,000-acre William O. Douglas Wilderness due south. The campground elevation is 3500 feet. (Reservations are required here. See special note on Naches Ranger District campgrounds, p. 181.)

Getting there: Lodgepole is 45 miles northwest of Naches (about 8 miles east of the Mount Rainier National Park boundary), near milepost 76 on SR 410.

11 Pleasant Valley ★ ★ ★ ◀

SITES	RESERVATIONS	CONTACT
🏕️ 🚐	Required; (877) 444-6777 or www.recreation.gov	Wenatchee National Forest Naches Ranger District (509) 653-1400
	OPEN	
16 sites, no hookups, RVs to 32 feet	Mid-May to November	

Like nearby Lodgepole and several other campgrounds, Pleasant Valley is a, well, pleasant Forest Service site on the American River in the Wenatchee National Forest, near the Norse Peak and William O. Douglas wildernesses. Unlike its neighbors, though, this campground has longer, more modern spaces that are better able to accommodate lengthy RVs. A recent renovation spiffed the place up considerably. The campground also has an RV dump station, as well as hand-pumped water and pit toilets. A trailhead at the campground leads up Kettle Creek to the American Ridge Trail, a 26.5-mile ridgetop path in the William O. Douglas Wilderness. The camp is very popular with RVers, and reservations are a good idea. The campground elevation is 3300 feet. (Reservations are required here. See special note on Naches Ranger District campgrounds, p. 181.)

Getting there: Pleasant Valley is 41.5 miles northwest of Naches, at milepost 80.2 on State Route 410.

12   Hells Crossing ★★★

SITES	RESERVATIONS	CONTACT
🏕️ 🚐	Required; (877) 444-6777 or www.recreation.gov	Wenatchee National Forest Naches Ranger District (509) 653-1400
	OPEN	
18 sites, no hookups, RVs to 16 feet	May to November	

Another in the string of Wenatchee National Forest camps along the American River, Hells Crossing is most popular among tent campers (most sites are too small for RVs) who like the dry, pine forests. Three sites are double-sized, multifamily camps. Like most campgrounds in this area, this one offers great access to day-hiking and backpacking trails, particularly to American Ridge and Goat Peak, a William O. Douglas Wilderness summit with a memorable fire lookout. The river through here is particularly beautiful in the fall, when red and gold leaves reflect in its peaceful waters. The campground, close enough to State Route 410 to hear the noise (traffic usually isn't that heavy), has pit toilets and hand-pumped water (at the west end only). The elevation is 3250 feet. (Reservations are required here. See special note on Naches Ranger District campgrounds, p. 181.)

Getting there: The campground is 38 miles northwest of Naches, at milepost 83.4 on SR 410.

13   Cedar Springs ★★★◂

SITES	RESERVATIONS	CONTACT
🏕️ 🚐	Required; (877) 444-6777 or www.recreation.gov	Wenatchee National Forest Naches Ranger District (509) 653-1400
15 sites, no hookups, RVs to 22 feet	**OPEN**	
	Late May to late November	

The first of several Wenatchee National Forest camps in the scenic Bumping River drainage, Cedar Springs is set right along the small, scenic river, where trout fishing is allowed during the summer. This is also a popular picnic spot for day-trippers headed for Bumping Lake, 11 miles farther southwest on Bumping Lake Road. Many good hiking trails are found a short distance down Bumping Lake Road. The campground has hand-pumped water and pit toilets. Two of the sites here are multifamily units. The elevation is 2800 feet. (Reservations are required here. See special note on Naches Ranger District campgrounds, p. 181.)

Getting there: From Enumclaw, drive 47 miles east on State Route 410 to Chinook Pass and proceed another 19 miles east (about 33 miles northwest of Naches) to Bumping Road (Forest Road 1800, at milepost 88.4). Turn right (south) and drive about half a mile to the campground.

14 Soda Springs ★ ★ ★ ◀

SITES	RESERVATIONS	CONTACT
🏕 🚐	Required; (877) 444-6777 or www.recreation.gov	Wenatchee National Forest Naches Ranger District (509) 653-1400
	OPEN	
26 sites, no hookups, RVs to 30 feet	May to late November	

Soda Springs is a well-known camp in the Bumping River drainage, and probably the best RV camp along this stretch of the river. It's certainly the most developed. This area provides an interesting lesson in geology: Soda Springs really is a spring—a nearby spring keeps pumping out minerals from deep inside the earth, a reminder of the geologic forces that created this South Cascades outdoor adventureland. Some of that geology lesson is described on an interpretive trail across the river, via a suspension bridge, from the campground—the rest you'll absorb on your own by hiking local trails and driving the scenic Chinook Pass and White Pass highways. The campground has hand-pumped water, pit toilets, an RV dump station, and some beefy CCC-constructed picnic shelters for day-trippers headed for Bumping Lake (or for bike campers caught in a rainstorm). Elevation at this campground on the Bumping River is 3100 feet. (Reservations are required here. See special note on Naches Ranger District campgrounds, p. 181.)

Getting there: From Enumclaw, drive 47 miles east on State Route 410 to Chinook Pass and proceed another 19 miles east to Bumping Road (Forest Road 1800, at milepost 88.4). Turn right (south) and continue 5 miles to the campground.

15 Cougar Flat ★ ★ ★

SITES	RESERVATIONS	CONTACT
🏕 🚐	Required; (877) 444-6777 or www.recreation.gov	Wenatchee National Forest Naches Ranger District (509) 653-1400
	OPEN	
12 sites, no hookups, RVs to 20 feet	Late May to mid-September	

Another pleasant campground along the Bumping River, Cougar Flat is close to a wide range of good day-hiking and backpacking trails, such as the gut-busting Mount Aix

A footbridge crosses the Bumping River near Bumping Crossing.

Trail and the more pleasant Bumping Lake Trail (see Bumping Lake Campground, below). The small campground has hand-pumped water, pit toilets, and an RV dump station. The elevation is 3100 feet. (Reservations are required here. See special note on Naches Ranger District campgrounds, p. 181.)

Getting there: From Enumclaw, drive 47 miles east on State Route 410 to Chinook Pass and proceed another 19 miles east to Bumping Road (Forest Road 1800, at milepost 88.4). Turn right (south) and continue about 6 miles to the campground, on the left.

16 Bumping Crossing ★ ★ ✦

SITES	RESERVATIONS	CONTACT
🏕️ 🚐	None	Wenatchee National Forest Naches Ranger District (509) 653-1400
	OPEN	
12 sites, no hookups, RVs to 15 feet	Late May to November	

Bumping Crossing, the only campground in this valley not located directly on Bumping Lake or the Bumping River, isn't a bad consolation prize. The river runs nearby, and it's a lot quieter than the lakefront campground. Also more primitive. Bumping Crossing has pit toilets but no piped or pumped water, so bring your own. Watch for elk here and throughout the Bumping River Valley in the evenings. At this writing, at least, this camp at 3200 feet is free.

Getting there: From Enumclaw, drive 47 miles east on State Route 410 to Chinook Pass and proceed another 19 miles east to Bumping Road (Forest Road 1800). Turn right (south) and go about 10 miles to the campground, on the right.

17 Upper and Lower Bumping Lake ✦ ✦ ✦ ✦ ✦

SITES	RESERVATIONS	CONTACT
⛺ 🏕 🚐 68 sites, no hookups, RVs to 50 feet	Required; (877) 444-6777 or www.recreation.gov	Wenatchee National Forest Naches Ranger District (509) 653-1400
	OPEN	
	Mid-May to late November	

This is the main attraction in the Bumping River drainage—the place most campers, particularly those with boats, go to first in search of a place to set up shop. It's easy to see why. Both campgrounds here are more modern and—with paved driveways, ample privacy, and other modern niceties—better developed than the Forest Camps along Forest Road 18 in the valley below. The twenty-three-site lakefront (lower) campground has launching and moorage facilities and even a handful of sites directly on the lake. Its longer sites are preferred by RVers. The forty-five-site upper camp is a pleasant tent/RV area. For a true treat for the eyes, get yourself over here sometime on a clear weekend in October, when the larch trees lurking around this camp blossom into a brilliant golden color that almost seems too bright to be true. It's stunning.

Water-skiing and fishing are the primary activities on the Bumping Lake Reservoir in early summer, when the lake is still a lake (it shrinks to a giant mudflat by autumn,

Campsites are spacious and tidy in Upper Bumping Lake Campground.

when the reservoir is drawn down). The lake is stocked with trout in-season; boat rentals are available at a private resort nearby. But whenever you visit, don't overlook the great hiking trails in the valley. One, the Bumping River Trail, is an increasingly popular backpacking route, which can be hiked as a 20-mile, one-way hike between two separate trailheads. Watch for elk along the route. The campground has hand-pumped water and pit toilets. Several sites are barrier free. The elevation is 3400 feet. (Reservations are required here. See special note on Naches Ranger District campgrounds, p. 181.)

Getting there: From Enumclaw, drive 47 miles east on State Route 410 to Chinook Pass and continue another 19 miles east to Bumping Road (Forest Service Road 1800). Turn right (south) and drive 11.5 miles to the campground, on the right.

ı8 Little Naches ★ ★

SITES	RESERVATIONS	CONTACT
21 sites, no hookups, RVs to 32 feet	Required; (877) 444-6777 or www.recreation.gov	Wenatchee National Forest Naches Ranger District (509) 653-1400
	OPEN	
	Late May to November	

A small Forest Service camp near the confluence of the Little Naches and American rivers, Little Naches isn't very peaceful; it's near a major gateway for dirt bikes and off-road vehicle riders (see notes on Kaner Flat, below), and some sites are within sight of the highway. Still, if you catch it during a quiet time, kids will love short day-trips north to Horsetail Falls on the Little Naches, or south (via Forest Road 1706) to Boulder Cave, a 350-foot-long natural tunnel equipped with interpretive signs—and occupied by the rare, big-eared bat! Fishing in nearby streams also is a prime summer activity here. The campground has hand-pumped water and pit toilets. The elevation is 2562 feet. (Reservations are required here. See special note on Naches Ranger District campgrounds, p. 181.)

Getting there: Little Naches is 26.5 miles northwest of Naches on State Route 410.

ı9 Kaner Flat ★ ★

SITES	RESERVATIONS	CONTACT
41 sites, no hookups, RVs to 30 feet	None	Wenatchee National Forest Naches Ranger District (509) 653-1400
	OPEN	
	Mid-May to November	

Kaner Flat, on the Naches River, has a lot going for it: great scenery, spacious riverfront campsites, good location. It also has a lot going against it, namely, dirt bikes and off-road vehicles, which flock here to take advantage of the Naches Trail, an old wagon-train route that winds through the mountains. For campers, this campground marks

The gentle waters of the American River

a transition, of sorts, between the hiker-oriented wilderness experience to the west and the blue-smoke and loud-noise hubbub of lands in this immediate area and to the east. Tent campers will probably wish they'd chosen a more western destination for the night. The campground, 2.5 miles off State Route 410, has hand-pumped water and pit toilets. The elevation is 2678 feet.

Getting there: The campground is 30 miles northwest of Naches via SR 410 and Forest Road 1900.

20 Crow Creek ★ ✦

SITES	RESERVATIONS	CONTACT
🏕 🚐	None	Wenatchee National Forest Naches Ranger District (509) 653-1400
	OPEN	
15 sites, no hookups, RVs to 30 feet	Mid-April to November	

Like nearby Kaner Flats, Crow Creek is popular with dirt-bikers and off-road-vehicle jockeys, to which the Wenatchee National Forest dedicates large chunks of its forest. The campground has hand-pumped water and pit toilets. It's 3 miles off State Route 410, at an elevation of 2900 feet.

Getting there: The campground is 32 miles northwest of Naches via SR 410 and Forest Roads 1900 and 1904.

21 Sawmill Flat ★ ★

SITES	RESERVATIONS	CONTACT
🏕 🚐	Required; (877) 444-6777 or www.recreation.gov	Wenatchee National Forest Naches Ranger District (509) 653-1400
	OPEN	
24 sites, no hookups, RVs to 24 feet	April through November	

This is another good hiker's base camp for trails leading into the Wenatchee National Forest. Sawmill Flat, set near the Naches River, also offers good fishing access. It's also popular with dirt bikers and off-road vehicle drivers. It's a standard-issue Forest Service camp, with small sites in a pine forest, hand-pumped water, and pit toilets. Like some neighboring campgrounds, this one has a handful of double-wide "family" sites that will accommodate two vehicles. Whether you like the place or not might largely depend on your neighbors: When the off-road vehicle crowd hasn't taken it over, this is a popular family campground, thanks to its proximity to Boulder Cave and other natural attractions. The camp also has an old kitchen shelter built by the Civilian Conservation Corps (a truly lost art). The campground elevation is 2500 feet. One site here is barrier free. Halfway Flat, another Wenatchee National Forest campground, is nearby (see below). (Reservations are required here. See special note on Naches Ranger District campgrounds, p. 181.)

BEST FAMILY-FUN CAMPS

1. Wenatchee Confluence State Park, Central Washington
A lot of grass. A swimming beach. Courts and playfields. Hiking trails. A biking loop. It's all here at Confluence, found where the Wenatchee River meets the Columbia. See p. 243.

2. Millersylvania Memorial State Park, Tenino
One of the most diverse state parks in the system, this one offers fishing (dock or boat), hiking, cycling, even an exercise trail to work off those s'mores. See p. 62.

3. Fort Casey State Park, Whidbey Island
Big cannons and creepy old army bunkers to investigate, plus miles of saltwater beach and a blufftop kite-flying field to beat them all. See p. 40.

4. Mayfield Lake Park, Cowlitz River
This Tacoma Power park on Mayfield Lake is big, diverse and recreation-oriented with a BMX course, playgrounds, ball fields, and other amenities, plus of course, swimming in the lake. See p. 214.

5. Silver Lake Park, Northwest Washington
A hidden gem, this Whatcom County Park offers hiking, cycling, ball fields, and a lake that offers good fishing and rental canoes, kayaks, and pedal boats. See p. 123.

Getting there: The campground is 25 miles northwest of Naches on State Route 410, at milepost 93.2.

22 Halfway Flat ✦ ✦

SITES	RESERVATIONS	CONTACT
🏕️ 🚐	None	Wenatchee National Forest Naches Ranger District (509) 653-1400
	OPEN	
9 sites, no hookups, RVs to 27 feet	April through November	

For years, we thought this campground's biggest claim to fame was the correct answer to the *Jeopardy* question: How does Coke taste if you leave it sitting open on the counter for four hours? But a recent visit showed us this is a pleasant, although primitive, campground on the Naches River, with good hiking trails and stream fishing in the immediate area. Did you just get a new, totally self-contained motor home and want to go far, far away from the neighbor's barking dogs? Halfway Flat might fit the bill. But the dog might just be hiding from all the blue smoke: Beware the noise from off-road vehicles, which often seem to arrive here in great droves. The nine spaces are large enough for most RVs, and most have been recently renovated. The campground has pit toilets and hand-pumped water. The elevation is 2050 feet.

Getting there: The campground is 28.5 miles northwest of Naches via State Route 410 and Forest Road 1704.

A rustic kitchen shelter provides shade in Halfway Flat Campground.

23 Cottonwood ★ ★ ★

SITES	RESERVATIONS	CONTACT
 16 sites, no hookups, RVs to 22 feet	Required; (877) 444-6777 or www.recreation.gov	Wenatchee National Forest Naches Ranger District (509) 653-1400
	OPEN	
	April through November	

This camp on the banks of the Naches River is a grand place to visit in the fall, when the hordes of summer campers—and mosquitoes—have returned to wherever it is they hide out for the winter. It's a shady, scenic spot, with good river access for fishing and sore-feet soaking. The campground has hand-pumped water, vault toilets, and an RV dump station. The elevation is 2300 feet. (Reservations are required here. See special note on Naches Ranger District campgrounds, p. 181.)

Getting there: The campground is 22 miles northwest of Naches on State Route 410, at milepost 99.5.

Other Chinook Pass Corridor Campgrounds

American Forks, a small campground at milepost 88.4 on State Route 410, offers twelve sites and one shelter and accommodates RVs to 30 feet. There is no running water. Two group camps also operated by the Wenatchee National Forest are found along the SR 410 corridor. They are **Pine Needle** (maximum capacity sixty people, eight vehicles; 31 miles northwest of Naches on SR 410) and **Indian Flat** (maximum capacity sixty-five people, twenty-two vehicles; 24 miles northwest of Naches on SR 410). Reservations are required for both camps; call (877) 444-6777 or visit www.ReserveUSA .com. For more information on these three campgrounds, contact the Naches Ranger District, (509) 653-1400.

Eastern White Pass Corridor

24 La Wis Wis ★ ★ ★ ★

SITES	RESERVATIONS	CONTACT
🏕️ 🚐	(877) 444-6777 or www.recreation.gov	Gifford Pinchot National Forest Cowlitz Valley Ranger District (360) 497-1100
	OPEN	
122 sites, no hookups, RVs to 24 feet	Mid-May to late September	

This pretty Forest Service campground, set beneath a gorgeous, partially old-growth forest near the confluence of the Ohanapecosh and Cowlitz rivers, is one of the nicest in the U.S. Highway 12 corridor, and right up there on the list of great places to camp in the South Cascades. The sites are especially popular with tent campers; most are too small for RVs but have the unique, private feel that tent campers love. Not that overnighting RVers won't fit in here. Some sites are convenient, paved pull-throughs; others are double-wide "family" sites able to accommodate two vehicles. The premium spots here are on the riverfront Hatchery Loop, which offers a handful of gorgeous, walk-in tent sites. The campground has pit and flush toilets, piped water, a picnic area, and good river-fishing access. Short trails lead to the Blue Hole of the Ohanapecosh River and nearby Purcell Falls.

Best of all, the Ohanapecosh area of Mount Rainier National Park is a mere 7 miles up the road. All in all, a very nice place to camp. But be warned: This campground often serves as an overflow area for nearby Ohanapecosh. Reservations here are a good idea, any time in the summer. About two-thirds of the sites can be reserved. Note that there's a two-night minimum for reservations on weekends; three nights on holiday weekends. The elevation is 1243 feet.

Getting there: From Packwood, drive about 6 miles northeast on US 12. Turn north on Forest Road 1272 and proceed a half mile to the campground.

25 Summit Creek ★ ★ ◀

SITES	RESERVATIONS	CONTACT
🏕️	None	Gifford Pinchot National Forest Cowlitz Valley Ranger District (360) 497-1100
	OPEN	
6 sites	Mid-June to mid-September	

We've driven by Summit Creek several times on trips up (bumpy, rocky, occasionally torturous) Forest Road 4510. So far, we've never found a great reason to camp here. Which isn't a slam on the campground, a tidy, if primitive, spot along Summit Creek, found on the way to Soda Springs Trailhead and the William O. Douglas Wilderness. It's actually quite pretty. But there's not a lot to do here except stare at the bottom side of your big blue tarp for hours on end. But hey, if you're reading this during a management seminar and that thought sounds pretty enticing, have at it. The campground has pit toilets but no piped water or other facilities. Bring your water filter for the creek. At least it's a bargain: The campground, at least at this writing, is free. The elevation is 2400 feet.

Getting there: From Packwood, drive about 9.5 miles east on U.S. Highway 12 to Forest Road 45. Turn left (north) and proceed about 2.5 miles on Forest Roads 45 /4510 to the campground.

26 Soda Springs ★ ★ ✦

SITES	RESERVATIONS	CONTACT
	None	Gifford Pinchot National Forest Cowlitz Valley Ranger District (360) 497-1100
	OPEN	
8 sites	Mid-June to late October	

It's tough to get to, and once you arrive, there's not much there. But the primitive campsites at Soda Springs, north of U.S. Highway 12 between Mount Rainier and Rimrock Lake, might seem awfully plush to trekkers who stagger home from weeklong forays into the Dumbbell Lake area. That region, part of the beautiful William O. Douglas Wilderness, which lies just to the east, is typical of this high-Cascade, Mount Rainier "rain shadow" country: endless chains of scenic lakes and mountain peaks formed by ancient, violent volcanism, chock-a-block with modern, insatiable mosquitoes in the summer. Soda Springs is an "end-of-the-road" camp used largely by backcountry hikers and horse packers, who will find a loading ramp and hitch rail here. But it's definitely a quiet escape for the tent camper who's just looking to get far, far away from it all. The campground has pit toilets but no piped water. Summit Creek, which runs nearby, is the water source; bring a filter. And don't complain: As of this writing, at least, it's free. The elevation is 3200 feet.

Getting there: From Packwood, drive about 9.5 miles east on US 12 to Forest Road 45. Turn left (north) and proceed about 5 miles on Forest Roads 45/4510 to the campground, near the end of the road.

27 Walupt Lake ★ ★ ★ ★

SITES	RESERVATIONS	CONTACT
	(877) 444-6777 or www.recreation.gov	Gifford Pinchot National Forest Cowlitz Valley Ranger District (360) 497-1100
	OPEN	
44 sites, no hookups, RVs to 22 feet	Mid-June to early September	

A pretty alpine lake with a ban on big motors. A boat launch. A sandy swimming beach and clear views into the majestic Goat Rocks Wilderness. What's the catch? More than

20 miles of gravel roads, that's what. Walupt Lake, a central Gifford Pinchot National Forest camp well south of U.S. Highway 12, is a worthy reward for those who make the trek all the way down here. The campground is popular with swimmers and fans of lake fishing (selective-fishery rules are enforced; barbless hooks, no bait), as well as hikers bound for the Goat Rocks. One trail that begins right in the campground leads to the upper end of the lake and beyond to the Goat Rocks Wilderness, home of some of the most scenic mountain vistas and valleys in the Northwest. Many Walupt Lake visitors head that way on horseback; an adjacent horse camp has space for nine equestrian families. This is also a nice campground for canoe enthusiasts. The shallow launch and a ban on large motors on the lake (it's trolling motors only) make for calm, peaceful waters with great views. Most of the campsites can be reserved. Ten sites are walk-in; several are double "family" sites. The campground has pit toilets and piped water. The elevation is 3900 feet. Reservations are a good idea in July and August (and so is industrial-strength bug dope).

Getting there: From US 12 about 2.5 miles west of Packwood, turn south on Forest Road 21, proceed to Forest Road 2160, turn east and continue about 4 miles to the campground.

28 White Pass Lake (Leech Lake) ✦ ✦ ✦

SITES	RESERVATIONS	CONTACT
🏕️ 🚐	None	Wenatchee National Forest Naches Ranger District (509) 653-1400
	OPEN	
16 sites, no hookups, RVs to 20 feet	May to late October	

Talk about your multiple uses. The Forest Service gets twelve full months of duty out of this handy area along pretty little White Pass Lake. In the winter, it's White Pass Ski Area's

Boaters on White Pass Lake (Photo by Seabury Blair Jr.)

local cross-country venue, with trails that fan out around the (frozen) lake. But after the big thaw, the area reverts to White Pass Lake campground, a small, scenic spot that's a handy stopover for U.S. Highway 12 travelers. The campground, best suited for tents and small RVs, gets a fair amount of use from hikers as well. The Pacific Crest Trail passes very near here, offering great day-hiking opportunities in the William O. Douglas Wilderness to the north and the Goat Rocks Wilderness to the south. A worthy day hike can be made at the ski area across the road. Just follow the cat track (gravel road) up the main slope and keep climbing. You'll wind up on the ridge top, with splendid views south into the Goat Rocks, within a couple miles. However: Beware the killer mosquito hordes during summer! The campground has pit toilets but no piped water or showers. The lake, a decent trout fishery once the water warms, is reserved for fly fishers only. An adjacent horse camp has six campsites, hitching rails, and other equestrian facilities. The elevation is 4500 feet.

Getting there: The campground is 19 miles east of Packwood at the White Pass summit, directly across US 12 from the White Pass Ski Area.

29 Dog Lake ✦ ✦ ✦

SITES	RESERVATIONS	CONTACT
🏕 🚐	None	Wenatchee National Forest Naches Ranger District (509) 653-1400
	OPEN	
11 sites, no hookups, RVs to 20 feet	May to late October	

How in the world did they squeeze a campground in here? That's what you'll be wondering as you drive the short access road to Dog Lake, a small Wenatchee National Forest campground on a tiny lakeshore bench, squeezed between water and mountain in a rugged, rocky area east of White Pass. It's a pretty little lake, and not a bad place to camp, especially for hikers. A number of trails fan out into the William O. Douglas Wilderness north of here. However, RVers may find the place a bit rustic. The campground has pit toilets but no piped water, showers, or other services. The elevation is 3400 feet.

Getting there: The campground is on U.S. Highway 12, about 20 miles east of Packwood (about 2 miles east of White Pass Ski Area).

30 Clear Lake North ✦ ✦ ✦

SITES	RESERVATIONS	CONTACT
🏕 🚐	None	Wenatchee National Forest Naches Ranger District (509) 653-1400
	OPEN	
33 sites, no hookups, RVs to 22 feet	Mid-April to November	

Clear Lake North, one of a pair of nice Wenatchee National Forest camps on the east slope of U.S. Highway 12, sits on the shores of one of the more fascinating waterways in this part of the state. The lake actually is a portion of Rimrock Reservoir, an impound-ment of the Tieton River The water level varies dramatically from month to month. When it's full, the reservoir is a stunningly beautiful lake, reflecting the rugged peaks of the Goat Rocks Wilderness. But when it's dry, the entire place turns to a giant mudflat, riddled with channels and populated by dirt-bike and smoke-belching ATVs. Needless to say, aim for spring or early summer, when the reservoir is full. Clear Lake North, the first of two camps at the western end of this aquatic monstrosity, is by far the more primitive of the two campgrounds. Thus it gets much less use than Clear Lake South (see below). The campground has pit toilets but no piped water or showers. It does offer good bird-watching and fishing access to the lake. Watch for nesting bald eagles and ospreys in this area. An interpretive trail along the lake offers wildlife-viewing in-formation, and the North Fork Tieton, which flows out of the lake, is a great place to watch spawning kokanee (landlocked salmon; they'll be bright red). Note: Because this is a public water resource, no swimming is allowed in the lake; fishing only. The elevation is 3100 feet.

Getting there: From US 12 at the west end of Rimrock Lake (about 35 miles west of Naches, at milepost 158.5), follow signs a short distance south on Forest Road 1200.

Clear Lake is a popular boating and angling spot. (Photo by Seabury Blair Jr.)

31 Clear Lake South ✦ ✦ ✦ ✦

SITES	RESERVATIONS	CONTACT
⛺ 🚐	None	Wenatchee National Forest Naches Ranger District (509) 653-1400
	OPEN	
22 sites, no hookups, RVs to 22 feet	Mid-April to November	

This is the more developed of two campgrounds near one another at Clear Lake, a waterway connected to Rimrock Lake to the east. (See Clear Lake North, above, for recreation information.) Clear Lake South has hand-pumped water and pit toilets. The elevation is 3100 feet.

Getting there: From U.S. Highway 12 at the west end of Rimrock Lake (about 35 miles west of Naches, at milepost 158.5), follow signs a short distance south on Forest Road 1200.

32 Indian Creek ✦ ✦ ✦

SITES	RESERVATIONS	CONTACT
⛺ 🚐	Required; (877) 444-6777 or www.recreation.gov	Wenatchee National Forest Naches Ranger District (509) 653-1400
39 sites, no hookups, RVs to 32 feet	**OPEN**	
	Mid-May to mid-September	

RVers looking for a nesting spot on the east slopes of U.S. Highway 12 often wind up at Indian Creek, one of the most developed of the handful of Forest Service campgrounds on this side of White Pass. The camp, near Rimrock Lake (see Clear Lake North, above), has pit toilets, piped water, and an RV dump station. A private marina and resort are nearby, providing a store for major firewood and bug-dope purchases. Boaters camp here in the early summer, when the reservoir is full and boating and water-skiing commence at nearby Rimrock Lake. The elevation is 3000 feet. (Reservations are required here. See special note on Naches Ranger District campgrounds, p. 181.)

Getting there: The campground is 31 miles west of Naches on US 12.

33 Peninsula ✦ ✦ ✦

SITES	RESERVATIONS	CONTACT
⛺ 🚐	None	Wenatchee National Forest Naches Ranger District (509) 653-1400
	OPEN	
Dispersed camping, no hookups, RVs to 20 feet	Mid-April to late November	

Peninsula is one of two rustic Forest Service camps off the beaten path in the Rimrock Lake area. Like nearby South Fork (see below), Peninsula is on the southeastern shore of the big reservoir, the water level of which goes up and down dramatically throughout the year. It's a fairly primitive site, with pit toilets and no piped water or showers. But the views from the lakeshore of the incredible, volcano-hewn rocky peaks in this area are flat-out staggering. This is one of those places worth visiting and snapping a few photos even if you're not prepared to camp. The campground has a boat launch, which is the main draw for boaters (particularly water-skiers) in the summertime. The camp also gets some wintertime use by snowmobilers and cross-country skiers, thanks to a Sno-Park nearby. The elevation is 3000 feet. Note: Campers pay either a minimal fee ($5 at this writing), or must possess a Northwest Forest Pass parking permit.

Getting there: From U.S. Highway 12, about 22 miles west of Naches, turn south on Forest Road 1200 (Tieton Reservoir Road), proceed 3 miles, then follow signs a short distance west on Forest Road 711 to the camp.

34 South Fork ✦ ✦ ✦

SITES	RESERVATIONS	CONTACT
⛺ 🚐	None	Wenatchee National Forest Naches Ranger District (509) 653-1400
	OPEN	
Dispersed camping, no hookups, RVs to 20 feet	Late May to mid-October	

Welcome to *The Land of the Lost*. Fans of that cheesy 1970s dinosaur show will feel right at home at South Fork, a remote spot on the South Fork Tieton River, which runs through a valley so rugged and rocky it often looks like another planet. The South Fork Tieton Valley contains some of the most dramatic evidence you'll ever find of the unimaginably violent volcanic forces that forged this region. Explorers willing to rough it on questionable Forest Service roads can set out from this camp for days or weeks of discovery: Massive landslides, giant waterfalls, lava flows, and other gargantuan natural features (witness the notable Blue Slide, a large landslide area farther upstream on the South Fork, or the aptly named Goose Egg Mountain, which you'll pass along Forest Road 1200 on the way in) all are within reach. The campground itself has your basic Forest Service offerings: pit toilets and a dump station, but no other

A campsite at Hause Creek Campground, on the Tieton River

services. This is actually just a large parking area, mostly frequented by small RVs and campers. But it's a bargain—$5 at this writing. The elevation at South Fork, about a mile upstream from the river mouth at Rimrock Reservoir, is 3000 feet.

Getting there: From U.S. Highway 12, about 22 miles west of Naches, turn south on Forest Road 1200 (Tieton Reservoir Road), proceed about 4 miles, then follow Forest Road 1203 a short distance south to the campground.

35 Hause Creek ✦ ✦ ✦ ✦

SITES	RESERVATIONS	CONTACT
🏕️ 🚐	Required; (877) 444-6777 or www.recreation.gov	Wenatchee National Forest Naches Ranger District (509) 653-1400
	OPEN	
42 sites, no hookups, RVs to 30 feet	Late May to late November	

Bring your wet suit and helmet. Like most nearby campgrounds along the Tieton River, west of Naches, this one is river-rafting central in the fall, when the scheduled release of water from the Tieton Dam (just upstream) grabs the attention of the entire Northwest rafting community. Two reasons: (1) The Tieton drainage provides a gorgeous, clear-water-over-big-boulders ride, and (2) It's usually the only river in the state running at more than half-speed in the fall, the traditional river-rafting downtime. Fall is a good time to visit even if you're not rafting, as local aspens, alders, and larches turn a splendid gold and the canyon takes on an early-season bite of cold in the evening. It's hot and drier, but still nice, in the summertime. Hause Creek is the most developed campground on the Tieton below Tieton Dam, and the best RV campground in the area. It has flush toilets (!) and an RV dump station. One campsite is barrier free. The elevation is 2500 feet. (Reservations are required here. See special note on Naches Ranger District campgrounds, p. 181.)

Getting there: The campground is 22 miles west of Naches on U.S. Highway 12.

36 Willows ✦ ✦ ✦

SITES	RESERVATIONS	CONTACT
🏕️ 🚐	Required; (877) 444-6777 or www.recreation.gov	Wenatchee National Forest Naches Ranger District (509) 653-1400
	OPEN	
16 sites, no hookups, RVs to 20 feet	April through November	

Here's a nice spot along the Tieton River, especially for nature lovers. During the spring and fall, the Tieton drainage is one of the loveliest alpine river valleys in Washington, with vegetation and topography more reminiscent of the Colorado Rockies than the Evergreen State. It's particularly beautiful in the fall, when the river reaches full throttle as Rimrock Lake Reservoir is drawn down, and local larch, alder, and aspen trees (and yes, willow bushes) put on a goldenrod color show. Watch for wapiti in this area; the largest herd of Rocky Mountain elk in the state winters over in this valley, where a feeding station at Oak Creek is a popular wintertime tourist attraction. The campground has hand-pumped water and pit toilets. The elevation is 2400 feet. (Reservations are required here. See special note on Naches Ranger District campgrounds, p. 181.)

Getting there: The campground is about 19 miles west of Naches on U.S. Highway 12, near milepost 170.

37 Windy Point ★ ★ ★

SITES	RESERVATIONS		CONTACT
15 sites, no hookups, RVs to 22 feet	Required; (877) 444-6777 or www.recreation.gov		Wenatchee National Forest Naches Ranger District (509) 653-1400
	OPEN		
	April through November		

It opens early in the season, closes late, and provides great access to the scenic Tieton River. That's enough to keep faithful campers coming back to this small Wenatchee National Forest camp a short drive west of Naches. The campground has hand-pumped water and pit toilets. The elevation is 2000 feet. See Willows, Wild Rose, Hause Creek, Peninsula, South Fork, and Clear Creek North and South, above, for local recreation information. (Reservations are required here. See special note on Naches Ranger District campgrounds, p. 181.)

Getting there: Windy Point is about 13 miles west of Naches, near milepost 177.5, on U.S. Highway 12.

Other White Pass Corridor Campgrounds

Campers stuck on a mid-August night with no sites open at Ohanapecosh or La Wis Wis might resort to the private **Packwood RV Park** on U.S. Highway 12 at Packwood; (360) 494-5145. A private alternative in the Rimrock Lake area is **Silver Beach Resort** (about 30 miles west of Naches), with plentiful full hookup sites and other amenities; (509) 672-2500.

The view of Dog Lake from the shady Dog Lake Campground

38 Lewis and Clark State Park ✦ ✦ ✦ ✦

SITES	RESERVATIONS	CONTACT
	None	Washington State Parks (360) 902-8844
	OPEN	Lewis and Clark State Park (360) 864-2643
25 sites, no hookups, RVs to 60 feet	April through September	

Something about this place smells old. Actually, most of the star attractions here truly are. Lewis and Clark State Park, a short drive east of Interstate 5 south of Chehalis, contains a patch of old-growth forest, ancient volcanic caverns (now used to store natural gas), historic buildings, and a stretch of the old north spur of the Oregon Trail from the Cowlitz River Landing to Tumwater. The old-growth forest—one of the last lowland stands of ancient trees in Western Washington—is worth a visit all on its own. Historical legend has it that downed trees in the local stand of Douglas fir, western hemlock, and western red cedar were so huge—6 to 9 feet in diameter—that wagon-road builders had to build ramps over them, because they had no saws large enough to saw through. Although the horrific Columbus Day storm of 1962 blew nearly half of the

Hang gliding is a popular sport in the Cowlitz Valley.

remaining trees down, many still stand. Also worth a visit are the park's historic, Civilian Conservation Corps–constructed buildings and the John R. Jackson House (tours available), an 1845 pioneer log cabin that was the first north of the Columbia River.

Also on the premises is a Mount St. Helens visitor center, where the volcano crater is visible on clear days. The small campground is in a wooded area, with thick underbrush separating the sites. The 620-acre park also has a nature trail, wading pool, picnic sites with shelters, horseshoe pits, and two group campsites for up to 150 campers. A horse stable and riding trails are found on the east side of Jackson Highway, the park access road. You'll find 5 miles of horse trails and 8 miles of hiking trails nearby. Note: Although this historical campground is accessed via U.S. Highway 12, we include it in the campground-starved Mount St. Helens section—along with nearby Ike Kinswa State Park, Mayfield Lake County Park, and the Iron Creek, North Fork, and Tower Rock Forest Service campgrounds—because all are frequented by Mount St. Helens–area recreators, especially those arriving southbound from the greater Seattle area.

Getting there: From the US 12/Interstate 5 junction south of Chehalis, proceed about 2.5 miles east on US 12 to Jackson Highway. Turn right and drive about 1.5 miles to the park entrance.

39 Ike Kinswa State Park ✦ ✦ ✦ ✦

SITES	RESERVATIONS	CONTACT
🏕 🚻 🏠 103 sites, no hookups, 72 full or partial hookups, RVs to 60 feet, 5 cabins	(888) 226-7688 or www.parks.wa.gov	Washington State Parks (360) 902-8844
	OPEN	Ike Kinswa State Park (360) 983-3402
	Year-round	

This scenic, 454-acre park lies on the north shore of 14-mile-long Mayfield Lake, a Cowlitz River impoundment created by Tacoma Power's Mayfield Dam. It's a summer water-recreation heaven, packed to the gills in warm months with water-skiers, anglers, swimmers, and sunbathers. A boat launch, located on the west side of the bridge providing access to the main park area, gets heavy use. The campsites, in three wooded loops, are quite nice—a combination of back-in and pull-through sites—all near restrooms with flush toilets and coin-op showers. The park also has two primitive, walk-in sites (a good bet for cyclists), a picnic area near the mouth of the Tilton River, a non-patrolled swimming area, an RV dump station, and 46,000 feet of shoreline. Five cabins also are available for rent. This place is packed in the summer, so get a reservation if you can.

Historical note: The park occupies a site that once served as a Cowlitz Indian settlement. Several Cowlitz graves were removed from an area near the park's bridge before the area was flooded by the creation of Mayfield Dam. Two marked graves were left at the site and fenced for protection in 1974. Formerly known as Mayfield Lake State Park, it was renamed in 1971 to honor the late Ike Kinswa, a Cowlitz who owned property in the area.

Getting there: From Interstate 5 south of Chehalis, take Exit 68 (U.S. Highway 12) and drive 14 miles east to Silver Creek Road. Turn north and follow signs 3.5 miles to the park.

40 Mayfield Lake Park ★★★

SITES	RESERVATIONS	CONTACT
⛺ 🚐	(888) 226-7688 or www.mytpu.org/	Mayfield Lake Park
	OPEN	(360) 985-2364
55 sites, 55 water/electrical hookups, RVs to 40 feet	Mid-April to mid-October; year-round for day use	(888) 502-8690 for lake levels

It's not spectacular, large, or all that well known to U.S. Highway 12 travelers or Mount St. Helens visitors, but this fifty-acre park, a longtime county facility now run by Tacoma Power, is a good alternative to Ike Kinswa State Park for lake lovers, and to Lewis and Clark and Seaquest state parks for campers heading toward Mount St. Helens. The campground, with some waterfront sites on the 2250-acre Mayfield Lake, has a dump station, an expansive picnic and swimming area, a boat launch, flush toilets, and coin-op showers. Sites are nicely spaced, with average to above-average privacy. The park also has a twelve-site group camp, available by reservation. Fishing in the lake for planted trout or coho can be good. Sites at this writing were $25–$27 per night.

Note: This is one of three popular parks now operated by Tacoma Power, as part of its Cowlitz River Project, which includes Mayfield and Mossyrock dams and their resulting reservoirs, Mayfield and Riffe lakes. The others—both much larger—are Mossyrock Park and Taidnapam (below). Remember that the beachfront campsites might cease to be beachfront when the reservoirs are drawn down. Call the toll-free number for information.

Getting there: From Interstate 5 south of Chehalis, take Exit 68 (US 12) and drive about 17 miles east to Beach Road. Turn left (north) and drive about a quarter-mile to the park.

41 Mossyrock Park ★★★★

SITES	RESERVATIONS	CONTACT
⛺ 🚐	(888) 226-7688 or www.mytpu.org/	Mossyrock Park
	OPEN	360-983-3900
152 sites, 76 water/electrical hookups, RVs to 40 feet	Year-round, except December 20 through January 1	(888) 502-8690 for lake levels

Mossyrock, the second of Tacoma Power's triad of lakefront parks in this area, is the power company's camping powerhouse. A big park developed on the grassy, southwest shore of Riffe Lake in 1971, it has a little something for everybody—especially if they're anglers. The lake is open year-round and stocked with coho, steelhead,

Tree stumps appear to morph into spiders escaping the waters of Riffe Lake near Mossyrock Park.

and rainbow trout. Other fishing venues in the area include the North Shore Fishing Access behind Mossyrock Dam, and Swofford Pond, which is stocked with rainbow and brown trout, largemouth bass, channel catfish, and bluegill. The campground is equally diverse with a lakeside main camping loop featuring twenty-four water/electrical hookups and a wealth of pull-through sites. Also on hand are a sixty-site reservable group camp with a large kitchen shelter and thirty-five electric hookups, and a ten-site primitive group camp with no hookups. (We detect a theme here. By all means, get a group together.) Tent campers will enjoy the dozen walk-in tent sites. The camp, a great family place, also has a store, playfields and playground equipment, and just about everything else you'll need—except for solitude. There's very little privacy between sites in this open, grassy campground. And it's a busy place in summer. Sites at this writing were $14–$25.

Getting there: From Interstate 5 south of Chehalis, take Exit 68 (U.S. Highway 12) and drive about 21 miles to Williams Street in the town of Mossyrock. Turn right and continue several blocks to a T intersection. Turn left on State Street and proceed 3.5 miles to the park. (Note: Outside of Mossyrock, State Street becomes Mossyrock Road East, then Ajlune Road. The route is well marked.)

42 Taidnapam Park ✦ ✦ ✦ ✦

SITES	RESERVATIONS	CONTACT
🏕️ 🚐	(888) 226-7688 or www.mytpu.org/	Taidnapam Park
	OPEN	360-497-7707
67 sites, 51 full or partial hookups, RVs to 40 feet	Year-round, except December 20 through January 1	(888) 502-8690 for lake levels

One of the newest and nicest campgrounds in Western Washington, Taidnapam, southeast of Morton, was built in 1994 by Tacoma Power, which did some things right. It's

Anglers cast for Kokanee (land-locked salmon) from a bridge near Taidnapam Campground

a beaut of a location, with sites set in Doug fir and broadleaf maples near the Cowlitz River, at the head of Riffe Lake reservoir. The lake is open year-round for fishing (see Mossyrock Park, above), and this park offers great access via a high, pedestrian- and barrier-free fishing bridge across the Cowlitz. Fishing for kokanee and other species can be productive here, and the bridge is often jammed with anglers. (Note that when the lake is drawn down, you'll be fishing in a river far below you.)

But there's plenty more to do here than wet a line. The fifty-acre park is surrounded by the Cowlitz Wildlife Area, a 14,000-acre habitat on the lake's north shore that includes nesting grounds for ospreys and bald eagles. Look for hang gliders landing here in the open grassy area after launching from nearby peaks. Inside the park, family campers will appreciate the twin fish-cleaning stations, sandy swimming beach, boat launch, kids' playground, horseshoe pits, and other niceties. Campsites (your choice of paved pull-through or back-in) are set amidst Oregon grape, salal, and ferns with nice tree cover, in one main loop. Also available are a group camp with a large kitchen shelter (twenty-two sites, all with full or partial hookups) and a twelve-site primitive group camp. Tenters have their own walk-in sites in a secluded, wooded area. The campground has an RV dump station and hot showers. It's a pleasant spot any time of the year. And it's getting bigger: During our last visit, Taidnapam was undergoing a significant expansion, with nearly 100 new campsites being built. The new area will likely be open by the time you get there. Sites at this writing were $14–$26.

OK, now for the name. The moniker *Taidnapam* (pronounced tide-nuh-pom) honors the original campers here, the Upper Cowlitz Tribe, aka Taidnapam. Their history is highlighted at the park with a replica shovel-nose canoe (it was missing from its stirrups when we last visited; if you have it, please return!) and a kiosk detailing archaeological finds made here, with some artifacts dating back 4600 years.

Getting there: From Interstate 5 south of Chehalis, take Exit 68 (U.S. Highway 12) and drive about 37 miles east (about 5 miles east of Morton) to Kosmos Road. Turn right, then left onto Champion Haul Road. Proceed about 4 miles to the park entrance, on the right.

43 Iron Creek ★ ★ ★ ★

SITES	RESERVATIONS	CONTACT
🏕️ 🚐 98 sites, no hookups, RVs to 42 feet	(877) 444-6777 or www.recreation.gov	Gifford Pinchot National Forest Cowlitz Valley Ranger District Randle office (360) 497-1100
	OPEN Mid-May to late September	

Iron Creek, a very popular Gifford Pinchot National Forest site near the Cispus River, is a handy riverfront overnight spot for U.S. Highway 12 travelers or eastside Mount St. Helens visitors. It's located right on the main access route for visitors bound for the more remote northeast side of the volcano (via Forest Roads 25 and 99), where popular hikes along Norway Ridge and an awesome view from Windy Ridge Viewpoint are found about 25 miles to the southwest. The campground is in a pretty spot, set in a forest of tall fir and hemlock at an elevation of 1083 feet. Because it's one of only a few Cowlitz Valley Ranger District campgrounds accessible by primarily paved roads, this is a favorite RV camp for this area. Spaces are wide and easily maneuverable for trailers or motor homes. Also note that seventeen sites here are double-sized "family" sites, able to accommodate two vehicles. Reservations are a good idea. The campground, set near the Cispus River, has pit toilets and piped water.

BEST HIKER CAMPS

1. Cougar Rock, Mount Rainier
It's a short distance from here to Mount Rainier's Paradise area, which, for day hikers, truly is. But you don't have to go anywhere to connect to the national park's diverse trail system, segments of which run right next to the campground. See p. 186.

2. White River, Mount Rainier
It is to Mount Rainier Sunset-area hikers what Cougar Rock is to Paradise hikers—base camp central. See p. 188.

3. Salmon La Sac, Cle Elum River
A well-developed Forest Service camp, Salmon La Sac is conveniently located next to a number of trails that enter the Alpine Lakes Wilderness area. See p. 174.

4. Beverly, Teanaway River
A small Forest Service camp on the North Fork Teanaway River, Beverly is situated close to some of the state's most beautiful alpine hikes, especially in the Stuart Range of the Alpine Lakes Wilderness. See p. 177.

5. Panorama Point, Baker Lake
One of the best campgrounds in the Baker River drainage south of Mount Baker, this camp offers good access to the wealth of wonderful day-hiking and backpacking trails on the mountain's southern slopes. See p. 129.

Getting there: From US 12 at Randle, follow State Route 131/Forest Road 25 about 10 miles south (following signs to Mount St. Helens National Volcanic Monument) to the campground, a short distance beyond the bridge over the Cispus River.

44 Tower Rock ★ ★ ✦

SITES	RESERVATIONS	CONTACT
🏕️ 🚐	(877) 444-6777 or www.recreation.gov	Gifford Pinchot National Forest Cowlitz Valley Ranger District Randle office (360) 497-1100
	OPEN	
22 sites, no hookups, RVs to 22 feet	Mid-May to late September	

Here's an option to the oft-full Iron Creek Campground (above) when you're making those summer Mount St. Helens vacation plans. It's another decent Forest Service camping option for RVers. Tower Rock, an older Forest Service camp, is set along the North Fork Cispus River, which is open for trout fishing in the summer. (If you're looking for better odds, visit the nearby private trout pond.) Campsites, in a mixed forest, are mostly flat, with ample space to pitch tents or spread out. Most sites can be reserved. The elevation is 1224 feet. Mount St. Helens visitors bound for hikes around Norway Pass or mountain-watching at Windy Point Viewpoint can stop for road and trail information at Woods Creek Information Center, on Forest Road 25 south of Randle.

Getting there: From U.S. Highway 12 at Randle, drive about a mile south on State Route 131/Forest Road 25 and veer left on (paved) Forest Road 23. Following signs to Tower Rock, proceed about 8 miles to Forest Road 28. Turn right and proceed 2 miles to Forest Road 76. Turn right and drive 2 miles to the park entrance.

45 North Fork ★ ★ ✦

SITES	RESERVATIONS	CONTACT
🏕️ 🚐	(877) 444-6777 or www.recreation.gov	Gifford Pinchot National Forest Cowlitz Valley Ranger District Randle office (360) 497-1100
	OPEN	
33 sites, no hookups, RVs to 32 feet	Mid-May to late September	

Another favorite spot for eastside volcano visitors, North Fork is a pleasant camp along the North Fork Cispus River south of Randle. This is another good bet for RVers; campsites are large, road access is easy, and sites can be reserved well in advance. Many good hiking trails and a few cycling trails are found in the area. Stop by the ranger district office in Randle for information. Note that this also is a good base camp for exploring the northeast side of Mount St. Helens, including the Norway Pass area and the Windy Ridge Viewpoint. The Woods Creek Information Center, on Forest Road 25, south of Randle, is a good information source. Campsites are set in a shady, forested

The cold, clear waters of old Gifford Pinchot forests hold plenty of trout. (Photo by Dan A. Nelson.)

area adjacent to the North Fork Cispus River. Several sites are double-wide "family" sites, and some sites are pull-throughs. A group camp with three sites can be reserved.

Getting there: From U.S. Highway 12 at Randle, follow State Route 131 a mile south, veer left (southeast) on (paved) Forest Road 23, and continue about 11 miles south to the campground.

46 Seaquest State Park ✶ ✶ ✶

SITES	RESERVATIONS	CONTACT
88 sites, full or partial hookups, RVs to 21 feet, 5 yurts	(877) 444-6777 or www.recreation.gov	Washington State Parks (360) 902-8844
	OPEN	Seaquest State Park (360) 274-8633
	Year-round	

What in the world is going on here? An uninformed camper stumbling upon Seaquest State Park in the peak tourist season might be asking that, given the sell-out crowds at this otherwise unremarkable campground. What they didn't know—and you will—is that this is the main spot for campers bound for Mount St. Helens up State Route 504 (Spirit Lake Memorial Highway), the only paved entrance road to the National Volcanic Monument. Seaquest is the only significant campground within a short drive of the volcano's main visitor centers. So expect large crowds here in the summertime, rain or shine, and get a reservation if you can. The campground is far from spectacular, with rather ordinary RV spaces spread through a flat, grassy area, and others (in the north and south loops) in the woods. It has coin-op showers, horseshoe pits, a baseball field, five yurts, several Adirondack (three-sided sleeping) shelters, and an RV dump station. Seven miles of hiking trails are nearby; 1 mile is barrier free.

Across the road is the Mount St. Helens Interpretive Center, the original visitor center built after St. Helens erupted in 1980. An interpretive trail from the campground leads to a field where, weather permitting, St. Helens comes into view. But the mountain isn't the only lure here. Across the highway is wide, flat Silver Lake, one of the state's most notable bass, spiny ray, and trout fishing venues. (The closest boat ramp is 5 miles east on Highway 504.)

Getting there: From Interstate 5 at Castle Rock, turn east on SR 504 and proceed 6.5 miles to the park.

47 Lower Falls Recreation Area ✦ ✦ ✦ ✦

SITES	RESERVATIONS	CONTACT
	None	Mount St. Helens National Volcanic Monument (360) 449-7800
	OPEN	
43 sites, no hookups, RVs to 60 feet	May through September	

Lower Falls, high in the South Cascades along the Lewis River, is a hidden gem. It's close to the south side of Mount St. Helens, but because road access to the volcano itself is difficult from this side, the camp doesn't get a lot of use by St. Helens visitors. The place has its own contingent of fans, however, and little wonder. The campground, set in tall firs, is very near three scenic waterfalls on the Lewis River, as well as a wealth of good Gifford Pinchot National Forest hikes, such as the Lewis River Trail. (Beware abrupt cliff edges and seemingly safe, calm river water above the numerous falls in the area.) Campsites are very nicely spaced and fairly private. Some are pull-throughs. This, combined with the fact that the road here is paved except for the last mile or so, makes Lower Falls an increasingly popular RV destination. The campground has composting toilets and hand-pumped water. Two group sites for up to twenty campers each are available. The elevation is 1535 feet.

Getting there: From Interstate 5 at Woodland, turn east on State Route 503 and proceed about 23 miles. Where SR 503 turns south toward Amboy, continue straight (northeast) on what is now SR 503 Spur (Lewis River Road). Proceed about 7 miles, passing through Cougar, until the road becomes Forest Road 90. Continue an additional 21 miles northeast on Forest Road 90 to the campground, near milepost 29.

Other Mount St. Helens Campgrounds

They're a bit out of the way for most auto travelers visiting the volcano, but four campgrounds operated by a Portland utility company are located on the Swift Creek and Yale reservoirs along State Route 503. They are **Cresap Bay** (seventy-three sites), **Cougar** (sixty sites), **Beaver Bay** (seventy-eight sites), and **Swift** (ninety-three sites). Contact Pacificorp, (503) 813-6666, for information. In the same general area is a free DNR camp, **Lake Merrill** (seven walk-in only sites), on Forest Road 8100, north of SR 503 at Cougar. Call the DNR's Southwest Region office in Castle Rock, (360) 577-2025.

An alternate National Forest campground is **Lewis River Horse Camp** (nine sites, access via Forest Roads 90/93 northeast of Cougar). Call the Mount St. Helens National Volcanic Monument, (360) 449-7800. Note: For Gifford Pinchot National Forest campgrounds south of North Fork Campground, see the Mount Adams section of this chapter.

Southern Gifford Pinchot National Forest

48 Beaver ★ ★ ★ ◀

SITES	RESERVATIONS	CONTACT
🏕 🚐 21 sites, no hookups, RVs to 25 feet	(877) 444-6777 or www.recreation.gov	Gifford Pinchot National Forest Mount Adams Ranger District (509) 395-3400
	OPEN Mid-April to late September	

We've never seen one here. A beaver, that is. But we suspect more than a few have made their way past this site on the Wind River, the first Forest Service camp north of Stevenson and Carson. The Gifford Pinchot National Forest campground has shady sites and a big, grassy day-use area for those (rare) sunny days. Beaver has pit toilets and piped water. Most of the sites offer easy RV parking. The elevation is 1053 feet. Note to hikers: Falls Creek Trail and the little-visited Trapper Creek Wilderness are just to the north. Contact the Mount Adams Ranger District in Trout Lake for trail information.

Getting there: The campground is 12 miles north of Carson on Wind River Highway.

49 Panther Creek ★ ★ ★

SITES	RESERVATIONS	CONTACT
🏕 🚐 33 sites, no hookups, RVs to 25 feet	(877) 444-6777 or www.recreation.gov	Gifford Pinchot National Forest Mount Adams Ranger District (509) 395-3400
	OPEN Mid-May to mid-September	

It's out of the way, it's lightly used, it's quiet. Three good reasons to drive up the scenic Wind River north of Carson (in the Columbia River Gorge) to check out Panther Creek Campground, a nice Gifford Pinchot National Forest site set in a very deep Douglas fir forest. The campground, which has creekside sites, hand-pumped water, and pit toilets, is close to a wide range of good hiking trails. The campground, at 912 feet, has paved sites and actually is quite well suited to self-contained RVs. Eight of the sites here are double-sized "family" sites, able to accommodate two vehicles. About two-thirds of the sites here can be reserved in advance. The Pacific Crest Trail passes over the creek on a bridge nearby. A horse camp is located adjacent to the campground.

Getting there: From State Route 14 at Carson, drive 6 miles north on Wind River Highway to Forest Road 65. Turn right and proceed about 4 miles northeast to the campground.

Big-leaf maples shimmer in the sunlight.

50 Paradise Creek ✦ ✦ ✦

SITES	RESERVATIONS	CONTACT
🏕️ 🚐	(877) 444-6777 or www.recreation.gov	Gifford Pinchot National Forest Mount Adams Ranger District (509) 395-3400
	OPEN	
42 sites, no hookups, RVs to 25 feet	Mid-May to mid-September	

When you think about the wild inland areas of the Gifford Pinchot National Forest, you think of deep, old- and second-growth forest, clear streams, and a wide range of rocky, volcanic formations. All are in evidence in and around Paradise Creek, near the confluence of the creek and the scenic Wind River. The lightly used campground, which sits in heavy forest, has pit toilets and hand-pumped water. It offers good access to the Wind River, and a nearby trail leads to the top of scenic Lava Butte. Most campsites can be reserved in advance; four are double-sized "family" sites able to accommodate two vehicles. The elevation is 1539 feet.

Getting there: The campground is 20 miles north of Carson on Wind River Highway.

51 Moss Creek ✦ ✦ ✦

SITES	RESERVATIONS	CONTACT
🏕️ 🚐	(877) 444-6777 or www.recreation.gov	Gifford Pinchot National Forest Mount Adams Ranger District (509) 395-3400
	OPEN	
17 sites, no hookups, RVs to 32 feet	Mid-May to late September	

Moss Creek is the first Gifford Pinchot National Forest camp encountered on the south-to-north journey up the Little White Salmon River, north of State Route 14 in the

Columbia River Gorge. The campground, reached via paved roads, is a pleasant spot along the creek, with small, private campsites great for tents and OK for smaller RVs. This is a pretty area; bring the camera. The campground has pit toilets and piped water. A majority of sites can be reserved in advance. Campground elevation is 1300 feet. Note: The otherworldly Big Lava Bed, one of the state's most fascinating geologic features, is a short drive to the north on Forest Road 66. It really is big. Check it out: It's 12,500 acres of lava, varying in height from 2000 to 3350 feet. Trouble is, all lava looks pretty much the same, and it's easy to get lost in there. Bring a compass—and signal flares!

Getting there: From the town of Cook on SR 14 (near Drano Lake), turn north on County Road 1800 and drive about 8 miles north to the campground on Forest Road 18 (aka Oklahoma Road).

52 Oklahoma ★★◀

SITES	RESERVATIONS	CONTACT
🏕️ 🚐	(877) 444-6777 or www.recreation.gov	Gifford Pinchot National Forest Mount Adams Ranger District (509) 395-3400
	OPEN	
23 sites, no hookups, RVs to 22 feet	Mid-May to mid-September	

It's where the wind goes whipping down the plain. Actually, the flat spaces in and around this Oklahoma, high on the Little White Salmon River in the volcanically warped Gifford Pinchot National Forest, are more like meadows. But this far off the main highway, who's checking? The campground is a bit rough around the edges, with gravel roads (although it's paved all the way here) and campsites, pit toilets, and hand-pumped water. On the other hand, being this far away from the nearest bait 'n' video store has its advantages: it's quiet. See the note on the Big Lava Bed in the listing for Moss Creek, above. And beware the killer mosquitoes in the summer. Many sites here can be reserved in advance. The campground elevation is 1683 feet.

Getting there: From Cook on State Route 14 (near Drano Lake), turn north on County Road 1800 and drive about 14 miles north to the campground near the end of the pavement on Forest Road 18 (aka Oklahoma Road).

53 Peterson Prairie ★★★★

SITES	RESERVATIONS	CONTACT
🏕️ 🚐	(877) 444-6777 or www.recreation.gov	Gifford Pinchot National Forest Mount Adams Ranger District (509) 395-3400
	OPEN	
30 sites, no hookups, RVs to 32 feet	May to late September	

Ooh. You've gotta see the stuff to be seen here. This is a truly grand place to come camping in the fall, when berries ripen and this area, southwest of Mount Adams, turns into the biggest wild huckleberry patch in the entire Northwest, and perhaps on the planet. Choice picking abounds in this region if you time it right (usually late August through mid-September). Watch for black bears, and check with the Mount Adams Ranger District for berry-ripeness reports; the time varies from year to year. If the berry festivities don't hold your attention, mosey over to the nearby Ice Cave, a lava tube discovered here long ago by early settlers. The tube, accessible by a stairway, for many years served as the ice supply for pioneers in Hood River and The Dalles, both in the Columbia River Gorge. Worth a look. The campground is in a mixed evergreen forest (not too dark), with a range of (gravel) pull-through sites for RVs and level back-in sites with good privacy for tents.

Taking in a bird's eye view of the South Cascades

It has pit toilets and piped water. Many sites can be reserved in advance. A group camp for up to fifty campers is available. Good fishing can be found 8 miles west at Goose Lake. The elevation is 2976 feet.

Getting there: From State Route 14 west of White Salmon (66 miles east of Vancouver), turn north on State Route 141 and proceed about 24 miles north to the town of Trout Lake. Proceed 4 miles beyond the Mount Adams Ranger Station to the end of SR 141. Continue 2.5 miles west on Forest Road 24 to the campground, on the left.

54 Goose Lake ★ ★ ◀

SITES	RESERVATIONS	CONTACT
🏕 🚐	(877) 444-6777 or www.recreation.gov	Gifford Pinchot National Forest Mount Adams Ranger District (509) 395-3400
37 sites, no hookups, RVs to 18 feet	**OPEN** Mid-June to late September	

Here's a nice spot to float your canoe, paddle your float tube, or set out on an air mattress in search of a few alpine-lake trout. A lot of campers do so in midsummer at Goose Lake, making this lakeshore fish camp a popular spot. That's in spite of somewhat primitive conditions, which include 8 miles of gravel roads; sketchy, hilly, ill-defined parking areas (most of the sites are walk-in, making them nice for tenters, but a royal pain for RV owners); pit toilets; and a lack of piped water. Other summer options include huckleberry picking and exploring the Big Lava Bed (see Moss Creek, above) and other local geologic features. The elevation is 3200 feet. This campground melts out slowly in

June. Note that a majority of the campground sites can be reserved in advance.

Getting there: From State Route 14 west of White Salmon (66 miles east of Vancouver), turn north on State Route 141 and proceed 25.5 miles to Forest Road 24 (about 5.5 miles beyond the town of Trout Lake). Follow Forest Road 24 about 2.5 miles west (near Peterson Prairie, see above) to Forest Road 60. Continue about 5 miles west to the campground on Road 60. (Note: This camp also can be accessed from Wind River Valley to the west via Wind River Road, Forest Road 65 [Panther Creek Road], and Road 60.)

55 Cultus Creek ★ ★ ★ ◄

SITES	RESERVATIONS	CONTACT
▲ 🚐	None	Gifford Pinchot National Forest Mount Adams Ranger District (509) 395-3400
	OPEN	
51 sites, no hookups, RVs to 32 feet	June through September	

Here's a perfect base camp for that long-considered, but never undertaken, backpacking expedition into the Indian Heaven Wilderness, one of the wildest portions of the very wild Gifford Pinchot National Forest. The somewhat rustic campground, which gets the most use during the fall huckleberry season, is pleasant all summer and receives only light use much of the time. The final 7 miles up here are on gravel road, and the campground roads are gravel. But the campsites are great, with nice level spaces for tents and just the right amount of sun in a Douglas fir and hemlock forest. Most sites are RV friendly, if you're willing to drive the beast all the way up here to 4000 feet. The campground has pit toilets and drinking water, but no garbage service. A Northwest Forest Pass parking permit is required in lieu of a camping fee. Local, um, "art" note: If he's still there, don't miss the campground's chainsaw-stump sculpture of "Smokey the forest worker." He looks a bit too much like the late former governor Dixie Lee Ray for our taste.

Getting there: From State Route 14 west of White Salmon (66 miles east of Vancouver), turn north on State Route 141 and proceed 25.5 miles to Forest Road 24 (5.5 miles beyond the town of Trout Lake). Follow Forest Road 24 (turning north at the junction near Peterson Prairie Campground) about 13.5 miles northwest to the campground.

56 Tillicum ★ ◄

SITES	RESERVATIONS	CONTACT
▲ 🚐	None	Gifford Pinchot National Forest Mount Adams Ranger District (509) 395-3400
	OPEN	
32 sites, no hookups, RVs to 18 feet	Mid-June to late September	

The Forest Service prospectus on this campground sounded dubious. "A few good camping spots," it said, "with numerous other poor ones." Let's just say the folks at

Gifford Pinchot get high marks for truth in advertising. This isn't a great place to camp. It's not even a very good place to camp. But in a pinch, such as during the great human berry-picking waves down here in the fall it might suffice. It also makes a decent base camp for backcountry hikes into the wilds of the Squaw Butte/Big Creek area north of the Indian Heaven Wilderness. The campground has pit toilets. The elevation is 4300 feet.

Getting there: From State Route 14 west of White Salmon (66 miles east of Vancouver), turn north on State Route 141 and proceed 25.5 miles to Forest Road 24 (5.5 miles beyond the town of Trout Lake). Follow Forest Road 24 (turning north at the junction near Peterson Prairie Campground) about 20 miles northwest to the campground (about 6.5 miles north of Cultus Creek, above).

Other Southern Gifford Pinchot National Forest Campgrounds

On the far west side of Gifford Pinchot National Forest, a small, alternative campsite is **Sunset Falls** (eighteen sites, on Forest Road 42). Call the Wind River Work Center, (509) 427-3200. In the Trout Lake area (upper White Salmon River drainage), more primitive, alternative sites include **Trout Lake Creek** (twenty-one sites for tents and RVs, on Forest Road 8810-011); **Smokey Creek** (three sites for RVs, on Forest Road 24, no fee; the Forest Service describes it as "hardly a campground"); **Little Goose** (twenty-eight sites for tents or RVs, used primarily during fall berry season, on Forest Road 24); **Saddle** (twelve tent sites, free, a poor campground with bad road access on Forest Road 2480 near Tillicum, above); and **Atkisson Group Camp** (space for fifty campers), reservations only, (877) 444-6777 or www.recreation.gov. It's on Forest Road 2400, which turns northwest from State Route 141 about 5 miles south of Trout Lake; Mount Adams Ranger District, (509) 395-3400.

An old kitchen shelter stands guard at American Forks, along the American River.

Mount Adams

57 Morrison Creek ★ ★ ★ ◀

SITES	RESERVATIONS		CONTACT
🏕	None		Gifford Pinchot National Forest Mount Adams Ranger District (509) 395-3400
	OPEN		
12 sites	July through September		

It's more a bivouac site than a campground, but Morrison Creek makes up for its lack of amenities with an awesome setting—the southern shoulder of 12,275-foot Mount Adams, second highest peak in Washington. It's a primitive site, with pit toilets but no piped water or anything else to speak of. Which is fine if you're here for what most Morrison Creek campers come for: A bit of rest before heading into the Mount Adams Wilderness for extended day hikes, backpack trips, or summit attempts. A grand day hike right from the campground is the Shorthorn Trail, a 5.6-mile round-trip hike to a scenic viewpoint on the mountainside. Farther up the road from here is Cold Springs, an even less official hike-in climber's campsite with one outhouse signaling its presence. Access to these camp-grounds, at 4600 feet and 5700 feet, respectively, is on rough Forest Service roads. Leave that pretty Lincoln Navigator in the garage and take somebody else's beat-up 4x4. Note: A Northwest Forest Pass parking permit is required here in lieu of a camping fee. Also, this camp was closed in 2008 due to a wildfire. Call before you head out.

Getting there: From State Route 141 at Trout Lake, turn north on County Road 17. Following signs for Mount Adams Recreation area, continue about 12 miles north on CR 17 and Forest Roads 80 and 8040.

58 Blue Lake Creek ★ ★

SITES	RESERVATIONS		CONTACT
🏕 🚐	(877) 444-6777 or www.recreation.gov		Gifford Pinchot National Forest Cowlitz Valley Ranger District Randle office (360) 497-1100
	OPEN		
11 sites, no hookups, RVs to 22 feet	Mid-May to mid-September		

This small campground, one of the least used in the area, is a nice spot for tents, with flat, open spaces in a pleasant mixed forest. Roads are paved to the campground; those driving RVs can park here but probably would prefer other local Forest Service camps, such as Iron Creek and North Fork, to the northwest. Blue Lake Creek is set along a creek near the trailhead to Blue Lake (3.5 miles). Whether you like the place or flee in terror is up to chance; a number of off-road-vehicle trails run nearby. If the blue-smoke belching machines are running, you won't want to stay long enough to

A trail leads along a massive lava flow near Mount Adams.

get the bottoms of your shoes dirty. The campground has a swank pit toilet and hand-pumped water. The elevation is 1814 feet.

Getting there: From U.S. Highway 12 at Randle, follow State Route 131 a mile south, turn left (southeast) on Forest Road 23, and proceed 16 miles to the campground. (See the access note about FR 23 on page 230.)

59 Adams Fork ★ ★ ┥

SITES	RESERVATIONS	CONTACT
🏕️ 🚐	(877) 444-6777 or www.recreation.gov	Gifford Pinchot National Forest Cowlitz Valley Ranger District Randle office (360) 497-1100
	OPEN	
24 sites, no hookups, RVs to 22 feet	May through September	

Adams Fork is a very pretty campground on the upper Cispus River, below the north-western flank of Mount Adams. Unfortunately, it can suffer from the same malady as nearby Blue Lake Creek (see above): off-road-vehicle pollution, both the noise and air varieties. If that's not a problem with you, or if you're lucky enough to be here when they aren't, this is a pleasant spot in a nice stand of fir and hemlock. A nearby trail leads to Blue Lake. The campground has pit toilets and hand-pumped water. Seventeen campsites can be reserved in advance. The elevation is 2600 feet.

Getting there: From U.S. Highway 12 at Randle, follow State Route 131 a mile south, turn left (southeast) on Forest Road 23, and proceed about 18 miles to Forest Road 21. Turn southeast (stay left) and continue about 5 miles to the campground, near the junction with Forest Road 56. (See the access note about FR 23 on page 230.)

60 Horseshoe Lake ★ ★ ★ ★

SITES	RESERVATIONS	CONTACT
	None	Gifford Pinchot National Forest Cowlitz Valley Ranger District Randle office (360) 497-1100
	OPEN	
10 sites, no hookups, RVs to 16 feet	Mid-June to late September	

Canoe lovers, this one's for you. Horseshoe Lake is a tiny, insignificant Gifford Pinchot National Forest camp on the northwestern flank of magnificent Mount Adams. But once you've been there, it looms large in the memory of those who love to pitch a tent next to a serene alpine lakeshore, with the family canoe parked within range of sight. Campsites are sort of ill defined here, but this dime-sized lake offers a billion-dollar view of Adams, and trout fishing can be good in season. Gas motors are prohibited on the lake. The serenity is spoiled from time to time by dirt bikes and other off-road vehicles in this general vicinity, but all in all, it's a nice spot. The campground has pit toilets, but no piped water. The elevation is 4150 feet. A National Forest road map will be a worthy investment to navigate the roads here, at least 12 miles of which will be gravel in various states of repair.

Getting there: From U.S. Highway 12 at Randle, follow State Route 131 a mile south, then turn left (southeast) on Forest Road 23. Continue 29 miles to a junction with Forest Road 2329. Turn left (northeast) and, proceeding around the north shore of Takhlakh Lake, drive 7 miles to Forest Road 078. Turn left and follow Forest Road 078 about 1.5 miles to the campground. (See the access note about FR 23 on page 230.)

BEST RIVERFRONT CAMPS
---

1. Ohanapecosh, Mount Rainier
There's something magical about the cold, clear waters of the Ohanapecosh River in Mount Rainier National Park, and this camp puts you as close as you can get. See p. 187.

2. Silver Fir, North Fork Nooksack
A quiet, out-of-the-way camp along the Mount Baker Highway, Silver Fir has very private sites where all you can see and hear is the North Fork Nooksack River. See p. 125.

3. La Wis Wis, Ohanapecosh River
Just outside Mount Rainier National Park is this fine Forest Service camp that sits on not one but two rivers. See p. 203.

4. Johnny Creek, Icicle River
The best-developed campground along the Icicle River drainage outside Leavenworth, which is stunning at almost any time of the year. See p. 162.

5. Nason Creek, Lake Wenatchee
Because it sits right next to sprawling Lake Wenatchee State Park, this pleasant Forest Service camp on Nason Creek often gets overlooked. See p. 154.

61 Takhlakh Lake ★★★★

SITES	RESERVATIONS	CONTACT
🏕 🚐	(877) 444-6777 or www.recreation.gov	Gifford Pinchot National Forest Cowlitz Valley Ranger District Randle office (360) 497-1100
	OPEN	
62 sites, no hookups, RVs to 22 feet	Mid-June through September	

If you've only got enough energy to get up close to Mount Adams once in your life, expend it here. Takhlakh Lake, the stunning campground with the funny name (it's pronounced "TOCK-lock"), is the flagship camping area in the Gifford Pinchot National Forest. Sites are spread nicely through a slightly hilly, beautifully forested shore of the lake, where gas motors are prohibited and the view straight across to Mount Adams will melt your Neoprene socks. This is a wonderful place to bring a canoe or kayak (small boats are allowed, but gas motors are prohibited) and spend a few days in awe of the mountain. That's about all most of us are capable of: sitting in the middle of the lake, staring up at the glaciers.

Not that there isn't plenty to do nearby. The campground has a great beachfront day-use area, with picnic sites right along the shore. It also has a boat launch, and a 1.5-mile trail that runs around the lake and makes for great morning exercise. On the far side of the lake, that trail connects with another path that leads up to an impressive lava flow just off Forest Road 2329 (you can also drive here). Local roads make great mountain-bike paths, although they're very dusty in midsummer. Back at the lake, many people spend the daytime hours fishing. Angling for trout can be productive here, especially early in the season, just after the campground opens for the summer. If you get bored with all that, a host of hiking trails, from trailheads in the immediate vicinity, lead southeast onto Mount Adams itself.

And now the bad news: The campground has pit toilets but no showers—and, in recent times, no piped water, as the campground water system has gone kaput. The necessity to bring your own, or filter from local sources, is a drag. But it might keep some people away from this camp, which would probably earn a 5-star rating if fully functional. The sites are paved, twelve are double-wide, "family" sites, and most are easily accessible by RVs. Most can be reserved, and it's a good idea to get a reservation almost anytime you're planning to come here. The campground elevation is 4416 feet.

Access note: The (long) drive down from Randle is mostly paved, with several miles of intermittent stretches of dusty gravel road. (It gets really narrow in a couple spots; use caution.) Forest Road 23 was heavily damaged by storms in the winter of 2006 and at press time, had not been fully repaired. Call for access information before you go.

Getting there: From U.S. Highway 12 at Randle, follow State Route 131 a mile south, then turn left (southeast) on Forest Road 23. Continue 29 miles to a junction with Forest Road 2329. Turn left and drive about 1.5 miles to the campground.

Opposite: Takhlakh Lake's shorelines offer otherworldly views of Mount Adams.

Takhlakh Lake's shorelines offer otherworldly views of Mount Adams.

Other Mount Adams–Area Campgrounds

Several other small, primitive, National Forest camps ring Mount Adams. These include **Chain of Lakes** (three dusty, scattered sites near the end of Forest Road 2329;

motorcycle trail nearby); **Cat Creek** (five sites for tents or RVs, on Forest Road 21); **Twin Falls** (eight sites, on Forest Road 90); **Killen Creek** (eight sites for tents or RVs, essentially a wilderness trailhead, on Forest Road 2329 south of Horseshoe Lake, above), nearby **Keene's Horse Camp** (dispersed camping for horse campers and sixteen sites in two areas for tents and RVs) and **Olallie Lake** (five sites for tents or RVs, a pretty, but very small, dusty, Adams-view campground, on Forest Road 5601). Call the Cowlitz Valley Ranger District, (360) 497-1100, for information.

On the east side of the mountain, the Department of Natural Resources operates **Island Camp** (six sites for tents or RVs up to 16 feet long) and **Bird Creek** (twelve sites for tents and RVs up to 22 feet long), both primitive campgrounds with access through the Goldendale area. Call the DNR's Southeast Region office in Ellensburg, (509) 925-8510.

Green ferns reach for spring sunlight.

Columbia River Gorge

62 Beacon Rock State Park ★ ★ ★ ★

SITES	RESERVATIONS		CONTACT
⛺ 🚐	None		Washington State Parks (360) 902-8844
	OPEN		Beacon Rock State Park (509) 427-8265
29 sites, no hookups, RVs to 50 feet	Year-round		

Let's just say you don't need to follow many road signs to find Beacon Rock. The aptly named stone, a massive, volcanic plug jutting from the soil along the banks of the lower Columbia River, is a wonder in itself: 850 feet high, with near vertical walls. It's believed to be the second largest monolith in the world, second only to that little rock called Gibraltar. A trail winds upward 1 mile—with fifty-three precarious switch-backs—to the top, where an unforgettable view awaits.

The rock is so impressive, its summit trail so popular, that most of us ignore the large, diverse state park just across the road. Beacon Rock, the park, is in many ways nearly as impressive as Beacon Rock, the rock. The 4650 acres contain a nice, albeit small, older campground that's really best suited for tents; a large group camp with Adirondack shelters for up to 200 guests; a picnic area with five shelters; coin-op show-ers; playground equipment; and other niceties. Above the park proper are many good hiking trails, including one up Hardy Creek to Rodney and Hardy falls (about 2 miles round-trip) and beyond to the top of Hamilton Mountain. More than 13 miles of gravel fire roads run through the wooded upland area, providing a trail-riding bonanza for horse and mountain bike riders. Below Beacon Rock is another strip of state park land with picnic facilities and a Columbia River boat launch.

Of course, all of this must wait until the entire camping party has made the obligatory march to the summit of the rock, which is believed to be a large an-desite plug from a long-since-eroded volcano vent. (Keep a tight rein on the kids here; the handrails make this steep

Hike the Beacon Rock trail—if you dare.

trail, which literally clings to the south face of the rock, fairly safe, but short people can slide underneath.)

Also take a moment to consider the fascinating history of Beacon Rock. It had legendary landmark status among Natives who, before the Columbia was tamed by two dozen dams, knew it marked the last rapids on the river and the first tidal influence from the Pacific Ocean, 150 miles to the west. Lewis and Clark are believed to have been the first white men to see the rock. They camped near its walls in the winter of 1805, and named it Beacon Rock in their journals. Years later, a man named Henry J. Biddle purchased the big rock and surrounding property. He built the impressive summit trail between 1916 and 1918. After his death, much wrangling occurred over the property. Oregon residents at one point even attempted to make it an Oregon State Park to prevent commercial development. It ultimately was turned over to Washington State in 1935.

Today, the rock has a new constituency group keeping careful watch: rock climbers, who prefer the south face for its long, uninterrupted pitches. The face contains some sixty routes, many among the more technically challenging in the Northwest, with ratings up to 5.10. The rock is closed from February 1 to July 15 to allow peregrine falcons to nest on the cliffs. Note: Good day trips from here include the Bonneville Dam Fishway and Visitor Center (spring chinook pass through in April and May, other salmon species later), and the Carson National Fish Hatchery, near the Wind River Ranger Station north of Carson.

Getting there: Beacon Rock is 35 miles east of Vancouver on State Route 14. You can't miss it.

63 Columbia Hills State Park ★ ★ ★ ✦

SITES	RESERVATIONS	CONTACT
🏕️ 🚐	None	Washington State Parks (360) 902-8844
	OPEN	Columbia Hills State Park
18 sites, no hookups, RVs to 30 feet	April through October	(509) 767-1159

In the past, I've urged people to petition Washington State Parks to change the name of this park, formerly called "Horsethief Lake" because some 1950s surveyors said the nearby canyon looked like a good hideout for horse thieves. Lo and behold, it has happened, and the new Columbia Hills State Park has only a remaining "Horsethief Lake" section. (While we're on a roll, how about world peace by the next edition? At least give it some thought, folks.)

In all seriousness, our main objection to the former name was that it didn't do this historically significant spot justice. The campground that lies on the shores of this ninety-acre lake, a Columbia River backwater created by a railroad-crossing landfill, was ground zero for a thriving Native population that lived, traded, and fished near here for centuries. Historians note that this spot was a gathering and trading spot for coastal tribes and inland tribes. Lewis and Clark wrote that the land also was home to a permanent settlement of fishermen, who fished with spears and nets for salmon in the rapids of the now-flooded Celilo Falls area. The park site also was one of the largest

The Columbia River slices through the Cascade Mountains near the Bridge of the Gods.

Native burial sites on the Columbia. Some graves remain in a small cemetery here, and rocks in its upland area contain some of the oldest known petroglyphs in the Northwest. Several are visible from a short trail that starts in the park. One of the more notable drawings, "She Who Watches," can be viewed on guided tours arranged with rangers by pre-scheduling at the number above. It's worth your time.

The campground itself is unremarkable, with exposed, grassy campsites on the lake's west shore. The park has an RV dump station. Two boat launches get heavy use. The surrounding region is a great spring-wildflower-viewing venue, with plentiful bright balsam root. The lake (no gas motors allowed) is a popular spot for trout and bass fishing. It also has become a practice area for up-and-coming windsurfers who aren't quite ready for the big waters of the adjacent Columbia River. Above the park, several trails lead up to 500-foot Horsethief Butte, where some rock-climbing pitches are available. Beware poison oak, rattlesnakes, and occasionally quite nasty Gorge winds.

Getting there: The park is 17 miles east of White Salmon and 28 miles west of Goldendale on State Route 14, near milepost 85 and the Dalles Dam.

64 Brooks Memorial State Park ✦ ✦ ✦ ✦

SITES	RESERVATIONS		CONTACT
	None		Washington State Parks (360) 902-8844
	OPEN		Brooks Memorial State Park
45 sites, 23 full hookups, RVs to 30 feet	Year-round; limited winter facilities		(509) 773-4611

We placed this lovely, forested state park in the Columbia Gorge section for two reasons: (1) It's truly a nice place to camp, especially for tenters, and (2) It's not really close to anything else. Brooks Memorial, 25 miles north of the Gorge on U.S. Highway 97, is in the unique type of dry pine forest that's typical of the beautiful Satus Pass area in the Simcoe Mountains, on the eastern slope of the South Cascades. The park, which has a large group camp (with cabins and teepees), substantial picnic shelters, and educational facilities, is most heavily used by organized groups. But it has a very pleasant campground in the portion of the park on the west side of US 97. It's equipped with flush toilets, piped water, RV hookups, horseshoe pits, a softball field, and coin-op showers. The tent-designated campsites, scattered through two ponderosa pine-forested loops, are tidy and pleasant. Hookup sites are in a grassy area with paved parking strips. The park also offers 9 miles of hiking trails to local beaver dams on the Little Klickitat River, among other attractions. The entire place is beautiful in the spring, when wildflowers burst into blossom in local meadows. The high elevation (3000 feet) makes this a popular cross-country skiing destination in the winter. Also note that the Goldendale Observatory, the largest telescope of its kind in the United States available for public use, is a short drive away, near Goldendale. (Call [509] 773-3141 for schedules and details.) Note: See important notice about this park's future on p. 25.

Historical note: The park was named for Nelson Brooks, a local citizen who helped establish and improve local roads.

Getting there: The park straddles US 97 13 miles north of Goldendale and 40 miles south of Toppenish, just south of Satus Pass summit.

Windsurfers ride the Columbia Gorge's stiff winds near Doug's Beach.

65 Maryhill State Park ★ ★ ★ ★

SITES	RESERVATIONS	CONTACT
⚠ 🚐	(888) 226-7688 or www.parks.wa.gov	Washington State Parks (360) 902-8844
70 sites, 50 full hookups, RVs to 50 feet	**OPEN** Year-round	Maryhill State Park (509) 773-5007

Maryhill has long been one of our favorite state parks. Not so much for what it contains, which is nice enough, but for the spirit that comes along with this odd corner of the Evergreen State. Most of that, of course, is the legacy of local legend Sam Hill, son-in-law of railroad tycoon James Hill. The eccentric/inspired (take your pick) character of this man, who lies buried in a tomb on the hillside above, lives on around Maryhill, named after Hill's wife, Mary. In the 1920s, he built a massive castlelike home on a bluff overlooking the river here, now known as Maryhill Museum. Hill, a Quaker and ardent pacifist, also built a near-scale concrete model of Stonehenge on the hillside above this park, dedicating it to the victims of World War I. He is buried nearby, not far from an intriguing Native American cemetery on the slopes below the Stonehenge monument.

The state park that bears Hill's family name is a pleasant spot on a broad, flat plain with 4700 feet of frontage on the Columbia River. Camping spaces are mostly shaded and grassy, nice for tents—assuming they're well tied down against the gusty winds. The beach area has breakwaters that cut the river current to provide swimming and windsurfing access. The park is also popular among fishermen, who launch here and pursue Columbia River salmon or sturgeon bigger than your car. The campground is nicely equipped with picnic facilities with two kitchen shelters, flush toilets, piped water, an RV dump station, and coin-op showers. Reservations are a good idea in the summer.

Getting there: The park is 12 miles south of Goldendale on State Route 14, immediately east of the Sam Hill (U.S. Highway 97) bridge over the Columbia River.

Other Columbia River Gorge Campgrounds

Visitors heading for the Columbia River Gorge can take advantage of two southwest Washington State Parks: **Paradise Point** near the East Fork Lewis River (seventy-eight sites, no hookups; 15 miles north of Vancouver and 6 miles south of Woodland; take I-5 exit 16), and **Battle Ground Lake** (forty-six sites, including six RV hookups and four rentable cabins for up to four people, northeast of Vancouver via State Route 503). Call Washington State Parks, (360) 902-8844.

6. CENTRAL WASHINGTON

You get the sense that something really big happened here once a long time ago. And by that we do not mean Dylan and the Dead at the Gorge.

More than any other place in Washington, the central slice of the state—the heartwood of the Evergreen, as it were—looks, feels, and sometimes acts disturbed. It has good reason. This is the scene of the crime—the big spurt that made the rest of our state what it is today. We're referring, of course, to the Great Flood. Not the one Noah allegedly rode out; the one that came booming across the West after a massive glacial ice dam packed its bags in western Montana and fled for good to the Northwest Territories. In the process, much of what we now know as Central and Eastern Washington lived up to what at that time must have been its highest and best use—as a sink drain for the head and shoulders of North America.

Some truly Big Waves came ripping through Central Washington in those days, between 10,000 and 40,000 years ago, when massive floodwaters poured across the central state, creating waterfalls that would make Niagara look like the stream from a Super Soaker. It's all over with now, thank heavens. But the result—gaping canyons and coulees now filled with kinder, gentler waters—is enjoyed, boated in, and camped upon today by millions of sun-drenched outdoor lovers, without so much as a thought about how it all got here.

Which is fine. We're here to point you toward campsites, not spew out lectures for skipping Natural History 104. Now that you're properly schooled in the geologic forces that created the Grand Coulee, sandblasted the Channeled Scablands, and paved the way for the world's biggest, juiciest apple crop, feel free to roam the area at will and select a good place to park the Itasca Land Yacht.

There's a surprising amount from which to choose over here on the dry side. Many Western Washingtonians are amazed when they see figures that show central-state parks as some of the busiest in the Northwest. They're less surprised once they visit and see the obvious lures: The white mountains and deep blue inland sea of Lake Chelan. The calm, flat waters of the middle Columbia River. The awesome cliffs and watery reservoirs of the Grand Coulee.

See the pattern? It's the sun, stupid. And the water it warms. In these dry, wind-whipped lands surrounded by the comforting arms of the Columbia River, consistently dry, sunny weather combines with hundreds of square miles of cool, clear water to create an unbeatable recreation double team. Sun and water lovers—be they water-skiers, anglers, swimmers, Jet Ski cowboys, windsurfers, bird-watchers, or just misplaced beach bums—can't get enough of Central Washington. That explains why many of its parks, particularly the state parks along the middle Columbia and in the Sun Lakes/Banks Lake area, are among the most consistently booked in Washington.

These parks draw hordes of repeat customers. If you don't believe it, visit North Bend on a Friday night and watch the long trail of boat trailers snake its way east over Interstate 90, then come back the same way Sunday night. It's like the water-toy-and-bass-boat tide going slowly in and out. Luckily, most of these parks are on the state reservation system, allowing you first-timers to make the trip over and see what all the commotion is about without worry.

We don't mean to suggest Central Washington ever gets crowded, cramped, or even upset. This is a big, tough area—one that is, after all, used to more large-scale commotion than all of us combined could ever muster. We might think we're big time when we load up the rig, but to Central Washington, we're just the gnat on the elephant's back. Pack the sunscreen, dig in, and hang on.

Opposite: *Daroga State Park, named after an apple, is a unique getaway in Central Washington.*

Dry hills and lots of water dominate the Middle Columbia region.

Middle Columbia

1 Wenatchee River County Park
2 Wenatchee Confluence State Park
3 Lincoln Rock State Park
4 Orondo River Park
5 Daroga State Park
6 Beebe Bridge Park
7 Entiat City Park
8 Alta Lake State Park
9 Bridgeport State Park

Lake Chelan and Stehekin

10 Lake Chelan State Park
11 Twenty-Five Mile Creek State Park
12 Lakeshore RV Park

Columbia Basin and the Grand Coulee

13 Ginkgo Petrified Forest/Wanapum
   Recreation Area
14 Potholes State Park
15 Sun Lakes State Park
16 Coulee City Park
17 Steamboat Rock State Park
18 Spring Canyon
19 Keller Ferry
20 Fort Spokane
21 Hawk Creek

Yakima Valley

22 Yakima Sportsman State Park

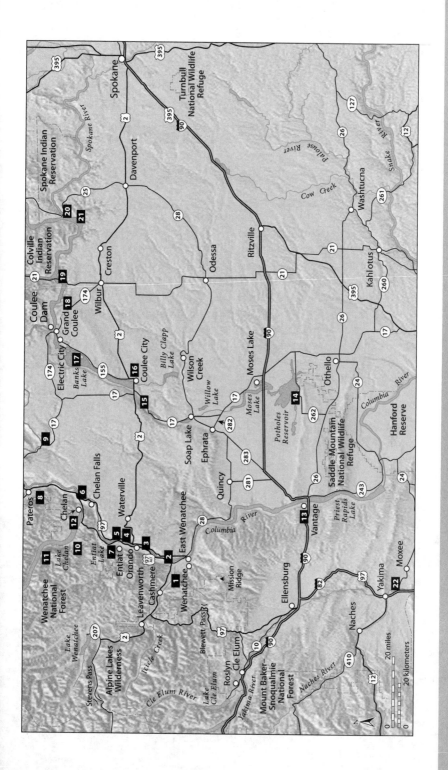

Middle Columbia

I Wenatchee River County Park ★ ★ ◄

SITES	RESERVATIONS	CONTACT
🚐	(509) 667-7503	Wenatchee River County Park (509) 667-7503
	OPEN	
49 sites, RV only, 43 partial or full hookups, RVs to any length	April through October	

Given its location—sandwiched between the rushing Wenatchee River and the roaring interstate—this campground doesn't exactly rate high on the serenity scale. And it has been an on-again, off-again affair over the years, as the county seems to struggle to decide what to do with it. But it's on again now, scaled down and improved with new features, including reservable sites.

Its main attraction is its convenience to U.S. Highway 2 travelers, particularly those in RVs. In fact, only in RVs. This is one of the few camps we've ever encountered whose rules declare: "Absolutely no tents of any kind allowed in the park!" They say it's to protect the grass. But we suspect someone in charge of Chelan County had a bad experience with coated nylon as a youngster.

The park is a stone's throw from the highway. Which, of course, is also its greatest drawback, due to the noise. The campsites are spread in four loops of a flat, grassy area

Kayaks await their turn during the Ridge to River race at Wenatchee River County Park.

on a medium-high bank above the Wenatchee River. Also on site are horseshoe pits, a kids' play area, a volleyball court, a small workout room, and a golfing cage (!), a day-use picnic area, flush toilets, and showers. The day-use area serves as a popular put-in site for rafters and kayakers. The park also advertises free Wi-Fi. Right next door is a cluster of small cabins. These are temporary housing for migrant workers. The campground would do in a pinch as a base for exploring the heart of Wenatchee Valley apple country. But if you plan to hang around camp very long, Wenatchee Confluence (see below) is a quieter destination. And you can put up a tent there without being handcuffed. Sites at Wenatchee River County Park were $19 to $29 at this writing.

Getting there: The campground is about 5 miles west of Wenatchee and 15 miles east of Leavenworth on US 2.

2 Wenatchee Confluence ★ ★ ★ ★ ◀
State Park

SITES	RESERVATIONS	CONTACT
⛺ 🚐	(888) 226-7688 or www.parks.wa.gov	Washington State Parks (360) 902-8844
59 sites, 51 full hookups, RVs to 65 feet	**OPEN** Year-round	Wenatchee Confluence State Park (509) 664-6373

For camping families who like to play, this is the Disneyland of the Washington State Parks system. The park, 200 acres of open, green space just north of the confluence of the powerful Wenatchee and Columbia rivers, was for many centuries a gathering place of Native peoples from both the east and west sides of the Cascades. The campground here today continues that tradition, offering visitors a wide choice of activities—land and waterborne—at a site fittingly located not far from the geographic center of Washington State. The campsites on this flat, sunny, riverside facility, built in the early 1990s, are tidy and beautifully manicured, although slightly antiseptic, since this is a new park and much of the vegetation is still only head high. Because of that, the park suffers from the same lack of shade as other new parks in this region. But cool breezes often emanate from the two rivers, and trees installed with the campsites will make this a more pleasant summer spot with the passage of each year. Besides, that very lack of rough natural vegetation makes this a completely wonderful place to pitch a tent, particularly for campers tired of fighting pine needles and mud. The sites are grassy, level, and clean. For RVers, full hookups, as well as pull-through sites, coin-op showers, and other niceties, make this a pleasant home away from home. Thankfully, Wenatchee Confluence escaped the fate of other, similar state parks that reside on lands leased by utility co-ops during state budget cuts in the past decade. Some of those parks were turned over to private operators; Confluence survived with the assistance of Chelan County Public Utility District.

The list of activities here makes this 197-acre park one of the best family campgrounds in the state. The park has playgrounds; basketball and tennis courts; dual boat-launch ramps; two picnic shelters; a Columbia River swimming area and bathhouse; and a delightful interpretive nature trail that winds through a riverside marsh, home to many resident and migratory birds. An even greater lure is the Apple Capital Loop Trail, a paved recreation path that runs through this campground on its way around a 14-mile loop. From the campground, the path crosses a bridge over the Wenatchee River, then rolls through some lovely green city and utility-company waterfront parks near the city of Wenatchee before crossing the Columbia on a railroad-bridge-turned-footbridge. On the east side, it follows the Columbia's shoreline north for 4 or 5 miles, then recrosses the river on a concrete highway bridge and returns to Wenatchee Confluence. The loop makes a great day trip for Wenatchee Confluence campers. It's all asphalt, with smooth riding, few hills, and plenty of walkers and in-line skaters for company. Even on hot days, a cooling breeze off the river makes this path a treat. Plans call for a northern extension of the trail to Rocky Reach Dam.

Getting there: Wenatchee Confluence is immediately north of the U.S. Highway 2/US 97A junction near Wenatchee. From US 2, follow signs north on US 97A.

3 Lincoln Rock State Park ★ ★ ★ ✦

SITES	RESERVATIONS	CONTACT
🏕 🚐	(888) 226-7688 or www.parks.wa.gov	Washington State Parks (360) 902-8844
	OPEN	Lincoln Rock State Park (509) 884-8702
94 sites, 32 full hookups, 35 water/electrical hookups, RVs to 65 feet	March to mid-October	

Lincoln Rock has long been one of our favorite state parks, mostly because of the amount of local character revealed by its namesake. History records that somewhere back around 1889, a local man, Billy Schaft, photographed a large rock outcrop across the river from this park and remarked how much it looked like a profile of Abraham Lincoln. Plenty of other local people who—let's face it, living in Wenatchee and all—had plenty of time to consider such things, agreed. Someone sent the picture to a photo contest in *Ladies' Home Journal*, and it won first prize. Voila! Lincoln Rock went on the maps, and public gatherings soon followed. The park, on a broad, flat Columbia River shoulder across the river from the rock, now bears its name. If you look through the little fixed pipe near the Lincoln Rock upper restroom, you can see it. By George, it does look like Abe. Wake the kids. The campground here is worthy of a visit on its own, however. It's the prototype for a series of Washington State Parks on the middle Columbia, all of which follow a wildly successful formula: sprawling grassy playfields; boat launches; a swimming area; and flat, open trailer and tent sites separated by young shade trees. All these parks are popular with boaters, who flock here in summer months to water-ski and soak up the sun. Lincoln Rock, on the Columbia's Entiat Lake behind Rocky Reach Dam, has all of these pleasures and more, including two boat launches, multiple moorage docks, tennis and basketball courts, coin-op showers, horseshoe pits, a large kitchen shelter, and an amphitheater. It's a very pleasant spot—

The Apple Capital Loop Trail winds through Wenatchee Confluence State Park.

too hot for some tastes in the summer, but just right for the lizard people among us. Just across the river is the popular Rocky Reach Dam Visitor Center, which you can only get to by driving back south to Wenatchee, crossing the river, and driving up U.S. Highway 97A.

Getting there: The campground is 7 miles north of East Wenatchee on U.S. Highway 2/97, on the east side of the Columbia River.

4 Orondo River Park ★ ★ ★

SITES	RESERVATIONS	CONTACT
🏕️ 🚐	(509) 784-2556	Port of Douglas County (509) 884-4700
	OPEN	
24 sites, 14 water/electric hookups, RVs to any length	Late May through late September	

This small (five-acre) park on the Columbia River near the town of Orondo is a mid-point stopover for U.S. Highway 97 travelers. Its campsites, like others on PUD-owned property in this area, are grassy, level, and pleasant, with large shade trees providing summertime relief. The park also has horseshoe pits, picnic shelters, a swimming area, showers, and a single-lane boat launch. It's not likely to be the quietest campground in these parts; Jet Ski rentals are available on-site. But it's a useful alternate to other, larger nearby parks such as Daroga, Lincoln Rock, and Beebe Bridge.

Getting there: Follow signs from U.S. Highway 2/97 3 miles north of Orondo, about 18 miles north of East Wenatchee, on the east side of the Columbia River.

5 Daroga State Park ★★★★

SITES	RESERVATIONS	CONTACT
🏕️ 🚐	For group camp only: (888) 226-7688 or www.parks.wa.gov	Washington State Parks (360) 902-8844
	OPEN	Daroga State Park (509) 664-6380
45 sites, 28 water/electrical hookups, RVs to any length	Early March to early October	

"KITE FLYING PROHIBITED." Now there's a welcome sign you don't see every day. About thirty seconds after arriving at Daroga State Park, however, you'll see why—a set of extremely high-voltage electric transmission lines runs right over the camping area at this diverse Columbia River park. Kite flying would be ill-advised, indeed. But you can get away with just about any other form of summertime fun here. Daroga, a relatively

BEST FISHING CAMPS

1. Sun Lakes State Park, Central Washington
Trout fishing typically is strong, particularly early in the season, at Sun Lakes' home pond, Park Lake, as well as a half dozen other top-producing lakes in the same region. See p. 259.

2. Taidnapam Park, Southwest Washington
This Tacoma Power Park on the Cowlitz River has great fishing in season for kokanee (landlocked salmon) and other species, all from a convenient fishing bridge a short walk from the campground. See p. 215.

3. Potholes State Park, Central Washington
The park sits on a productive, multispecies fishery, and many other good fishing lakes are within a short drive. See p. 258.

4. Deception Pass State Park, North Puget Sound
The key here is variety, from saltwater bank fishing for bottomfish and migratory salmon and steelhead, to freshwater fishing in separate lakes for trout and bass. See p. 42.

5. Curlew Lake, Northeast Washington
A little gem in the North Cascades north of Republic, Curlew Lake was famous for trout fishing long before it became famous for camping. See p. 281.

new, modern state park, is actually two parks in one. The RV camping area, which sits on a high bluff, is nicely equipped with hookups, paved pull-through sites, metal picnic tables, and fire pits. Most of the sites have nice views of the Columbia—and the unique walk-in camping area below. Daroga, a former ranch site, has a lagoon separated from the main Columbia by a narrow earthen bar, which has been equipped with seventeen walk-in campsites (the park provides wheelbarrow-type devices to help you move your gear). These are very nice spots, well worth the effort to get here. Note: This is a great place to set the kids up with a walk-in site and let Mom and Dad retreat to peaceful slumber in the RV. The entrance for the walk-in sites is a short distance south of the main park entrance on U.S. Highway 97. Daroga also offers boat launching and moorage, extensive picnic facilities, a gorgeous swimming area with a bathhouse, and a group camp for up to 100 campers. When the wind kicks up enough, the beach area here draws a few windsurfers.

Local trivia: You just had to ask about the name. Here goes: Former property owner Grady Auvil developed a new strain of peach, which was named "Daroga" by local nurseryman Pete Van Well, Sr. The name contains the first two letters of the names of three Auvil brothers, Dave, Robert and Grady, who began working the ranch in 1928.

Getting there: The park is 18 miles north of Wenatchee on US 97, on the east side of the Columbia River.

6 Beebe Bridge Park ★ ★ ★ ★

SITES	RESERVATIONS	CONTACT
	None	Chelan County Public Utility District (509) 661-4551
	OPEN	
46 sites, all have water/electrical hookups, RVs to any length	April through October	

Chelan County Public Utility District used a lot of its own water to turn this former dusty riverbank shelf into a gleaming gem of a campground with ample shoreline frontage on the Columbia River. Beebe Bridge's campsites, most of which are pleasant pull-throughs with modern hookups, tables, and fire pits, are so clean and well-manicured, you almost feel the need to take off your shoes before stepping onto the grass. Smart design helps keep it that way: Every site has a level, sandy tent pad to keep family campers from squishing the lawn. This is a clean, pretty spot, lacking, like most of its neighbors, summertime shade because the trees here are newly planted. Give it time, though, and Beebe Bridge's popularity is sure to grow. Amenities at the fifty-six-acre park include picnic shelters, a swimming area, a two-lane boat launch, tennis courts, horseshoe pits, hot showers, boat moorage, playfields, a shoreline trail, and an RV dump station. It's a winner.

Getting there: Beebe Bridge Park is about 34 miles north of Wenatchee and 4 miles east of Chelan on U.S. Highway 97, near the Beebe Bridge over the Columbia River.

7 Entiat City Park ★ ★ ★ ◀

SITES	RESERVATIONS	CONTACT
🏕 🚐	Recommended; (800) 736-8428	City of Entiat Parks Department (509) 784-1500
56 sites, 31 water/electrical hookups, RVs to any length	**OPEN** April through September	

Travelers who choose the U.S. Highway 97A route up the west side of the Columbia River have their choice of campgrounds: Entiat City Park or Entiat City Park. It's not all that bad a choice, actually. The riverfront park is close to downtown Entiat, but that's not exactly like being in downtown Pittsburgh. The forty-acre municipal park is quite nicely equipped, with hookup sites, a boat launch, pleasant picnic facilities, hot showers, playgrounds, a swimming beach, and an RV dump station. It's a very popular RV stopover, so reservations are recommended.

Getting there: The park is in the town of Entiat on US 97A, about 16 miles north of Wenatchee, on the west side of the Columbia River.

8 Alta Lake State Park ★ ★ ★ ★

SITES	RESERVATIONS	CONTACT
🏕 🚐	(509) 667-7503	Washington State Parks (360) 902-8844
200 sites, 32 electrical hookups, RVs to 38 feet	**OPEN** Late March to late October	Alta Lake State Park (509) 923-2473

Here's the deal: We won't tell our small RV/tent-camping friends about Alta Lake. And you don't either. This well-hidden, 181-acre state park, tucked into a bowl behind two hulking, sheer ridges above the west shore of the Columbia River, is a favorite of fans of the dry, pine-forested, rocky terrain common to the east-slope Central Washington Cascades. We have many fond memories of camping here in the brutally cold, crisp air of winter, tagging along while Dad went deer hunting in the Methow drainage. Today, the facilities here are definitely showing their age, but there's something about this park's setting and feeling that keeps bringing us back. Campsites are split into two groups: two loops in the sweetly scented pine forest above the lake, and one near the still waters of the lake itself. The campground has coin-op showers, a swimming beach, a boat launch, and a trail that leads 0.6 mile to a viewpoint of the Middle Columbia Valley. (Watch for snakes!) The lake is a popular trout-fishing venue; a private resort with a store and boat rentals is nearby. The park also has a group camp for twenty to sixty-four people; RVs are allowed, but there are no hookups. Call the park information number above for details.

Local trivia: This former federal land was donated to the City of Pateros in 1928 by a Forest Service supervisor grateful for the services of a local man who pulled the

A camper enjoys the dry heat and pine smell of Alta Lake State Park.

supervisor's car from the sand with a team of horses. When state auditors ruled the city couldn't own land outside its limits, the site was transferred to Washington State Parks in 1951. The lake was named for Alta Heinz, daughter of a jeweler from the town of Wilbur who was working a mining claim near here in 1900.

Getting there: From the U.S. Highway 97/State Route 153 junction near Pateros, drive about 2 miles northwest on SR 153 to Alta Lake Road. Turn left and proceed about 2 miles to the campground, at the end of the road.

9 Bridgeport State Park ★ ★ ⬧

SITES	RESERVATIONS	CONTACT
🏕️ 🚐	None	Washington State Parks (360) 902-8844
34 sites, 20 water/electrical hookups, RVs to 45 feet	**OPEN** Late March through October	Bridgeport State Park (509) 686-7231

If you get a chance to pause and prop up your feet at Bridgeport, a 750-acre state park just upstream from Chief Joseph Dam, say a word of thanks to the late Ralph Van Slyke, a retired Army Corps of Engineers employee who forged the beginnings of this park from the barren, rocky soil—using only common garden tools. With the help of some bigger equipment, the park has grown to a comfortable, shaded stop-over, with campsites scattered beneath cottonwood trees, all in view of the massive hydro dam to the west. The park has coin-op showers, picnic facilities, an RV dump station, and a boat launch and moorage docks. A pleasant, sandy swimming beach on the Columbia's Rufus Woods Lake will be popular with the kids. The park's group camp holds twenty to seventy-two people; call the park number above for details. The eighteen-hole Lake Woods Golf Course is nearby. Several trails run through the park, and windsurfers use the beach on occasion. Be on guard for rattlesnakes. And don't forget to check out the "haystacks"—some odd volcanic basalt formations on the premises.

Getting there: From U.S. Highway 97 about 21 miles south of Okanogan and 70 miles north of Wenatchee, turn south on State Route 17 and proceed 8 miles to the park entrance, 3 miles northeast of Bridgeport.

Other Middle Columbia Campgrounds

For a more "out-there" camping experience nearly the opposite of the sprawling, grassy, lower-valley state parks, tent campers and hikers might want to take a hard left turn from U.S. Highway 97A south of Entiat and explore the long, narrow Entiat Valley, which connects the Columbia River Valley to the alluring alpine country in the Glacier Peak Wilderness. A string of picturesque Forest Service campgrounds, between 1600 and 3100 feet in elevation, awaits in the upper valley. Sites are primitive but strategically located. The remote campgrounds are filled in summer months with small-stream anglers, horse or dirt bike riders, or hikers and backpackers headed into the wilderness; in the fall they're filled with hunters. Note that much of this valley was devastated by the massive Tyee Creek wildfire of 1994, one of the worst in modern history. The fire burned uncontrolled from midsummer to the first snows of October, stretching north nearly all the way to Lake Chelan. But vegetation and wildlife have been quick to spring back. The campgrounds, all accessed via Entiat River Road, are **Pine Flat** (six sites and a thirty to fifty-person group camp, 13 miles from the junction of US 97A and Entiat River Road); **Fox Creek** (sixteen sites, 27 miles); **Lake Creek** (eighteen sites, 28 miles); **Silver Falls** (fourteen sites and a thirty- to fifty-person group camp, 32 miles); **North Fork** (eight sites, 33 miles); **Spruce Grove** (two tent-only sites, 34 miles); **Three Creek** (two tent-only sites, 36 miles); and **Cottonwood** (twenty-five sites, 38 miles). All these campgrounds are open mid-May through October, all have pit toilets, and all except Spruce Grove and Three Creek have piped water. Most are suitable for tents and small RVs. Call or visit the Wenatchee National Forest's Entiat Ranger District, 2108 Entiat Way, (509) 784-1511.

In the Wenatchee area, **Squilchuck State Park**, near the Mission Ridge Ski Area, is a reservation-only group camp for up to 168 people. It reverts to a ski hill operated by Wenatchee Valley College on winter weekends. Follow Mission Street south from Wenatchee, then follow signs along Squilchuck Road. Contact Washington State Parks, (360) 902-8844 or (509) 664-6373 to make reservations for the group camp.

Opposite: An outline of Abe Lincoln's face can be seen at Lincoln Rock State Park near Wenatchee.

Lake Chelan and Stehekin

10 Lake Chelan State Park ✦ ✦ ✦ ✦

SITES	RESERVATIONS	CONTACT
🏕️ 🚐 144 sites, 30 full hookups, RVs to 30 feet	(888) 226-7688 or www.parks.wa.gov **OPEN** Year-round	Washington State Parks (360) 902-8844 Lake Chelan State Park (509) 687-3710

If you close your eyes and concentrate, you can almost hear the grinding of the glaciers. OK, so maybe it's just the septic pump in that guy's Winnebago next door. Never mind. Use your imagination, and conjure up the behemoth mass of ice it must have taken to carve the incredible gorge known as Lake Chelan. The glacier-carved trough, surrounded in some places by peaks approaching 9000 feet, is among the deepest gorges in all of North America. And the lake, 55 miles long and never more than 2 miles wide, is a wonder of nature. The water here gives new meaning to "deep and clear." Lake Chelan is 1500 feet deep in places, a mark surpassed in America only by Lake Tahoe and Crater Lake. Get away from the water, and it only gets better. To the south rise the magnificent, glacier-draped mountains of the Glacier Peak Wilderness. To the west are the rugged peaks of North Cascades National Park. And due north is the impressive Sawtooth Range and other peaks in the Lake Chelan–Sawtooth Wilderness.

Some Lake Chelan State Park campsites come with their own dock.

Many people choose to explore this Chelan's water wonderland via boat, either private pleasure craft or the commercial Lady of the Lake tour boats, which ferry visitors to Stehekin and North Cascades National Park. But others come here just to admire, and partake of, the lake itself. That makes Lake Chelan State Park, a 127-acre waterfront getaway built with boaters, water-skiers, and Jet Ski riders in mind, one of the very busiest in the state park system. Little wonder. The park has the best of both worlds when it comes to camping: full hookup sites (in an older, private-resort setting; walk-in lakeshore tent sites on the other). The RV sites are packed a bit too close together for our comfort; this is a much better place for tenters. The lakefront tent sites on the opposite side of the park are delightful, each with a flat tent pad, a table, a fireplace—and a view up the lake to die for. It's hard to imagine a more idyllic setting for campers with boats. Most sites are within a very short walk of modern moorage piers, placing the park in high demand among water-skiers and anglers.

But there's plenty to do right in the park, which is equipped with a swimming beach, a bathhouse, coin-op showers, a picnic shelter, a playground, an RV dump station, and a boat launch.

In the winter the park becomes a popular snow-play area, with cross-country skiers using it as a warming base for ski trips on local roads and trails. Get a reservation for this one. You'll need it.

Local trivia: The name Chelan is at least some approximation of the Salish word for the tribe that once lived here. It is believed to translate to "lake" and/or "blue water."

Getting there: Southbound from Chelan: From U.S. Highway 97A about 3 miles south of Chelan, turn right on South Lakeshore Road and proceed 6 miles to the park entrance, on the right. Northbound from Wenatchee: On US 97A, about 9 miles north of Entiat, turn left onto State Route 971. Continue 7 miles to Lakeshore Road. Turn right, then immediately left into park entrance.

ıı Twenty-Five Mile Creek ✦ ✦ ✦ State Park

SITES	RESERVATIONS	CONTACT
🏕️ 🚐	(888) 226-7688 or www.parks.wa.gov	Washington State Parks (360) 902-8844
67 sites, 13 full hookups, 8 water/ electrical hookups, RVs to 30 feet	**OPEN** Late March to early October	Twenty-Five Mile Creek State Park (509) 687-3710

You might think it looks more like an old resort than a state park. Give yourself a gold star. Twenty-Five Mile Creek *is* an old resort, converted to Washington State Parks use in 1975. Like Lake Chelan State Park just down the road, boating is the primary activity here; the 235-acre park has a boat launch, ample moorage, a fuel dock, and other services. But the campground is pleasant, too, with nicely wooded, fairly private (and fairly small) sites near the lake and along Twenty-Five Mile Creek, where fishing for trout is popular. The park also has coin-op showers, a group camp for up to forty people, an RV dump station, a shady picnic area, and even its own grocery store. Bring your mountain bike and ride down to Lake Chelan State Park, or up the hill and on to the wealth of backcountry roads in the Navarre Coulee, to the south.

Getting there: Southbound from Chelan: From U.S. Highway 97A about 3 miles south of Chelan, turn right on South Lakeshore Road and drive 15 miles to the park, on the right. Northbound from Wenatchee: On US 97A, about 9 miles north of Entiat, turn left onto State Route 971. Continue 7 miles to Lakeshore Road. Turn left and proceed 9 miles to the park.

12   Lakeshore RV Park ★ ★ ★ ★

SITES	RESERVATIONS	CONTACT
	Recommended; (509) 682-8023	Lakeshore RV Park (509) 682-8023
165 sites, 165 full hookups, RVs to 40 feet	**OPEN** Year-round	

Everything that's good about Lake Chelan—fun in the summer sun, swimming, boating, tanning, paddling, and kid-sister-teasing—can be found at Lakeshore, the city of Chelan's pleasant camping and day-use park that becomes a bustling activity zone in summer months. The campsites are pleasant, in partially shaded, grassy blocks near the lake. RV sites have full hookups with free Wi-Fi and cable TV (!), even many tent sites have electricity and water; twenty-two of them have 16-by-16-foot tent pads. This is a big, modern park, with six main camping areas, a large marina, coin-op showers, an RV dump station, a covered picnic area, a boat launch, and other niceties. Prices are a bit steep in the peak season ($38 for RVs, $29 for tents when this guide went to press). But that does little to stem the flow of Lakeshore fans, many of whom book summer vacations here far, far in advance. Reservations for the summer are accepted beginning January 2 each year. Start dialing early. Note that some sites have a seven-night minimum during July and August.

Getting there: From downtown Chelan, follow signs to State Route 150 and Manson, proceeding about a half mile to the campground on the left.

Boat-in/Hike-in Lake Chelan National Recreation–Area Campgrounds

Adventurers with hiking boots, boats, tents, and sleeping bags are in luck on Lake Chelan, whose waters lead to the greatest wealth of boat-in and hike-in campsites in Washington State. Many summertime visitors make use of both, ferrying by private watercraft to a shoreline campsite, then setting out on foot for hike-in sites in the same area. (One popular example: boating to Lucerne, riding the shuttle to Holden Village, then setting out on foot into the Glacier Peak Wilderness.) The starting points are a dozen small, primitive Forest Service campgrounds all with floating docks or fixed moorage piers, that ring the lake. They are **Big Creek** (four campsites, four-boat moorage capacity); **Corral Creek** (two sites, six boats); **Deer Point** (four sites, eight boats; at this writing, temporarily closed because of a summer 2002 wildfire); **Domke Falls** (three sites, six boats); **Graham Harbor** (five sites, ten boats); **Graham Harbor Creek** (four sites, six boats); **Lucerne** (two sites, eleven boats); **Mitchell Creek** (six sites, seventeen boats); **Moore Point** (four sites, three boats); **Prince Creek** (six sites, three boats); **Refrigerator Harbor** (four sites, four boats); and **Safety Harbor** (two sites, six boats).

The Forest Service also maintains a half dozen primitive walk-in sites along the Chelan Lakeshore or Prince Creek trails. They are **Cub Lake** (three sites, 6.5 miles from Lake Chelan on Prince Creek Trail); **Boiling Lake** (three sites, 10 miles from Lake Chelan on Prince Creek Trail); **Domke Lake** (eight sites, 2 miles from Lucerne via Trails 1230 and 1280); **Moore Point** (four sites, 5.5 miles south of Stehekin on Chelan Lakeshore Trail); **Prince Creek** (six sites, 18 miles south of Stehekin on Chelan Lakeshore Trail); and **Surprise Lake** (three sites, 6 miles from Lake Chelan on Trail 1246). Another possible destination is **Holden Ballpark** (two sites), near the Lutheran camp/mining burg of Holden Village, reached by boating to Lucerne and riding the shuttle bus. All the lakeshore campsites can be reached either by private watercraft or floatplane (call Chelan Airways, (509) 682-5555). Or arrangements can be made for drop-offs by the Lady of the Lake, the passenger boat that ferries visitors from Chelan to Stehekin in North Cascades National Park. Call (509) 682-4584 for Lady of the Lake boat schedules. Or visit the Lady of the Lake website, www.ladyofthelake.com, for full schedules and North Cascades National Park Stehekin Valley shuttle bus information. (The most popular drop-off camps are Prince Creek, where Chelan Lakeshore Trail walkers depart for an 18-mile walk north to Stehekin, and Lucerne, the drop point for hikers bound for Holden Village along Railroad Creek in the Glacier Peak Wilderness.) Call the Wenatchee National Forest's Chelan Ranger District, (509) 682-2576, for more information.

Hike-in/Shuttle-in Stehekin–Area Campgrounds

In the Stehekin area, North Cascades National Park visitors, most of whom will have ferried up the 28-mile-long lake on boats operated by the Lady of the Lake company, have their choice of walk-in sites, all reached by trail along the north end of Lake Chelan, or via the shuttle bus moving people up the Stehekin Valley Road (call the national park, (360) 856-5700, ext. 340, for bus information). Campers will need to stop at Stehekin's Golden West Visitor Center for overnight permits. Choose from **Purple Point**, a short walk from the Stehekin landing; **Weaver Point**, a boat-in site; or **Harlequin, Rainbow Bridge, High Bridge, Tumwater, Dolly Varden, Shady, Bridge Creek, Flat Creek, Cottonwood**, or a half dozen other walk-in sites. Consult with rangers, and remember that upper-valley campsites don't melt out until early July, and winter flooding often closes portions of Stehekin Valley Road. Call (360) 873-4590 for updates and (509) 682-4584 for Lady of the Lake boat schedules. Or visit the Lady of the Lake website, www.ladyofthelake.com, for current conditions, full schedules, and North Cascades National Park Stehekin Valley shuttle bus information.

BEST FULL-SERVICE RV CAMPGROUNDS

1. Lakeshore RV Park, Lake Chelan
Almost like a private park run by a public entity (the city of Chelan), Lakeshore has all the amenities—down to cable TV and internet access. See p. 254.

2. Taidnapam Park, Cowlitz River
The flagship park of the Tacoma Power parks, Taidnapam just got bigger and better. Pull-through sites and full hookups abound. See p. 215.

3. Grayland Beach State Park, Grayland
In our experience, it's the state's best, flattest, most convenient campground with full hookups that's within a short walk of the Pacific Ocean. See p. 102.

4. Millersylvania Memorial State Park, Tenino
With forty-eight full hookups in an open area with many pull-through sites, Millersylvania, near Tenino, is not only convenient to Interstate 5 travelers but historic and pleasant, as well. See p. 62.

5. Fort Worden State Park, Port Townsend
A big park with easy RV access and many full hookups, Fort Worden's sites also offer stunning views of Admiralty Inlet. See p. 78.

Other Lake Chelan–Area Campgrounds

A handful of primitive, tents-only, Forest Service campgrounds are scattered in the rugged hills above Lake Chelan's southern shore. All are on or near Forest Road 5900, reached by continuing beyond Twenty-Five Mile Creek State Park (see above) on South Lakeshore Drive. These campgrounds, most of which have pit toilets but no piped water or other services, are, in order: **Ramona Park** (eight sites; closed at this writing due to flood damage); **Windy Camp** (two sites, 15 miles southwest of Ramona Park on Road 8410); **Grouse Mountain** (four sites, 8 miles west of Twenty-Five Mile Creek State Park on Road 5900); **Junior Point** (five sites, 14 miles west of Twenty-Five Mile Creek State Park Road 5900); **Antilon** (dispersed sites, 14 miles northwest of Chelan on Road 5900); **Handy Springs** (one site, 15 miles west of Twenty-Five Mile Creek State Park on Road 5900); and **South Navarre** (four sites at 6475 feet, 40 miles northwest of Chelan on Road 5900). Campers who seek RV shelter before taking on the boat ride to Stehekin, and find Lake Chelan State Park or Lakeshore RV Park already booked, might consider **Lakeview Park** on State Route 150, (509) 687-3612 (reservations suggested).

Columbia Basin and the Grand Coulee

13 Ginkgo Petrified Forest/Wanapum Recreation Area ★ ★ ★

SITES	RESERVATIONS	CONTACT
50 sites, all have full hookups, RVs to 60 feet	(888) 226-7688 or www.parks.wa.gov	Washington State Parks (360) 902-8844
	OPEN	Ginkgo Petrified Forest/Wanapum Recreation Area (509) 856-2700
	Year-round	

It's hot, it's dry, and it's occasionally gusty and dusty. For West Siders, it's the perfect introduction to the Columbia Basin. But hey, it's a short walk from 27,000 feet of shoreline on the Columbia River and a short drive from the Gorge Amphitheater summer concert venue. And that's more than enough to keep this geologically fascinating state park packed with visitors in the summer, when it serves as one of very few regional campgrounds for music and sun lovers. The park has come into such demand, in fact, that it's a good idea to get reservations in the summer.

High cliffs of the Columbia River dominate views from Ginkgo Petrified Forest/Wanapum Recreation Area.

The Wanapum campground, on the west side of the Vantage Bridge over the Columbia, has a nice spread of picnic sites, a swimming area and bathhouse, a boat launch, and fifty partially shaded (thank heavens) campsites, all with full hookups to run the air conditioner in the Winnie. These sites work OK for tenters, but they're really designed for the RV crowd. Make time to visit the nearby Ginkgo Petrified Forest State Park, one of Washington's more fascinating geological oddities. It contains fossil remnants of an ancient forest, including the petrified remains of ancient Ginkgo trees, now extinct. Several miles of trails lead through the petrified forest, discovered by highway workers in the 1930s. Watch for snakes! Note: Wanapum is one of only a handful of Washington State Parks that does not have an RV dump station. Also note: This park is "subject to high winds, especially in the evening," State Parks cautions correctly, adding, "Campers should secure tents and lightweight articles"—such as your children. You've been warned.

Getting there: The campground is 30 miles east of Ellensburg on the Columbia River; follow signs from Interstate 90 Exit 136 at Vantage.

14 Potholes State Park ★ ★ ★ ◂

SITES	RESERVATIONS	CONTACT
🏕️ 🚙	(888) 226-7688 or www.parks.wa.gov	Washington State Parks (360) 902-8844
121 sites, 60 full hookups, RVs to 50 feet	OPEN Year-round	Potholes State Park (509) 765-7271

Bring the binoculars, the oars, and a fly rod. Potholes State Park is the hub of waterborne activity in the Columbia Basin. The 640-acre splash of green amid the rather harsh surrounding desert won't be everyone's idea of a grand vacation getaway, but if fishing or canoeing are even medium-high on your list, the place deserves a visit. The water, naturally, is the star here. Most of the water in Potholes Reservoir (the actual Potholes Lakes are a half-hour's drive away) is seepage from the grandiose Columbia Basin Irrigation Project, which pumps millions of gallons of water from Banks Lake onto surrounding fields. When earthen O'Sullivan Dam was completed here in 1949, the water backed up and filled a series of low-lying glacial depressions: the Potholes. At about 29,000 acres when full in the spring, Potholes Reservoir is by far the largest body of water here. But literally hundreds of other small ponds and water canals are linked to it by the artificial water table, creating a serendipitous, navigable paradise for anglers and paddlers.

The campground, on the southwest shore of the reservoir, is a nice mix of pleasant waterfront RV and rougher-cut tent sites (they're set in sand and sagebrush, exposed to the wind). The park also contains a mondo boat launch and day-use parking area, picnic facilities, an RV dump station, and a playground. This is a very popular springtime destination for Washington anglers and, increasingly, bird-watchers. Hundreds of species of birds migrating on the Pacific Flyway make stops here and at nearby Columbia Wildlife Refuge.

Dry Falls, a fascinating Grand Coulee feature, once was the most powerful waterfall on the planet.

Getting there: From Interstate 90 at Moses Lake, take Exit 179 and follow State Route 17 about 9 miles south to State Route 262 (O'Sullivan Dam Road). Turn right (west) and drive about 11 miles to the park.

15 Sun Lakes State Park ✦ ✦ ✦

SITES	RESERVATIONS	CONTACT
191 sites, 39 full hookups, RVs to 65 feet	(888) 226-7688 or www.parks.wa.gov	Washington State Parks (360) 902-8844
	OPEN	Sun Lakes State Park (509) 632-5583
	Year-round	Sun Lakes State Park Resort (509) 632-5291

Close your eyes and imagine the flow. One of the most cataclysmic natural events ever to hit North America—the flooding of Missoula Lake, a glacier-dammed inland sea that covered huge portions of Northwest Montana during the last ice age—created all of the many lakes within Sun Lakes State Park, as well as the amazing natural features all around it. These include the Grand Coulee, itself an ancient meander scar from one of the Columbia Basin's many incomprehensible ancient floods, as well as hundreds of other local lakes—wet and dry—that linger as flood scars in this area known as the Channeled Scablands. The upper Grand Coulee north of here is water-filled once more. It's now Banks Lake, a storage basin for irrigation water piped from the Columbia. But the Lower Coulee remains in more of a natural (dry) state. And in between is Sun Lakes, a series of small lakes all believed to have been former splash pools for Dry Falls, the awesome, 3.5-mile-wide, 400-foot-tall former waterfall north of

Sun Lakes State Park attracts more than its share of sun worshippers.

here that dwarfed Niagara—and every other waterfall on Planet Earth—when water last flowed over it 10,000 to 15,000 years ago. A trip to the nearby Dry Falls Interpretive Center is a must.

That said, the campground here near the foot of Dry Falls, wildly popular for generations of Washingtonians, leaves a bit to be desired. Many of the spaces are quite closely packed, with little privacy and dusty floors that can be downright dirty in summer months. Tent sites lack tent pads, RV sites lack fire pits. Some sites are grassy, and some are near the south shores of Park Lake. But the entire place is a bit busy for some campers' tastes: The adjacent Sun Lakes State Park Resort lends a commercial, Palm Springs-ish air, adding rental cabins and trailers, a golf course, boat ramps and rentals, a store, a laundromat, a horse stable, and 110 full-hookup RV sites to the mix. If that's OK with you, the rest of this big (4000-acre) park will be, as well. The public portion of the park is similarly well outfitted, with a large group camp, picnic facilities, coin-op showers, an RV dump station, a boat launch, and more than 16 miles of hiking trails, one of which leads to nearby Lake Lenore Caves. The caves have produced some significant archaeological finds, such as pictographs still visible on the walls. Watch for snakes on trails here.

Sun Lakes is a summer watersport and angling hotspot. Lakes in this park, and the area in general, are among the very best in Washington for trophy trout. Park Lake, right at the park, and Blue Lake, just to the south, both are notable hotspots on opening day of trout season (in late April; check state regulations), with good bank access and, often, easy limits. Other good fishing spots include Deep, Perch, Rainbow, and

Dry Falls lakes. The latter is a selective fishery, with bait and barbed hooks prohibited. Needless to say, campground reservations are a must here. But if you call well in advance, the wealth of sites at the dual campgrounds gives you a good chance to land a site. Tenters: Be prepared for occasional strong winds.

Getting there: From Interstate 90 at Moses Lake, follow State Route 17 about 38 miles north to the park, 17 miles north of Soap Lake and 6 miles south of Coulee City.

16 Coulee City Park ★ ★ ★ ◀

SITES	RESERVATIONS	CONTACT
⛺ 🚐	None	Coulee City Park (509) 632-5331
	OPEN	
160 sites, 55 full hookups, RVs to 35 feet	April to late October	

This campground at Coulee City, on the south shore of Banks Lake, is a good alternative to the oft-booked Sun Lakes State Park nearby. It's not exactly scenic, but it is conveniently located near the lake, and its launch and moorage facilities make it very popular among anglers and boaters. Note that 100 sites here are designated tent sites, and the full-hookup RV sites are drive-throughs. The partially-shaded campground also has a playground, store, and showers. It can get quite windy here; batten down the hatches. Avoid the place during the big Memorial Day weekend rodeo. (Unless of course you're going to the rodeo, which sounds pretty fun.)

Getting there: The campground is in Coulee City, 2 miles east of the Dry Falls junction of State Route 17 and U.S. Highway 2.

17 Steamboat Rock State Park ★ ★ ★ ★ ◀

SITES	RESERVATIONS	CONTACT
⛺ 🚐	(888) 226-7688 or www.parks.wa.gov	Washington State Parks (360) 902-8844
	OPEN	Steamboat Rock State Park
126 sites, 100 full hookups, RVs to 50 feet	Year-round; limited winter facilities	(509) 633-1304

Steamboat Rock is Fun Central in the Grand Coulee. It's hard to imagine a better way to immerse oneself in the intriguing natural environs of the Columbia Basin than putting in some serious camping time at Steamboat Rock, named after the massive, prow-shaped basalt bluff jutting up from Banks Lake. The lake, an old Columbia River coulee (floodwater scar), was turned in the 1940s into a massive reservoir for Columbia Basin irrigation water. This turned Steamboat Rock—once likely an island in the ancient, flooding Columbia—into a mighty peninsula. At the same time, a grand outdoor playground was created. Steamboat Rock State Park takes advantage of all its offerings. The park, one of Washington's premier sunny-side vacation getaways, is

Banks Lake, near Steamboat Rock State Park, is a favorite with anglers.

a huge place—3500 acres—with a very well-groomed, very well-attended campground. Steamboat was one of the first parks in the state to leap onto reservation status, and if you're seeking a campsite between Memorial Day and Labor Day, it's a good idea to get one. Most of the sites are clean, comfortable RV spaces, but you'll also find a dozen isolated, boat-in campsites at the north end of Steamboat Rock. Most sites are on flat, grassy land that's well suited to tents (be warned, however, about nasty winds and predatory late-night sprinklers).

Most of the best things to do here are immediately obvious: For canoeists and water-skiers, the 27-mile-long, 4-mile-wide lake is paradise. Steamboat Rock is a water-sports recreation hub, with boat launches and moorage, a sandy-bottom swimming area, a water-ski float, bathhouses, and extensive waterfront picnic facilities. Also on the premises are a bathhouse, coin-op showers, picnic facilities, an RV dump station, a group camp for up to fifty people, and a nice playground. Anglers probably already know about this 30,000-acre reservoir's reputation as a hotspot for bass, walleye, perch, and other warm-water species.

If the weather's not baking hot, you can take to the park's trail system, which contains 25 miles of paths on, around, and over Steamboat Rock. The access trail to the top is only about a mile, but gains 800 feet in elevation. Be sure to carry plenty of water, and to stay back from crumbly basalt cliffs. And do watch for rattlesnakes along the way. A more obscure attraction near here is across the highway from the park's northern rest area/boat launch (about 3.5 miles north of the main entrance): Northrup Canyon, the only natural forest in Grant County. The 3120-acre area is filled with forested ravines between coulee walls, where bald eagles and other raptors sometimes are spotted. In the winter the park keeps hopping, with ice fishing and cross-country skiing drawing small but happy crowds of Steamboat Rock visitors.

Getting there: The park is on State Route 155, 11 miles south of Electric City, 16.5 miles north of Coulee City.

18 Spring Canyon ★ ★ ★ ◆

SITES	RESERVATIONS	CONTACT
🏕 🚐	(877) 444-6777 or www.recreation.gov	Lake Roosevelt National Recreation Area (509) 633-9441
	OPEN	
87 sites, no hookups, RVs to 26 feet	Mid-April to mid-October, weather permitting	

Spring Canyon, a national park site operated as part of the massive Franklin D. Roosevelt Lake National Recreation Area, is the closest public campground to the tourist-magnet of Grand Coulee Dam. That makes it the most popular of many campgrounds scattered along the shores of the 130-mile-long reservoir. Luckily, it's also among the largest and best-equipped. Campsites are spread through a series of loops in this dry, sagebrush-speckled area above the lake. The park also has a boat launch, making it a favorite home base for anglers, water-skiers, and, in the winter, bald-eagle-watchers. Lake Roosevelt is open year-round for a variety of game-fish species. Check the state fishing regulations book for information. Spring Canyon also has a very popular swimming area, with a lifeguard on duty in the summer. (Even if you don't usually swim, you'll want to get in here on sweltering summer days.) The campground has piped water and an RV dump station, but no hookups or showers. A group site holds up to twenty-five people.

Getting there: From Grand Coulee, drive 3 miles east on State Route 174 to the campground, on the shores of Lake Roosevelt.

19 Keller Ferry ★ ★ ★

SITES	RESERVATIONS	CONTACT
🏕 🚐	(877) 444-6777 or www.recreation.gov	Lake Roosevelt National Recreation Area (509) 633-9441
	OPEN	
55 sites, no hookups, RVs to 16 feet	Mid-April to mid-October, weather permitting	

If you close your eyes and use your imagination, you might think you were back on Puget Sound. Well, OK. Not really. But you almost have to take a ferry to get here. Keller Ferry, at the south side of the Lake Roosevelt ferry crossing on State Route 21, is off the beaten path unless you're taking the ferry to somewhere else. But the Colville Confederated Tribes' boat ramp and moorage facility is nearby, and there's a playground here for kids. The lake is increasingly popular among walleye anglers. A lifeguard is on duty at the swimming area from July through Labor Day weekend.

Getting there: From U.S. Highway 2 near the town of Wilbur, turn north on SR 21 and drive 14 miles to the campground, near Keller Ferry crossing.

20 Fort Spokane ✦ ✦ ✦ ◀

SITES	RESERVATIONS	CONTACT
🏕️ 🚐	(877) 444-6777 or www.recreation.gov	Lake Roosevelt National Recreation Area (509) 633-9441
	OPEN	
67 sites, no hookups, RVs to 25 feet	Mid-April to mid-October, weather permitting	

Lake Roosevelt National Recreation Area's second-largest campground (the largest is Spring Canyon, above) also has a fascinating history. There actually was—and is—a fort here, built in the late 1800s and occupied by the U.S. Army for about twenty years. The fort, strategically located near the confluence of the Spokane and Columbia rivers, today is home to interesting historical exhibits describing the late nineteenth-century Indian wars. Fort Spokane has a noted swimming area (lifeguard included during summer months), a boat launch, and other goodies. The large park, with spaces in dry, sagebrushy loops, has no hookups, but it's popular through the summer, thanks to its swimming area, boat launch, and central location on 130-mile-long Lake Roosevelt. Rangers often host campfire programs in the evening. Two group sites here host up to thirty campers each; reserve at (877) 444-6777 or www.recreation.gov.

Getting there: From U.S. Highway 2 at the town of Davenport, turn north on State Route 25 and proceed about 22 miles to the campground.

21 Hawk Creek ✦ ✦ ✦

SITES	RESERVATIONS	CONTACT
🏕️ 🚐	None	Lake Roosevelt National Recreation Area (509) 633-9441
	OPEN	
21 sites, no hookups, RVs to 16 feet	Year-round; limited winter facilities	

This small, somewhat out-of-the-way Lake Roosevelt campground is a good alternate site if Spring Canyon and Fort Spokane, the two largest public campgrounds in this region, are booked. It has no hookups. A boat launch is nearby, and it is popular with anglers who troll around the mouth of Hawk Creek.

Getting there: From U.S. Highway 2 at the town of Davenport, turn north on State Route 25 and proceed about 23 miles to Miles–Creston Road. Turn left and proceed about 10 miles to the campground.

Other Columbia Basin/Grand Coulee Campgrounds

In the Vantage area, most tent campers avoid RV-geared Ginkgo Petrified Forest/ Wanapum State Parks, scooting instead over to the nearby **Vantage Riverstone Resort** (formerly Vantage KOA), which offers more than 100 campsites (fifty with full hookups) and the usual private-campground amenities. It's north of Vantage off Interstate 90

Exit 136; (509) 856-2800 or www.vantagewa.com. Gorge Amphitheater visitors also might consider another private campground, **Shady Tree RV Park** in Quincy, which offers seventy-one campsites (forty-one with full hookups). At the State Route 281/ State Route 283 junction, 2 miles east of George; (509) 785-3101.

In the Potholes area, a notable private development, **Mar Don Resort**, offers 300 sites with full hookups, a store, a motel, and extensive boating and fishing services. It's on O'Sullivan Dam Road (State Route 262) at the west end of O'Sullivan Dam; (509) 346-2651 or (800) 416-2736; mardonresort.com.

To the north, in the thriving hub of Ephrata, **Oasis Park Resort** on State Route 28 is a quiet spot, complete with shaded picnic facilities, a swimming area, fishing ponds, and more than 100 campsites, sixty-eight with utilities. It's a good possible stopover spot for travelers bound to or from Grand Coulee; (509) 754-5102 or for reservations, (877) 754-5102. In Soap Lake, **Smokiam Campground** (fifty-two sites, forty-five with utilities) is a city facility that makes a decent RV stopover. On East Beach in Soap Lake; (509) 246-1211.

Steamboat Rock State Park operates a stash of primitive campsites on Banks Lake, at **Jones Bay** (forty-four sites, no water), and **Osborn Bay** (thirty-six sites, no water). In addition, twelve boat-in campsites are located near the main park itself, and five equestrian sites are available by reservation only at **Northrup Canyon**; (509) 633-1304.

In the upper Grand Coulee, nearly three dozen small waterfront campgrounds, managed either by the National Park Service (because they lie within the Lake Roosevelt National Recreation Area) or the Colville Confederated or Spokane tribes, ring Lake Roosevelt, the 130-mile-long reservoir behind Grand Coulee Dam. Four of these—Spring Canyon, Keller Ferry, Hawk Creek, and Fort Spokane—are profiled above. Contact the **Lake Roosevelt NRA** office in Coulee Dam, (509) 633-9441, for current information on others. All these campgrounds provide water access, most are open year-round, and some have boat launches. Some of the campgrounds are so far up the lake that they land in a separate chapter of this guide (see Kettle Falls, Colville, and the Pend Oreille section, in the Northeast Washington chapter).

Yakima Valley

22 Yakima Sportsman State Park ✦ ✦ ✦

SITES	RESERVATIONS	CONTACT
▲ 🚐	(888) 226-7688 or www.parks.wa.gov	Washington State Parks (360) 902-8844
	OPEN	Yakima Sportsman State Park (509) 575-2774
67 sites, 37 full hookups, RVs to 60 feet	Year-round	

This just might be the best public campground in or around Yakima. Never mind that it's the only public campground in or around Yakima. It's not that bad a place to be, all things considered. And besides, you can't be too choosy in these parts, one of the least campsite-infested regions in all of Washington State (and yes, we're including the Palouse!). The park, which has good access to the Yakima River and its increasingly impressive (and popular) Yakima River Greenway Trail, has convenient pull-through RV sites, a playground, a horseshoe pit, kids' fishing ponds, and extensive (shady) picnic facilities. Two sites are barrier free. Some of the campsites are very near the Yakima, a pretty river with good fishing, even in this semi-urban setting. More than 140 species of birds have been recorded at this park, which gets heavy use during events at the Yakima fairgrounds or Sun Dome. A short, barrier-free trail begins in the campground.

Historical note: The park owes its existence to members of the Yakima Sportsman's Association who, noting the lack of public parks in Yakima, purchased the land and began development here in the 1940s. The park was later turned over to Yakima County and, subsequently, Washington State Parks, in 1949.

Getting there: From Interstate 82 near Yakima, take Exit 34 and follow signs about 2 miles mile east to the park, on Keys Road.

Other Yakima Valley Campgrounds

Private campgrounds in the area include Yakima's **Circle H RV Ranch**, (509) 457-3683; **Trailer Inns RV Park**, (509) 452-9561; and **Yakama Nation RV Resort**, (800) 874-3087.

Far west of Yakima, in the Ahtanum Creek drainage, the Department of Natural Resources maintains four small, primitive campgrounds. Unless you're riding a dirt bike or really enjoy the exhaust from other people's, don't bother.

Opposite: *Stone "hoodoos" jut from hillsides in the Okanogan Highlands.*

7. NORTHEAST WASHINGTON

Let's dispense with the really important stuff right off the bat. If you ever want to be considered a serious or even capable Washington camper, do not—repeat, do not—walk into a meeting of The Mountaineers and tell the assembled masses you're taking the Pathfinder and tent over to "Penned Oriole" for the weekend.

It's understandable. It's probably even happened. But just so you know, the river running through Northeast Washington—that goofy thing spelled Pend Oreille—is pronounced "POND o-ray." The sooner you get that off your tongue without hurting yourself, the sooner people will stop asking to see your real driver's license—the California one—and the sooner you'll be out there in Washington's wildest corner, living happily with the ornery moose and largely indifferent bighorn rams.

This is the very problem with far-out places marked by far-out names, like Northeast Washington. Nobody ever goes there, and if they do, they can't even explain where they've been once they get back. Anonymity is preserved. The cycle continues.

All of this, of course, works to your advantage. The fact is that, for whatever reason, Northeast Washington, from year to year, stays right up there on Mr. Black's Top Ten Most Remote list. This means, among other things, that you can go there without a reservation—yes, even on a Friday—and still snare a campsite at many of the region's fine campgrounds. (The catch: You have to leave home by Wednesday.)

Once the shock from all that solitude wears off, take a look around. The northeast corner of Washington, aka "that big area up around Metaline Falls," hides in its second-growth pine trees a wide array of camping splendors. You can sip drinks festooned with umbrellas from a chaise lounge along sun-baked Franklin D. Roosevelt Lake, the giganto, 130-mile-long waterway created by that little dam downstream at Grand Coulee. You can hike up a rocky peak east of Sullivan Lake and come face to face with your creator—assuming your creator is a Rocky Mountain bighorn sheep. Or you can drive far, far up badly maintained Forest Service roads into the heart of the Salmo–Priest Wilderness and shake hooves with a woodland caribou, a bona fide endangered species. Don't be surprised if you hear, but never see, some wolves along your way.

All around and in between, you can camp in relative solitude at a wide range of campgrounds, most operated by the federal government. It's a fine example of your tax dollars at work. Uncle Sam's long reach, which extends to the Columbia River (through the Lake Roosevelt National Recreation Area) and into the mountainous Okanogan Highlands, the Kettle Range, and the Selkirks (courtesy of the Okanogan and Colville national forests), has strewn outhouses, fire pits, and picnic tables across this land. It's your land. My land. Our land. Go forth, multiply, and camp upon it.

Okanogan Valley and Highlands

1 American Legion Park
2 Conconully State Park
3 Sugarloaf
4 Cottonwood
5 Oriole
6 Kerr
7 Salmon Meadows
8 Crawfish Lake
9 Osoyoos Lake State Park
10 Bonaparte Lake
11 Beaver Lake
12 Beth Lake
13 Lost Lake
14 Ten Mile
15 Ferry Lake
16 Swan Lake
17 Long Lake
18 Curlew Lake State Park
19 Sherman Pass Overlook
20 Canyon Creek

Lake Roosevelt

21 Kettle Falls
22 Kamloops Island
23 Marcus Island
24 Evans
25 North Gorge
26 Gifford

Kettle Falls, Colville, and the Pend Oreille

27 Pierre Lake
28 Little Twin Lakes
29 Lake Gillette/East Gillette
30 Lake Thomas
31 Big Meadow Lake
32 Edgewater
33 East and West Sullivan Lake
34 Noisy Creek

Spokane

35 Riverside State Park
36 Mount Spokane State Park
37 Pend Oreille County Park

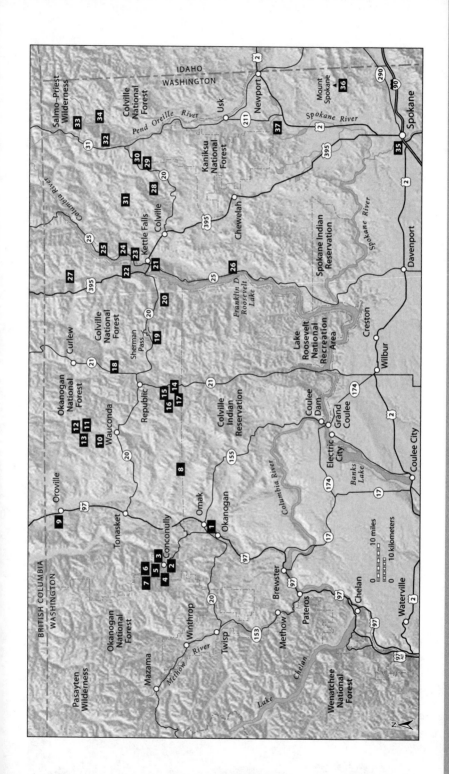

Okanogan Valley and Highlands

1 American Legion Park ✦ ✦

SITES	RESERVATIONS	CONTACT
🚐	None	City of Okanogan (509) 422-3600
	OPEN	
35 sites, no hookups, RVs to any length	May to October	

A small municipal park in Okanogan, American Legion is primarily an RV stopover along the Okanogan River. Sites are clustered in a gravel area with little shade or greenery. But it's close to the highway if you're just looking for a place to pull over for the night. The Okanogan Historical Museum is nearby.

Getting there: The park is on State Route 215 in Okanogan.

2 Conconully State Park ✦ ✦ ✦ ✦

SITES	RESERVATIONS	CONTACT
⛺ 🚐	None	Washington State Parks (360) 902-8844
	OPEN	Conconully State Park (509) 826-7408
82 sites, no hookups, RVs to 60 feet	April through October	

Many private resorts and cabins ring Lake Conconully, an impoundment managed by the Federal Bureau of Reclamation. But public camping is found here, too, both

Lake Conconully, a reservoir, is a popular trout-fishing spot. (Photo by Washington State Parks)

on the lakeshore and the surrounding hillsides. Leading the way is Conconully State Park, an eighty-acre site with 5400 feet of shoreline on the reservoir. The park, a very popular fishing spot, has broad lawns shaded by massive willow trees, making it a favorite summer lounging spot. Don't get too used to the location of the beach, however: Waterfront areas for swimming and boating are affected by broad fluctuations in lake levels as the water is drawn down. The camping area is divided between a main campground and a second, more primitive section closer to the lake. The campground has coin-op showers, a swimming beach, and a boat launch. Also within the property is a half-mile nature trail.

Historical note: The name *Conconully* comes from *Conconulp*, an early English name for the area. That name was taken from the Native *konekol'p*, which meant "money hole"—a reference to the region's former status as a large producer of beaver pelts, which were traded to whites at an old trading post here.

Getting there: From U.S. Highway 97 at Omak, follow signs 22 miles northwest to the campground, on Conconully Road.

3 Sugarloaf ★ ★

SITES	RESERVATIONS	CONTACT
🏕️	None	Okanogan National Forest Tonasket Ranger District (509) 486-2186
	OPEN	
4 sites	Mid-May to mid-September	

You'll need to bring a big ol' stack of paper plates to make a sign trail long enough to enable your friends to find you at Sugarloaf, a tiny, lakefront campground north of Conconully. The National Forest camp, elevation 2400 feet, is primitive with pit toilets and not much else. Strictly for the roughin' it campers among us, although you'll find plenty of privacy here in late summer, when the small lake shrinks away from the shore. If you're looking for more creature comforts, try Conconully State Park (above) or the other local Forest Service camps to the northwest, along Salmon Creek (below).

Getting there: From the town of Conconully, follow Sinlahekin Road (County 4015) northeast about 5 miles to the campground.

4 Cottonwood ★ ★ ★

SITES	RESERVATIONS	CONTACT
🏕️🚐	None	Okanogan National Forest Tonasket Ranger District (509) 486-2186
	OPEN	
4 sites, no hookups, RVs to 16 feet	Mid-May to mid-October	

If booming downtown Conconully comes across as just too much civilization for you, help is at hand along the sparkling water of Salmon Creek, northwest of town.

A canoe awaits paddlers in the Okanogan Highlands.

Cottonwood, the first campground encountered along Forest Road 38, is small but somewhat pretty, with four streamside sites set in a mixed forest. The campground has piped water and pit toilets, but no other amenities. It's open year-round, with no garbage service or water in the winter. The elevation is 2700 feet.

   Getting there: From Conconully, drive 2 miles northwest on FR 38 to the campground.

5 Oriole ★ ★ ✦

SITES	RESERVATIONS	CONTACT
🏕️ 🚐	None	Okanogan National Forest Tonasket Ranger District (509) 486-2186
	OPEN	
10 sites, no hookups, RVs to 16 feet	Mid-May to mid-October	

If you visit during the dog days of summer, you just might find a wily old local stomping around in Salmon Creek near Oriole Campground, looking to land a rainbow on a dry fly. Whip out your gear and join him somewhere along the stream, then settle into your tent or small RV in this remote, quiet campground, set amidst some lovely larch and fir trees. You'll find the Forest Service basics here: pit toilets, but few other amenities. But there's plenty of solace to go around. The elevation is 2900 feet. Note: The water system here was damaged when this guide went to press. Call for current information.

Getting there: From Conconully, drive 3 miles northwest on Forest Roads 38 and 38025 to the campground.

6 Kerr ★ ★ ★

SITES	RESERVATIONS	CONTACT
🏕️ 🚐	None	Okanogan National Forest Tonasket Ranger District (509) 486-2186
	OPEN	
13 sites, no hookups, RVs to 16 feet	Mid-May to mid-October	

Kerr, the third of four campgrounds along Salmon Creek northwest of Conconully, is a quiet spot along the creek, a bit more primitive than other campgrounds on this road. It has pit toilets but no piped water or other services. The campground has good fishing access to the creek—the main reason many people visit here, although the fishing is usually marginal. The elevation is 3100 feet.

Getting there: From Conconully, follow Forest Road 38 4 miles northwest to the campground.

7 Salmon Meadows ★ ★ ★

SITES	RESERVATIONS	CONTACT
🏕️	None	Okanogan National Forest Tonasket Ranger District (509) 486-2186
	OPEN	
7 sites	Mid-May to mid-October	

Ever have a hankering to pack up your entire work group and head way, way, way, way into the hills—away from even the most determined gearhead's cell-phone range—

The Okanogan region is studded with alpine lakes, such as Tiffany. (Photo by Seabury Blair Jr.)

to talk about birds, fish, the unmitigated gall of the U.S. Forest Service to charge day-use hiking fees, and just life in general? Here's a good candidate for extreme solitude. Salmon Meadows, 9 miles beyond Conconully and 200 years beyond civilization, is high on Salmon Creek. The scenic campground has a group site with a community kitchen, around which all the campground citizens can gather to introduce legislation or just play cards. The campground has piped water and pit toilets and remains open in the winter with no water or garbage service. Note: Give your CEO the space next to the john. (Let's just say that on our last visit, at least, it was not one of those newfangled, vented odorless jobs.) The elevation here is 4500 feet—bring a sweater in the off-season. You'll need to pack out your own garbage, but you can't beat the price: At this writing, sites were $5 here and at nearby Cottonwood, Oriole, and Kerr campgrounds.

Getting there: From Conconully, follow Forest Road 38 about 7 miles northwest to the campground.

8 Crawfish Lake ✦ ✦ ✦

SITES	RESERVATIONS	CONTACT
🏕️ 🚐	None	Okanogan National Forest Tonasket Ranger District (509) 486-2186
	OPEN	
19 sites, no hookups, RVs to 31 feet	Mid-May to mid-October	

The Forest Service lists crawfish hunting as one activity at this scenic, lakefront campground, halfway to nowhere in the hills beyond the town of Riverside. We can't vouch for that, but we can vouch for summer days of fun in the canoe, kayak, or motorboat. That's what most campers make their way all the way out here to do, and it can get a bit noisy at times when the water-skiers and Jet Ski jockeys are doing their thing. Fishing can be productive in season. The campground is primitive, with no piped water or garbage service. You'll find pit toilets, a lot of trees, and not much else here. The elevation is 4500 feet.

Local trivia: the far side of the lake actually is inside the northern border of the massive, seldom-trod Colville Indian Reservation. The best news: this campground, at this writing, is free.

Getting there: From U.S. Highway 97 at the town of Riverside (north of Omak and south of Tonasket), drive about 18 miles east on County Road 9320. After the road becomes Forest Road 30, continue 2 miles east to Forest Road 30100, turn right, and proceed a half mile to the campground.

9 Osoyoos Lake State Park ✦ ✦

SITES	RESERVATIONS	CONTACT
🏕 🚐	(888) 226-7688 or www.parks.wa.gov	Washington State Parks (360) 902-8844
	OPEN	Osoyoos Lake State Park
86 sites, no hookups, RVs to 45 feet	Year-round; primitive winter camping	(509) 476-3321

We have strong childhood memories of a particularly bad summer stopover here, during which: (1) It was so hot, the sun baked the ground in the campground to an asphalt-like surface, so replete with surface cracks and dust that we expected to see rhinos and giraffes galumphing through at any moment; (2) It was so crowded, we had to prey on departing families to snare a spot; and (3) The lifeguard yelled at us. Chances are, budget cuts have all but taken care of that lifeguard. But we can't vouch for remedies for the other two problems. Osoyoos, the long-ago site of the Okanogan County Fair, is an unimpressive state park that gets plenty of use by virtue of its location—on a major highway, close to the Canadian border. Swimming, fishing (trout,

The American dipper, or water ouzel, is a frequent visitor to Northwest wild places.

kokanee, smallmouth bass, perch), water-skiing, and dumping ice on one's head to avoid wandering around in a heatstroke stupor are the primary summer activities. The campground, on a 14-mile lake that stretches into British Columbia, has coin-op showers and an RV dump station. In the winter, RVs can park in the day-use parking lot. About the name: It comes from the Native word *sooyos,* which means "narrows." Note: See important notice about this park's future on p. 25.

Getting there: The park is about 1 mile north of Oroville and 4 miles south of the Canadian border on U.S. Highway 97.

10 Bonaparte Lake ★ ★ ★ ◂

SITES	RESERVATIONS		CONTACT
⛺ 🚐	None		Okanogan National Forest Tonasket Ranger District (509) 486-2186
	OPEN		
28 sites, no hookups, RVs to 31 feet	Mid-May to mid-October		

Bonaparte Lake is the first, and most popular, of a handful of small Forest Service camps in the Five Lakes area, north of State Route 20 and east of Tonasket. It's a remote, quite pretty campground, set in the kind of picturesque, dry forest the Okanogan National Forest is known for. It's a good place for groups: ten of the camping spaces are double sites, which can accommodate two cars or RVs. The campground also has a group site for up to thirty people, and three of the sites are walk-in sites for hikers and bikers. The campground, equipped with pit toilets and piped water, is popular with hunters in the fall. For much of the year, however, the primary draw is fishing. Brook and rainbow trout can be plentiful, and Bonaparte also holds some massive Mackinaw (lake) trout.

Fallen trees reach into the waters of a lake in the Okanogan Highlands. (Photo by Seabury Blair Jr.)

A handful weighing over twenty pounds have been caught here. Boat rentals are available at nearby Bonaparte Lake Resort. The area also offers some nice hiking trails, including the South Side Bonaparte Trail, an 11-mile round-trip hike to a stunning view atop 7258-foot Bonaparte Peak, site of a pair of fire lookouts. A trail to the lookout begins in the campground, but you can shave several miles—and a lot of vertical— off the climb by driving to the upper trailhead at Lost Lake Campground (below). The elevation at Bonaparte Lake is 3600 feet.

Getting there: From SR 20, about 20 miles east of Tonasket, turn north on County Road 4953 (Bonaparte Lake Road), which becomes Forest Road 32, and proceed about 6 miles to the campground, on the left.

11   Beaver Lake ★ ★ ★

SITES	RESERVATIONS		CONTACT
	None		Okanogan National Forest
	OPEN		Tonasket Ranger District (509) 486-2186
11 sites, no hookups, RVs to 31 feet	Mid-May to mid-October		

It's small, quiet, and out of the way—and that makes it a perfect destination for what many campers come here for: solitude in the cracklin' dry forests of the Okanogan Highlands. Beaver Lake is a great place for hikers, thanks largely to the Beth Lake Trail, an easy, 3.8-mile loop that begins in the campground and follows a nearly flat course along both Beaver Lake and nearby Beth Lake (where there's another campground; see below). Other great local hikes include the 2-mile round-trip Pipsissewa Trail, and the Big Tree Botanical Loop, which begins on Forest Road 33 and weaves through an old-growth forest of larch and pine trees. The campground, which has pit toilets and no piped water, is OK, but not remarkable. Two of the spaces are double sites that can accommodate two vehicles. The lake is stocked with trout in the spring. The elevation is 2700 feet.

Getting there: From State Route 20, about 20 miles east of Tonasket, turn north on County Road 4953 (Bonaparte Lake Road), which becomes Forest Road 32. Proceed about 12 miles north to the campground.

12   Beth Lake ★ ★ ★

SITES	RESERVATIONS		CONTACT
	None		Okanogan National Forest
	OPEN		Tonasket Ranger District (509) 486-2186
15 sites, no hookups, RVs to 31 feet	Mid-May to mid-October		

Another in the cluster of campgrounds in this Five Lakes region of the Okanogan National Forest, Beth Lake is a peaceful Forest Service camp on the north shore of a tiny alpine lake in the North Fork Beaver Creek drainage. It's a familiar Forest Service facility, with pit toilets, piped water, and a boat launch. One of the sites is a multiple site for two families. Fishing in this and other nearby lakes can be productive. (See Beaver Lake and Bonaparte Lake campgrounds, above, for local hiking options.)

Getting there: From State Route 20, about 20 miles east of Tonasket, turn north on County Road 4953 (Bonaparte Lake Road), which becomes Forest Road 32. Continue about 12 miles north to Beaver Creek, and turn left (northwest) on County Road 9480. Proceed about a mile to the campground.

13 Lost Lake ★ ★ ★ ◀

SITES	RESERVATIONS	CONTACT
🏕️ 🚐	Group camp only, (877) 444-6777 or www.recreation.gov	Okanogan National Forest Tonasket Ranger District (509) 486-2186
	OPEN	
19 sites, no hookups, RVs to 31 feet	Mid-May to mid-October	

Another campground high in the Okanogan's Five Lakes area, Lost Lake is a peaceful spot with good access to local hiking trails, most notably the South Side Bonaparte Trail, which climbs from Forest Road 100 north of here to spectacular views and fire lookouts atop 7258-foot Bonaparte Peak. Fishing also is productive in this lake and the other four in the area. The campground has pit toilets, piped water, and a popular group-camp area that must be reserved in advance at the number above. No gas motors are allowed on the lake.

Getting there: From State Route 20, about 20 miles east of Tonasket, turn north on County Road 4953 (Bonaparte Lake Road). Continue north beyond Bonaparte and follow signs about 6 miles to the campground, on Forest Road 33-050.

14 Ten Mile ★ ★ ★

SITES	RESERVATIONS	CONTACT
🏕️ 🚐	None	Colville National Forest Republic Ranger District (509) 775-7400
	OPEN	
9 sites, no hookups, RVs to 21 feet	Mid-May to mid-October	

Ten Mile is one of four uncrowded, high-country campgrounds in the Sanpoil River drainage, which drains a giant slice of Northeast Washington, and the Colville Indian Reservation, into the Columbia River. The campground, on the west side of the 1.1-million-acre Colville National Forest, is easy to reach from Republic, making it a good overnight stopover for State Route 20 travelers. It's also a good base for exploring the chain of local lakes in this area, each of which has its own Forest Service camp (see Ferry Lake, Swan Lake, and Long Lake, below). The campground has pit toilets but no piped

A mallard drops the gear on landing approach.

water. Sites, set in trees with ample underbrush, are fairly private—good for tenters.

Getting there: From State Route 20 about 2 miles east of the town of Republic, turn south on State Route 21 and drive 10 miles to the campground.

15 Ferry Lake ✦✦✦

SITES	RESERVATIONS	CONTACT
▲ 🚐	None	Colville National Forest Republic Ranger District (509) 775-7400
	OPEN	
9 sites, no hookups, RVs to 20 feet	Mid-May to mid-September	

Intrepid campers who make it this far into the heart of the sprawling lodgepole pine and clear-streamed lands south of Sherman Pass won't be displeased with Ferry Lake, a scenic—if rough-around-the-edges—Forest Service campground in the Sanpoil River drainage. The small lake is a popular fishing spot, with a boat launch near the campground (gas motors are prohibited). The campground has some rather pretty lakefront sites, which is a good thing, because there's no piped water here. The campground has pit toilets and no other amenities. In general, this entire area is decent mountain-biking terrain. Three other local Forest Service camps in the area make nice day trips. Get up early and watch for loons on the lake!

Getting there: From State Route 20 about 2 miles east of the town of Republic, turn south on State Route 21 and proceed about 7 miles to Forest Road 53 (Scatter Creek Road). Turn right (southwest) and drive 6 miles to Forest Road 5330. Turn right (north) and continue just over a mile to Forest Road 100. Turn right and proceed about a mile to the campground.

BEST LAKEFRONT CAMPS

---

1. Lake Chelan State Park, Central Washington
The main camping area on the longest, deepest lake in the state isn't quiet, but if you're a boater or angler, it's tough to beat. See p. 252.

2. Steamboat Rock State Park, Banks Lake
One of the bigger, more diverse, and more interesting state parks on the dry side, Steamboat Rock puts you in touch with the many recreation offerings of the Banks Lake Reservoir. See p. 261.

3. Lake Wenatchee State Park, Central Cascades
Most campsites are not on the shore itself, but Lake Wenatchee still makes our list just because the lake is so big, so alpine-like, and so stunning, and you can stroll to it from your lazy chair next to the campfire. See p. 155.

4. Willaby, Lake Quinault
An Olympic National Forest campground on the shores of Lake Quinault, Willaby is set in a beautiful forest, with good access to nearby rain forest hiking trails. See p. 95.

5. Glacier View, Lake Wenatchee
A quiet camp for tenters only, most of Glacier View's shady sites are right on the waters of Lake Wenatchee. See p. 157.

16 Swan Lake ★ ★ ★

SITES	RESERVATIONS	CONTACT
🏕 🚐	None	Colville National Forest Republic Ranger District (509) 775-7400
	OPEN	
25 sites, no hookups, RVs to 31 feet	May through September	

Please, no ballet jokes. Swan Lake is the largest and most developed of four Colville National Forest camps in the Sanpoil River drainage south of Republic. It's also the only one in the area able to comfortably accommodate RVs longer than 21 feet. It's a pretty spot, with lakefront sites popular with anglers on the lake. A ban on gas motors keeps things peaceful here, and fishing can be good at times. A boat launch and mooring docks are nearby. The campground has pit toilets and, unlike others in the area, piped water. The elevation is 3700 feet. If the campground is full, note the presence of Ferry Lake, Long Lake, and Ten Mile, three similar, if smaller, Forest Service camps in the same area.

Getting there: From State Route 20 about 2 miles east of the town of Republic, turn south on State Route 21 and proceed about 7 miles to Forest Road 53 (Scatter Creek Road). Turn right (southwest) and drive 8 miles to the campground.

17 Long Lake ★ ★ ★ ✦

SITES	RESERVATIONS	CONTACT
🏕️ 🚐	None	Colville National Forest Republic Ranger District (509) 775-7400
	OPEN	
12 sites, no hookups, RVs to 21 feet	May through September	

Long Lake is one of the nicest of a cluster of four Forest Service camps in the Sanpoil River drainage south of Republic. It's a bit out there, but the camp has some great sites on tiny, scenic Long Lake, a noted cutthroat fishing spot. The campground has pit toilets and hand-pumped water. A 1.25-mile trail around the lake is level and easy enough for the whole family, and a ban on gas motors at this fly-fishing-only lake keeps the shorelines quiet, even at the peak of fishing season. Sites are generally clean, level, fairly private, and like most in this region, covered with nice, soft, pine-needle flooring.

Getting there: From State Route 20 about 2 miles east of the town of Republic, turn south on State Route 21 and proceed about 7 miles to Forest Road 53 (Scatter Creek Road). Turn right (southwest) and drive 8 miles to Forest Road 400. Turn south and proceed about 1.5 miles to the campground.

18 Curlew Lake State Park ★ ★ ★ ★

SITES	RESERVATIONS	CONTACT
🏕️ 🚐	None	Washington State Parks (360) 902-8844
	OPEN	Curlew Lake State Park (509) 775-3592
84 sites, 18 full hookups, 7 water/ electrical hookups, RVs to 40 feet	April through October	

There's gold in these hills. And some of it spreads to the shores of Curlew Lake, where one of Washington's more obscure—and more pleasant—state parks awaits on the east shore. The lake, long ago a center of local gold-panning activity, is a recreation center these days. And the 123-acre park, a favorite fishing, swimming, and water-skiing spot in the dry, lodgepole pine forests north of the groovy mountain town of Republic, is a nice one, with campsites spread through a hilly area with green grass and shade trees along the lakeshore. This is one of the region's most notable rainbow trout fisheries, and the lake can be crowded with boats (both from the state park and from two private resorts on the lake) during peak fishing-season weeks in early summer. (The lake receives annual plants of trout, supplemented by fish raised here in net pens.) The park has coin-op showers, a swimming beach, a boat launch and mooring facilities, an RV dump station, and ten picnic sites. Good mountain-bike trails are found in the area. The main camping area, to the right as you enter the campground, has particularly pleasant sites with grassy lawns and some shade trees. Some of the prime

The day-use area at Curlew Lake State Park is a rare patch of green in the area.

spots are walk-in tent spaces near the lake. The campground is located near what archaeologists believe was a Native American village; artifacts and some skeletons have been unearthed here. The campground is open summers only, but cross-country skiing and ice fishing are popular winter day-use activities. And watch for the park's active osprey nest.

Note: If Curlew Lake seems a long way out there, get chummy with your favorite pilot. This 123-acre park has five primitive "fly-in" sites with tie-downs for planes landing at adjacent Merritt Field.

Getting there: From State Route 20, about 2.5 miles east of the town of Republic, turn north on State Route 21 and proceed 7 miles to the campground.

19 Sherman Pass Overlook ✦ ✦

SITES	RESERVATIONS	CONTACT
9 sites, no hookups, RVs to 21 feet	None	Colville National Forest Three Rivers Ranger District Kettle Falls office (509) 738-7700
	OPEN	
	Mid-May to mid-October, weather permitting	

They don't just hand out those National Scenic Byway plaques to every little road that applies. That's obvious after a trip across State Route 20, aka Sherman Pass National Scenic Byway. The road, which parallels the Canadian border between north-central and northeastern Washington, climbs to 5575 feet—higher than any other mountain pass in Washington—to take visitors on a journey into some of the state's wildest natural areas, as well as some of its oldest and most colorful history. Modern outdoor explorers will find a tiny-but-convenient roadside campground right near the summit of Sherman Pass (road noise is evident, although we're hardly talking about I-90 traffic levels here). Sherman Pass Overlook offers nine tidy sites and pit toilets but no reliable water. Thus, it has no showers, even of the homemade kind—a bummer, given the wealth of great hiking opportunities in this area. A good example is the Kettle Crest Trail, which follows the top of the Kettle Range (a sub-group of the Rockies) 29 miles north and 29 miles south of the highway. Campsites are in a wooded, somewhat dark area just off the highway. The campground elevation is 5300 feet—bring a sweater. You'll need to pack out your own garbage.

Getting there: The campground is on SR 20 near Sherman Pass, about 20 miles west of Kettle Falls.

20 Canyon Creek ✦ ✦ ✦

SITES	RESERVATIONS	CONTACT
12 sites, no hookups, RVs to 30 feet	None	Colville National Forest Three Rivers Ranger District Kettle Falls office (509) 738-7700
	OPEN	
	Late May to early September	

Canyon Creek is a small but pretty campground just off the Sherman Pass Scenic Byway. It's a popular fishing spot, thanks largely to the Canyon Creek Trail, an easy, 2-mile-round-trip path along the clear, rushing waters of Canyon Creek. Some campsites here are barrier free, as is the trail, which provides great angling access and makes a great short walk for camping families. The campground has pit toilets but no piped water. The elevation is 2200 feet.

Getting there: The campground is on Forest Road 136, just south of State Route 20, about 9 miles west of Kettle Falls.

A large wildfire scar casts a ghostly image near Sherman Pass.

Other Okanogan Valley/Highlands Campgrounds

In the southern Okanogan Valley, **Rock Creek** (six sites, on Loup Loup Canyon Road), **Rock Lakes** (eight sites, no piped water, on Rock Lakes Road north of Rock Creek), **Leader Lake** (sixteen sites, no piped water, on Leader Lake Road), and **Sportsman's Camp** (six sites, no piped water, on Sweat Creek Road) all are small, primitive DNR camps north of State Route 20, east of Loup Loup Summit. Contact the DNR office in Colville, (509) 684-7474.

In the northern Okanogan River drainage, **Toats Coulee** (nine sites, no piped water, on Toats Coulee Road), **Cold Springs** (five sites, no piped water, on Cold Creek Road), **North Fork Nine Mile** (eleven sites, near Toats Coulee), **Chopaka Lake** (sixteen sites, off Toats Coulee Road), and **Palmer Lake** (six sites, no piped water, 8.5 miles north of Loomis) all are small, primitive DNR camps in the Chopaka Mountain/Toats Coulee Creek/Palmer Lake area northwest of Tonasket. Contact the DNR's Northeast Region office in Colville, (509) 684-7474. **Tiffany Springs** is a high (6800-foot), remote Forest Service camp northeast of Winthrop (four sites, no piped water, 1 mile from Tiffany Lake off Forest Road 39). Far to the east, an equally remote camp high in the Sanpoil River drainage is **Lyman Lake** (four sites, no piped water, on Forest Road 3785 southeast of Tonasket). Contact the Okanogan National Forest's Tonasket Ranger District, (509) 486-2186.

On the east side of Sherman Pass, two small, primitive Colville National Forest sites are **Trout Lake** (four sites, on Trout Lake Road, north of SR 20), and **Lake Ellen** (fifteen sites, on County Road 412, south of SR 20). Call the Three Rivers Ranger District, Kettle Falls office; (509) 738-7700.

Lake Roosevelt

21 Kettle Falls ★ ★ ★ ✦

SITES	RESERVATIONS	CONTACT
 76 sites, no hookups, RVs to 26 feet	(877) 444-6777 or www.recreation.gov	Lake Roosevelt National Recreation Area (509) 633-9441
	OPEN	
	Mid-April to mid-October	

It's a long, long way from Kettle Falls to Grand Coulee. But you can paddle there from here, thanks to Grand Coulee Dam, which created the massive, 130-mile-long Franklin D. Roosevelt Lake. The damming of the Grand Coulee turned this lowland portion of northeastern Washington into a summer aquatic playground, and a series of campgrounds administered by the National Park Service rings the long, shimmering waterway. One of the most popular of the bunch is Kettle Falls, a large, well-developed camp 2 miles west of the town of Kettle Falls. Campsites are shaded and spread through three loops. Summer watersports—water-skiing, fishing, swimming, and boating—draw faithful legions to this camp's lakefront sites every summer. Kids, especially, love feeding the flocks of ducks and geese down at the marina (food is sold at the local store). Get there early if you're planning to spend a weekend. The campground has a boat launch and moorage. Note: The water level varies substantially on Lake Roosevelt throughout the year. Most Lake Roosevelt waterfront campgrounds, therefore, are left high and dry in the fall and winter, when the lake is drawn down.

Getting there: The campground is 2 miles west of Kettle Falls on U.S. Highway 395.

A tent camp above the banks of Lake Roosevelt.

22 Kamloops Island ✦ ✦ ✦ ✦

SITES	RESERVATIONS	CONTACT
🏕️	(877) 444-6777 or www.recreation.gov	Lake Roosevelt National Recreation Area (509) 633-9441
	OPEN	
17 sites	Year-round	

Tenters, this one's for you. And only for you. Tent campers seeking respite from the RV- and boat-trailer-dominated world of camping on upper Lake Roosevelt will appreciate Kamloops, a smaller, peaceful waterfront site on Kamloops Island. The campground has pit toilets but no piped water or showers. Nearby boat docks make this a decent place to launch a canoe. Squint really hard and try to imagine what the Columbia looked like here when it was still a real river. Note that there's no drinking water available if the lake level is drawn below 1272 feet.

Getting there: Kamloops campground is 7 miles west of Kettle Falls on U.S. Highway 395.

23 Marcus Island ✦ ✦ ✦

SITES	RESERVATIONS	CONTACT
🏕️ 🚐	(877) 444-6777 or www.recreation.gov	Lake Roosevelt National Recreation Area (509) 633-9441
	OPEN	
27 sites, no hookups, RVs to 20 feet	Year-round	

Marcus Island is another popular waterfront site on the north end of Franklin D. Roosevelt Lake. It's more remote and less crowded than Kettle Falls (see above) but still offers shore access as well as boat launching and moorage. The campground has pit toilets and a boat dock. Drinking water is available if the lake level is not drawn below 1265 feet. Another Lake Roosevelt National Recreation Area camp, Evans (see below), is just north of here.

Getting there: Marcus Island is 4 miles north of Kettle Falls on State Route 25.

24 Evans ✦ ✦ ✦

SITES	RESERVATIONS	CONTACT
🏕️ 🚐	Group camp only; (877) 444-6777 or www.recreation.gov	Lake Roosevelt National Recreation Area (509) 633-9441
	OPEN	
43 sites, no hookups, RVs to 26 feet	Mid-April to mid-October	

Evans is the largest and most developed Lake Roosevelt National Recreation Area campground north of Kettle Falls. It's easy to see why: The camp offers great lake access for anglers, water-skiers, swimmers, and other water lovers. The campground has a boat launch and moorage, an RV dump station, and a swimming area. Some of the sites are barrier free. Evans also has a group camp for up to twenty-five people.

Getting there: Evans is 8 miles north of Kettle Falls on State Route 25.

25 North Gorge ★ ★ ◆

SITES	RESERVATIONS	CONTACT
⛺ 🚐	None	Lake Roosevelt National Recreation Area (509) 633-9441
	OPEN	
12 sites, no hookups, RVs to 26 feet	Year-round	

Another National Park Service site on the northeast shores of Franklin D. Roosevelt Lake, North Gorge is small and a bit remote, but a suitable overnight spot that usually becomes more popular when all the waterfront camps closer to Kettle Falls are full. The campground has pit toilets and a boat launch. Drinking water is available unless the lake is drawn down below 1265 feet. A group site for forty-three campers is available by reservation only.

Getting there: North Gorge is 20 miles north of Kettle Falls on State Route 25.

26 Gifford ★ ★ ★ ◆

SITES	RESERVATIONS	CONTACT
⛺ 🚐	None	Lake Roosevelt National Recreation Area (509) 633-9441
	OPEN	
42 sites, no hookups, RVs to 20 feet	Year-round	

Gifford, located about halfway up the eastern shore of Franklin D. Roosevelt Lake, the 130-mile-long impoundment behind Grand Coulee Dam, is one of the lake's largest waterfront campgrounds and the major campground in this seldom-visited part of the state between the Columbia River and Chewelah. The campground is just far enough from civilization to make it a nice getaway for boaters, water-skiers, anglers, and canoeists who want to set up camp for a while and stay on the banks of the Columbia. It offers pit toilets, an RV dump station, boat docks, and moorage. Drinking water is available unless the reservoir drops substantially.

Getting there: The campground is on State Route 25, 60 miles north of the junction with U.S. Highway 2.

Other Lake Roosevelt Campgrounds

Many smaller and/or more remote campsites, administered by the Lake Roosevelt National Recreation Area, ring the northern shores of Lake Roosevelt. These include westside camps such as **Kettle River** (thirteen sites), **Barnaby Island** (four sites), and **Cloverleaf** (nine sites), and eastside camps such as **Haag Cove** (sixteen sites), **Bradbury Beach** (four sites), and **Hunters** (thirty-nine sites). Contact the Lake Roosevelt National Recreation Area, (509) 633-9441.

Rocky cliffs surround the Pend Oreille River.

Kettle Falls, Colville, and the Pend Oreille

27 Pierre Lake ★ ★ ★

SITES	RESERVATIONS	CONTACT
	None	Colville National Forest
	OPEN	Three Rivers Ranger District Kettle Falls office
15 sites, no hookups, RVs to 24 feet	Mid-April to mid-October	(509) 738-7700

It's not quite in Canada. But you can almost see it from here. Pierre Lake, a small camp on a small (105-acre) lake in the northern Colville National Forest, is known primarily to anglers, who use the boat launch here to pursue trout. But it's a pretty spot, with the added attraction of a nice day hike: The Pierre Lake Trail (easy, 1.6 mile round-trip), leads through a nice forested area on the shore of the lake. The trail begins in the campground and follows the west shore. It's a good family walk, with the added advantage of bank-fishing access to the entire lake. The campground has pit toilets and nine picnic sites. There's no piped water or garbage service, but at this writing, it is a steal at six bucks a night. The elevation is 2100 feet.

Getting there: Pierre Lake is 20 miles north of Kettle Falls via U.S. Highway 395 and County Road 4013.

28 Little Twin Lakes ★ ★ ★

SITES	RESERVATIONS	CONTACT
	None	Colville National Forest
	OPEN	Three Rivers Ranger District Kettle Falls office
20 sites, no hookups, RVs to 30 feet	Mid-May through October	(509) 738-7700

Leave the big Winnebago at home. It wouldn't fit if you could get it here, and the thing is, you can't. Access roads to this remote camp on a tiny lake in the Colville National Forest are rough, especially up high. When it's in bad shape, in fact, it's probably not even a good idea for passenger cars. The campground, used largely by anglers, has pit toilets, a fishing dock (cutthroat fishing can be decent), and a boat launch but no piped water, showers, or anything else—except the occasional moose (seriously!) and osprey and bald eagles fishing in the lake. It's pretty rough around the edges, even for those who really, really want to get away from it all. But that's what you come up here for, right? Plus, at this writing, the campground is free, and the sites offer decent privacy for tenters. You'll need to pack out your own garbage.

Getting there: From Colville, follow State Route 20 about 12.5 miles east to County Road 4915. Turn north and proceed 1.5 miles to Forest Road 4939. Turn north and proceed just over 4 miles to the campground.

29 Lake Gillette/East Gillette ★ ★ ◀

SITES	RESERVATIONS	CONTACT
 44 sites, no hookups, RVs to 31 feet	None	Colville National Forest Three Rivers Ranger District Kettle Falls office (509) 738-7700
	OPEN	
	Mid-May to mid-September	

Here's a pretty spot: pretty noisy. Which is too bad, because Lake Gillette and East Gillette, two Colville National Forest camps right across the road from one another in the chain of seven Little Pend Oreille Lakes (see also Lakes Thomas and Leo, below), are in a beautiful setting. Unfortunately, they're also popular with off-road-vehicle riders, even one of whom can destroy solitude for hundreds of people for many square miles. Still, if you can get here at a time when they're all at a convention in Yakima or something, this is a nice spot. Lake Gillette campground has fourteen sites, East Gillette, thirty. Five of the sites are multiple-family sites with room for two or more vehicles. Both campgrounds have pit toilets and access to a boat launch and moorage. An interpretive trail runs through the area, and cutthroat trout-fishing in the lake is a major activity in season. You'll find a boat launch and dock on the premises. The elevation is 3200 feet.

Note: RVers seeking hookups and other modern amenities might prefer the private Beaver Lodge Resort, (509) 684-5657, just to the north on the shore of Lake Gillette. Tent campers seeking quieter climes likely will prefer Lake Thomas (below).

Getting there: From Colville, follow State Route 20 about 20 miles east, turn right on Lake Gillette Road, and follow signs about a half mile north to the campground.

30 Lake Thomas ★ ★ ★ ◀

SITES	RESERVATIONS	CONTACT
 16 sites, no hookups, RVs to 31 feet	None	Colville National Forest Three Rivers Ranger District Kettle Falls office (509) 738-7700
	OPEN	
	Mid-May to early October	

Here's the quieter alternative to Lake Gillette/East Gillette for campers seeking solitude in the chain of seven Little Pend Oreille Lakes, in the Colville National Forest. The tent and small RV campground, with walk-in sites on the shores of scenic Lake Thomas, is easy to reach from State Route 20. This is a nice place to bring the mountain bikes, the fishing rod, and the camera and stay for a while, exploring each of the lakes in the Little

A squirrel enjoys a camper's fireplace leavings.

Pend Oreille drainage. It's pretty country. The campground has pit toilets and piped water. The elevation is 3200 feet.

Getting there: From Colville, follow State Route 20 about 20 miles east, turn right on Lake Gillette Road, and follow signs about a mile north to the campground.

31 Big Meadow Lake ★ ★ ★ ✦

SITES	RESERVATIONS	CONTACT
🏕️ 🚻 🚐	None	Colville National Forest Three Rivers Ranger District Colville office (509) 684-7010
	OPEN	
16 sites, no hookups, RVs to 32 feet	May through November	

This remote Colville National Forest campground doesn't earn high marks because of its creature comforts. But it does get extra credit for its comfort to creatures. The campground is primitive, with pit toilets and no garbage service, piped water, showers, or other amenities. And the road up here can establish all new levels of hell in the springtime, when the ground is soft. But the campground is in a gorgeous, waterfront location on seventy-acre Big Meadow Lake. And campground builders have taken full advantage of the large amount of wildlife in the area. The camp has an interpretive trail and a wildlife viewing platform from which deer, beaver, osprey, and—loosen your lens caps—moose(!) are sometimes spotted. This is only one of several grand wildlife observation posts in this remote corner of the state. See Sullivan Lake and Noisy Creek (below) for other places to spot moose, mountain goats, and bighorn sheep. The elevation is 3400 feet.

Getting there: From State Route 20, 1.1 miles east of Colville, turn northeast on Aladdin–Northport Road and continue about 20 miles to (rough and rocky) Meadow Creek Road. Turn right (east) and drive about 6 miles to the campground.

32 Edgewater ★ ★ ◀

SITES	RESERVATIONS	CONTACT
🏕 🚐	None	Colville National Forest Sullivan Lake Ranger District (509) 446-7500
	OPEN	
20 sites, no hookups, RVs to 20 feet	Late May to early September	

Look at the bright side: If not for Box Canyon Dam, a couple miles downstream from here, they would have had to call Edgewater something like High Above the Water. As it is, the small Forest Service campground makes proper use of this reservoir on the Pend Oreille River, which drains north to meet the upper Columbia River in British Columbia. The campground, a popular fishing base camp, has pit toilets and no garbage service. Its facilities are a bit worn around the edges, but the water is beautiful here. The elevation is 2200 feet.

Getting there: Edgewater is 2 miles northeast of the town of Ione via State Route 31 and County Roads 9345 and 3669.

33 East and West Sullivan Lake ★ ★ ★ ★

SITES	RESERVATIONS	CONTACT
🏕 🚐	(877) 444-6777 or www.recreation.gov	Colville National Forest Sullivan Lake Ranger District (509) 446-7500
	OPEN	
48 sites, no hookups, RVs to 50 feet	Late May through September	

Everything you need to know about what first brought people to the harsh northeast corner of Washington—and what keeps them coming back—can be found within a short distance of East and West Sullivan, adjacent campgrounds on the north shore of Sullivan Lake. In other words, if you're just passing through the area and only have a day or two to spare, spend them here. The campgrounds themselves are nice with sites nicely spaced between pleasant, shady pine and fir trees. Amenities include piped water, pit toilets (unusually clean!), an RV dump station, and great access to the 3-mile-long lake, which is a very popular water-skiing, swimming, and fishing venue (rainbow and brown trout) in the summer. But you'd be remiss if you wasted all your time sitting in these campgrounds east of Metaline Falls.

Much of the best of the northeast—whether manmade or wild—is within a short distance of your tent or trailer door. Three miles to the east, you'll encounter the western border of the 40,000-acre Salmo–Priest Wilderness, a vast, unspoiled area filled with 6500-foot rocky peaks. The wilderness contains the last old-growth forest in Eastern Washington and a wealth of rare animals, including woodland caribou, mountain goats, Rocky Mountain bighorn sheep, and the occasional moose. Not all this wildlife stays up in the hills, out of sight, either. Local bighorn sheep, in particular, often are viewed from trails around and to the top of Hall Mountain, which looms above the eastern shore of the lake. In the fall and winter, the same sheep are easily viewed from a platform near Noisy Creek Campground (see below), on the south shore of the lake. Don't get too close: The rams are upwards of 300 pounds and can be aggressive. Note that you can walk to Noisy Creek on the Sullivan Lake Trail, an easy, 4.1-mile (one-way) hike along the lake. Even in the summer, bighorn sheep usually can be viewed by those willing to hoof it up the Hall Mountain Trail, a strenuous, 5-mile round-trip hike to the 6325-foot top of the mountain. To supplement the sheep's diets, wildlife managers sometimes place salt licks near the summit.

Other local attractions include a wide range of beautiful, unpeopled trails in the Salmo–Priest Wilderness, as well as the short, fascinating (barrier-free) Millpond

Swimmers enjoy Sullivan Lake.

Interpretive Trail at nearby Millpond Campground, just up Sullivan Lake Road. Signs along the trail explain the creation of the lake and its connecting waterway: Sullivan Lake was raised 40 feet by a dam built in 1910 to supply water to Metaline Falls. The way the water got there was unique—via a massive wooden flume, wide enough to drive a car through. A boardwalk atop the flume, which was considered an engineering marvel in its day, provides a path between the lake and Metaline Falls. The elevation of the two campgrounds is 2600 feet. Note: East Sullivan is by far the larger campground, with thirty-eight sites in three loops, while West Sullivan has ten sites. A group camp for up to thirty campers is also reservable at East Sullivan. Also, a rough, grass airstrip between the East and West Sullivan Lake campgrounds allows pilots to "fly-in camp" here.

Getting there: From the power house in Metaline Falls, follow State Route 31 about 1.5 miles north, turn east on Sullivan Lake Road (County Road 9345) and proceed about 6.5 miles to the campground.

34 Noisy Creek ★★★✦

SITES	RESERVATIONS	CONTACT
🏕️ 🚻🚐	(877) 444-6777 or www.reserveusa.com	Colville National Forest Sullivan Lake Ranger District (509) 446-7500
19 sites, no hookups, RVs to 45 feet	**OPEN** Late May to early September	

Noisy Creek is a smaller, somewhat less crowded version of Sullivan Lake (see above), and it shares the wide variety of great activities in this area. The campground has vault toilets, piped water, and a boat launch. Reservations are a good idea; about 60 percent of the sites can be reserved in advance through the National Recreation Reservation Service. Note that Sullivan Lake shrinks away from the camping area when the reservoir is drawn down. See East and West Sullivan Lake, above, for recreation information.

Getting there: From the power house in Metaline Falls, follow State Route 31 about 1.5 miles north, turn east on Sullivan Lake Road (County Road 9345) and proceed about 9.5 miles to the campground, on the south end of Sullivan Lake. Alternatively, turn right (east) on Sullivan Lake Road from SR 31 near Ione and proceed about 8 miles northeast.

Other Kettle Falls/Colville/Pend Oreille Campgrounds

An alternative to the popular East and West Sullivan and Noisy Creek camps on Sullivan Lake is **Millpond** (ten sites with drinking water and restrooms, 5 miles northeast of Metaline Falls). Contact the Sullivan Lake Ranger District, (509) 446-7500. An alternative to popular camps at Lake Thomas and Lake Gillette in the Little Pend Oreille Lakes chain is **Lake Leo** (eight sites for tents and RVs up to 16 feet long, no drinking water, popular with cross-country skiers in winter). Contact the Colville Ranger District, (509) 684-7010 or (509) 684-7000.

BEST QUIET TENT CAMPS

1. Alta Lake State Park, Pateros
Hidden in a hanging valley above the town of Pateros, Alta Lake is almost always a quiet getaway that makes you feel like you're going back in time. See p. 248.

2. Bonaparte Lake, North Central Washington
A small, pleasant Forest Service camp in the Okanagan Highlands of north central Washington, Bonaparte is a great getaway from the RV world. See p. 276.

3. Silver Fir, Nooksack River
Great, private campsites, many of them on the North Fork Nooksack River. See p. 125.

4. Lower Loop, Salt Creek Recreation Area
Keep right on going through the open-field RV spots here for a stunning loop of tent sites set right on the Strait of Juan de Fuca. See p. 83.

5. Klipchuck, North Cascades
High, dry, and lonesome in the Upper Methow Valley, Klipchuck is camping like it used to be—warts and all. See p. 139.

Farther south in the Newport Ranger District are four additional Colville National Forest camps, **Panhandle** (thirteen sites for tents or RVs up to 38 feet long), **Browns Lake** (18 sites for tents and RVs up to 28 feet long, no drinking water, vault toilets), **South Skookum Lake** (twenty-five sites for tents or RVs up to 30 feet long), and **Pioneer Park** (seventeen sites for tents and RVs up to 38 feet long). Call the ranger district at (509) 447-7300 or make reservations at (877) 444-6777.

A handful of primitive DNR camps allow campers to really rough it in this region. They are **Sheep Creek** (eleven sites for tents or RVs up to 30 feet long, on Sheep Creek Road, just off State Route 25 near the Canadian border); **Upper Sheep Creek** (two sites, no piped water, 1.2 miles up the road, near Sheep Creek Falls); **Douglas Falls Grange Park** (twelve sites for tents or RVs up to 30 feet long, drinking water and vault toilets, on Douglas Falls Road north of Colville); **Williams Lake**, (eight sites for tents or RVs up to 30 feet long, drinking water and vault toilets, on Williams Lake Road north of Kettle Falls); **Rocky Lake** (seven unimpressive sites for tents and RVs up to 30 feet long, drinking water and vault toilets—and a lot of dirt bikes—off Highway 395 south of Colville, near the Little Pend Oreille Wildlife Area); **Flodelle Creek** (eight sites for tents or RVs up to 30 feet long and, again, a lot of dirt bikes, off Highway 20 northeast of Colville); **Starvation Lake** (six small sites and canoe/ fishing access, restrooms, and RV sites, east of Colville off State Route 20); **Sherry Creek** (three sites, no piped water, 24.2 miles east of Colville off SR 20); and **Skookum Creek** (nine sites on the Pend Oreille River near Usk, well water/hand pump and vault toilets, with access to a Native American painting interpretive site). Most of these campgrounds are free. For details, call the DNR's Northeast Region office in Colville; (509) 684-7474.

Spokane

35 Riverside State Park ★ ★ ★ ★

SITES	RESERVATIONS	CONTACT
 56 sites, 37 full or partial hookups, RVs to 45 feet	(888) 226-7688 or www.parks.wa.gov	Washington State Parks (360) 902-8844
	OPEN	Riverside State Park (509) 456-3964
	Year-round; Nine Mile Falls open May 15 through September 15	

It's not often that the very best place to camp, explore, and relax in a given place is close to the urban core of the same area. But such is the case in Spokane, where sprawling Riverside State Park takes care of an amazingly wide range of city recreational needs. The 10,000-acre park is scattered in separate parcels along 9 miles of the Spokane River. The camping area lies in a broad meander curve, in a park section called the Bowl and Pitcher, named for unique rock formations along the river. Recently upgraded to include utilities, the camping area has fewer sites in better condition. The thirty-two sites in the Bowl and Pitcher area are split into two areas, an upper campground with sixteen standard sites (one barrier free) and two hookup sites. They're about 100 yards from the river. The lower campground, parts of which can be reserved for groups, offers thirteen hookup sites and two grassy sites for thirty to sixty group campers, as well

A footbridge spans Spokane Falls, along the Centennial Trail.

as a kitchen shelter and an amphitheatre. There's a ten-day camping limit here in summer. The remaining campsites, most with full or partial hookups, are in a single loop in the Nine Mile Recreation Area, open summers only. It's a short drive to the north.

Camping, however, is only one of a dozen good reasons to visit. Inside Riverside's 10,000 acres are 36 miles of hiking and equestrian trails, a large group camp, multiple picnic areas, fascinating rock formations, Native American petroglyphs, white-water rapids on the Spokane and Little Spokane Rivers (novice paddlers should keep to the latter), a 600-acre off-road-vehicle park, a scenic river gorge, and the Spokane House Interpretive Center. The latter, near Nine Mile Falls, is on the site of Spokane House, explorer David Thompson's 1810 fur-trading outpost.

If none of that is enough to goad you from your lawn chair, you can seriously recreate from here by hoofing or pedaling up the Centennial Trail, the 37-mile paved multisport path between Nine Mile Falls and Coeur d'Alene, Idaho. The trail, perhaps the best urban-to-rural walking-and-cycling path in the Northwest, follows the Spokane River. By Washington standards, the trail isn't wildly scenic. But it's a walk with plenty of historical flavor. Native American petroglyphs are visible from the trail near Long Lake, and the trail itself follows a route pounded out over the centuries by native peoples—and after that, white fur traders. The entire length is open to strolling and cycling, with some portions also open to horseback riding. The trail passes by Riverfront Park, raging Spokane Falls, Gonzaga University, Mission Park, and other local attractions. For details and trail events, contact Friends of the Centennial Trail; (509) 624-7188 or see www.spokanecentennialtrail.org.

Getting there: To reach the park's Bowl and Pitcher area from Interstate 90 near Spokane, take Exit 280, Maple Street North. Cross the Maple Street Bridge and proceed about a mile to Maxwell Street (at the second stop light). Turn left (west) and drive about 2 miles (it becomes Pettit Drive, then Downriver Drive), passing Downriver Golf Course, to the park entrance. To reach the Nine Mile Recreation area from Interstate 90 near Spokane, take Exit 280, Maple Street North. Cross the Maple Street Bridge to Northwest Boulevard. Turn left and follow the road to Francis Avenue (State Route 291). Turn left. The road becomes Nine Mile Road. Continue 6 miles. After the town of Nine Mile Falls, turn left on Charles Road, crossing the dam. Continue west on Charles Road for 1.3 miles and turn right (across from the church) into the park entrance.

36 Mount Spokane State Park ✦ ✦ ✦

SITES	RESERVATIONS		CONTACT
🏕️ 🚐	None		Washington State Parks (360) 902-8844
	OPEN		Mount Spokane State Park (509) 238-4258
12 sites, no hookups, RVs to 30 feet	June through September		

Mount Spokane's main claim to fame is that it is the closest ski mountain to downtown Spokane. As such, it doesn't get much attention as a summertime getaway. But this is a nice day-trip destination out of Spokane that can turn into a pleasant overnighter, or a longer stay for equestrians making use of horse trails that ring this 5883-foot mountaintop—the most southerly peak in the Selkirk chain. Although the park is massive (almost 14,000 acres, encompassing the ski hill), the small campground is unremarkable. But the park has an extensive, 100-mile hiking, biking, and horse trail system, and the view from the Vista House at the summit is memorable. A group camp can accommodate up to 100 people. A state Sno-Park pass is required here from November 1 through May 1, when Mount Spokane turns into a popular area for cross-country skiing, on 25 kilometers of groomed trails, and alpine skiing, via five lifts.

Getting there: Mount Spokane State Park is 30 miles northeast of Spokane via Division Street (U.S. Highway 2) and State Route 206.

37 Pend Oreille County Park ★ ★ ◄

SITES	RESERVATIONS	CONTACT
▲ 🏕🚐	(509) 292-0121	Pend Oreille County Department of Public Works (509) 447-4821
	OPEN	
35 sites, no hookups, RVs to 30 feet	Memorial Day through Labor Day	

It's nothing to write home about, but 440-acre Pend Oreille County Park is a good stopover point in a pinch for Eastern Washington travelers. These are mostly tent sites, although two are described as RV sites. The campground, close enough to U.S. Highway 2 to hear it, has flush toilets and hot showers—a rarity for a campground geared for the tent crowd. There's not much to do in the local area, so most people use this as a one-night stopover.

Getting there: From Interstate 90 near Spokane, turn north on US 2 and proceed about 31 miles to the campground, on the west side of the highway.

Other Spokane-Area Campgrounds

Three DNR campgrounds in the area offer primitive alternatives. They are **Long Lake**, also known as Lake Spokane (twelve sites for tents and RVs up to 21 feet long, on Long Lake Dam Road north of Reardon); **Dragoon Creek** (twenty-two sites, on Dragoon Creek Road north of Spokane); and **A. J. Pat Kehn** (four sites, restrooms, and RV sites, on Bruce Road east of Chattaroy). For details, call the DNR's Northeast Region office in Colville; (509) 684-7474.

Private campgrounds within Spokane city limits include **KOA Spokane**, (800) 562-3309 or (509) 924-4722; and **Trailer Inns RV Park**, (509) 535-1811. Also, a number of private resorts are located west of town in the Medical Lake region. They include **West Medical Lake Resort**, (509) 299-3921; **Picnic Pines on Silver Lake**, (509) 299-6902; **Mallard Bay Resort**, (509) 299-3830; and **Rainbow Cove Resort**, (509) 299-3717. A private resort west of town is **Yogi Bear's Camp Resort**, (800) 494-7275 or (509) 747-9415.

Opposite: Towering cumulus clouds reflect in the Snake River downstream from the confluence of the Palouse, Tucannon, and Snake rivers. (Photo by Alan L. Bauer)

8. SOUTHEAST WASHINGTON

Let's be honest. The closest most of us West Siders want to get to summer in Southeast Washington is that bag of Walla Walla Sweets we brought home from QFC. Just thinking about the place makes the brain start squinting from the sun. Southeast—isn't that where Washtucna is? Not much out there except sand, sun, and the campus of Washington State University. And we all know what the combination of those three poisons can do to an otherwise sound mind.

That may be a bit harsh. But, well, so's the climate. That's why camping in the southeast corner of the state—where peas and lentils are often the most vibrant living creatures for miles—requires a bit of an attitude adjustment. Don't call it a campout. Consider it an expedition. Would Lawrence of Arabia have had a chance if he'd told his troops they were going for a restful weekend over at Aqaba? Precisely. To quote everybody's junior-high football coach: You've gotta want it.

And even in far-flung Southeast Washington, he or she who wants it shall find it indeed. In the most forlorn corner of this splendid state, a few nuggets of pure gold emerge from the billions of tons of rough ore. Camping can be good in the southeast corner, if you know where to look, when to go, and how to keep the rattlesnakes out of your boots once you've arrived. Not surprisingly, most of these oases in the great desert of the southeast are found along the banks of the life-giving rivers that cross the region, particularly the Snake. From the sun-and-water riverfront playgrounds of the Tri-Cities to the solemn, historic gravesites at Chief Timothy Park near Clarkston, the Snake can be a savage but beautiful land to visit. Speaking of Chief Timothy: It and three other former state parks in this corner—Lyons Ferry, Central Ferry, and Crow Butte—have fortunately survived, in spite of falling off the state parks' roles during a budget meltdown. All are now operated by other public agencies.

Bottom line: You can still find places to get lost in the region. A lot of wide-open space lies north and south of the Snake River. It's marked by a few notable getaways where time has stood still since long before white people came to this region. There's something reassuring about that. Last time we stood in the Blue Mountains of the Wenaha–Tucannon Wilderness east of Walla Walla, things looked a lot like they must have 1000 years ago. Here's hoping they'll look just the same when you get there next summer—and 1000 years after you leave.

Tri-Cities Area
1 Crow Butte Park
2 Plymouth Park
3 Hood Park
4 Charbonneau Park
5 Fishhook Park

The Palouse and Snake River
6 Lyons Ferry Park
7 Palouse Falls State Park
8 Central Ferry Park
9 Wawawai County Park
10 Kamiak Butte County Park
11 Chief Timothy Park

Walla Walla and the Blue Mountains
12 Lewis and Clark Trail State Park
13 Fields Spring State Park
14 Tucannon

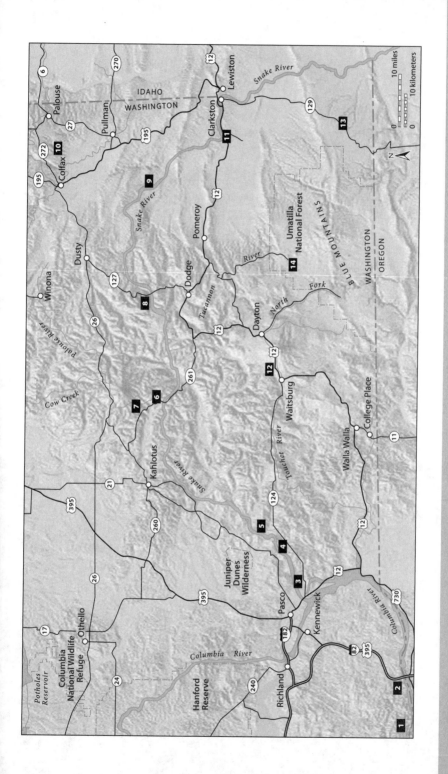

▮ Crow Butte Park ★ ★ ★ ★

SITES	RESERVATIONS	CONTACT
 50 sites, all have full hookups, RVs to 60 feet	(509) 875-2644	Crow Butte Park (509) 875-2644
	OPEN	
	March 15 through October 15	

Crow Butte is one of several campgrounds in this region that formerly operated as Washington State Parks but were turned over to local port districts (in this case, the Port of Benton) or their landowner, the U.S. Army Corps of Engineers, during a budget crunch in the past decade. It was sad to lose them from the state parks roster, but the good news is that parks such as Crow Butte proved to be too good of an asset to go to waste and are still operating. It's more than worth the drive south from the Tri-Cities to check out Crow Butte, one of Washington's most unique parks. The park sits on an island in the middle of a portion of the Columbia River called Lake Umatilla because of the flooded backwater from John Day Dam. The 1300-acre property is situated on what once was a very high river bluff.

The campground's fifty sites are in a grassy area with some shade. Fortunately, windbreaks have been constructed to cut through the stiff breezes that buffet this

A coyote takes a sip from the Columbia River along Hanford Reach (Photo by Janice Ohlsen).

large, flat knoll. The park also has a spiffy boat launch and moorage in a protected basin, a sixty-person group camp, a swimming area, and an RV dump station. Electric service was being upgraded from 30 amp to 50 amp for the spring of 2009. Sites are $15 to $25 at this writing.

Short hiking trails lead to the top of 670-foot Crow Butte, which offers views of Mount Hood. Watch for rattlesnakes! The land on the park's eastern border is a portion of the Umatilla National Wildlife Refuge, a significant migratory waterfowl nesting (and, sometimes, hunting) site.

Local trivia: Don't waste too much time looking for crows. The park's name comes from the Crowe family, homesteaders who moved to this area in the 1850s. The original homestead site, like a whole lot of other Columbia River history, now is underwater.

Getting there: From State Route 14, about 13 miles west of Paterson, cross the bridge southwest to the island.

2 Plymouth Park ✦ ✦ ✦

SITES	RESERVATIONS	CONTACT
32 sites, 16 full hookups, 16 water/electrical hookups, RVs to 40 feet	(877) 444-6777 or www.recreation.gov	U.S. Army Corps of Engineers Portland District (509) 783-1270
	OPEN	
	April through October	

Plymouth, one of many campgrounds in this area run by the Army Corps of Engineers, is a quality, mostly-RV stopover about a quarter-mile from the Columbia, with good shade from summer sun. Its location near the Umatilla Bridge to Oregon makes it a strategic stopover for road-trippers heading down the nearby Interstate 82 route to northeast Oregon, southern Idaho, and Utah. The campground has an RV dump station and coin-op showers, as well as a nearby launch ramp and tie-up dock at the day-use area. All of the campsites are pull-throughs.

Getting there: From I-82 at Richland, drive south for about 30 miles and take State Route 14 west 2 miles to the Plymouth exit. Proceed to Christy Road, turn right and follow signs to the park.

3 Hood Park ✦ ✦ ✦

SITES	RESERVATIONS	CONTACT
69 sites, all have electrical hookups, RVs to any length	(877) 444-6777 or www.recreation.gov	U.S. Army Corps of Engineers (509) 547-2048
	OPEN	
	April through September	

Everybody must get wet. The Tri-Cities, situated nicely in the oven-baked climate of southeastern Washington, fortunately also are situated nicely in a rich water world, thanks to the many dams on the Columbia and Snake Rivers. Lake Wallula, the 64-mile-long Columbia impoundment behind McNary Dam near Umatilla, Oregon, makes for a broad, smooth boating track. So does Lake Sacajawea, the Snake River backup created by the Ice Harbor Dam, 9 miles east of Pasco. That's why you'll find—no joke—three actual yacht clubs in town, and it's not difficult to find boating supplies and services. Major public launches are found at all the local public waterfront parks—some of which also welcome campers.

Hood Park is the most centrally located of a number of Army Corps of Engineers campgrounds on Tri-Cities impoundments (see Charbonneau Park and Fishhook Park, below). The ninety-nine-acre park provides good river access, basketball courts, horseshoe pits, flush toilets, piped water, showers, and an RV dump station. Like most parks in this area, it also has a boat launch and moorage facilities. More than two dozen of the sites here are paved pull-throughs with utilities—great for RVs. And the biggest bonus in this sun-baked camp: Mature shade trees and grass in most sites. The campground is popular with swimmers, anglers, water-skiers, and sunbathers. Sacajawea State Park, a popular day-use area at the confluence of the Snake and Columbia rivers, is nearby, as is the McNary Wildlife Refuge. An overflow area at Hood Park has an additional ninety sites. It's a good base camp for exploring Tri-Cities-area wineries and other sights.

Getting there: From Pasco, drive about 5 miles southeast on U.S. Highway 12 to junction with State Route 124. Turn east and follow signs to the campground.

BEST SUNNYSIDE GETAWAYS FOR WATERLOGGED WEST SIDERS

1. Daroga State Park, Central Washington
A newer, pleasant waterfront camp on the Middle Columbia, Daroga is a great spring destination for people who can't take one more rainy day. See p. 246.

2. Steamboat Rock State Park, Banks Lake
It's a bit of a drive, but there are two good reasons this park on Banks Lake near Grand Coulee is one of the first to fill up every year on the state reservations system: sun and water. See p. 261.

3. Alta Lake State Park, Pateros
We can't recall ever being here in the rain. Snow, maybe. But not rain. See p. 248.

4. Wenatchee Confluence State Park, Wenatchee
Conveniently located in Wenatchee, not far from a major supermarket, in case you've forgotten your sunscreen. Acres of pleasant, grassy sites and good water access to the Columbia and Wenatchee rivers. See p. 243.

5. Yakima Sportsman State Park, Yakima
It's not all that scenic, but how bad can a park near the "Palm Springs of the Northwest" be for sun-starved Western Washingtonians? See p. 266.

Deer cooling off in the Columbia River shallows (Photo by Janice Ohlsen)

4 Charbonneau Park ✶ ✶ ✶

SITES	RESERVATIONS	CONTACT
🏕️ 🚐	None	U.S. Army Corps of Engineers (509) 547-2048
	OPEN	
54 sites, 15 full hookups, 39 electrical hookups, RVs to 60 feet	April through October; day-use area open year-round	

Next time you're in the Tri-Cities area, stop by here to see what all this lingering controversy about dams on the Columbia and Snake rivers is all about. Charbonneau Park, an Army Corps of Engineers site, is very near one of them: Ice Harbor Dam. It's one of a series of dams built on the Snake between the Tri-Cities and Lewiston, Idaho, from the late 1960s through the 1970s. The dams and locks—Ice Harbor, Lower Monumental, Little Goose, and Lower Granite—are used mostly for barge navigation. They accomplished the seemingly impossible, turning Lewiston into a seaport, of sorts. They also helped snuff out what was left of the struggling Snake iver salmon runs, which long have been listed as endangered. Not a good tradeoff, perhaps, but one that reaped many recreational benefits for this area. Charbonneau Park, a 244-acre complex on 31-mile long Lake Sacajawea, is but one example. Its fifty-four sites all have full or partial hookups, and eighteen are drive-through sites favored by big-RV drivers. But it also offers some tent pads, making this a nice, mixed-use park, with some shade from the summer sun. The park also has showers, boat launching and moorage, and a nice playground. The primary activities are fishing, boating, water-skiing, and touring the dam, which is open daily April through October.

Getting there: From Pasco, drive about 5 miles southeast on U.S. Highway 12 to State Route 124. Turn northeast on SR 124 and proceed 8 miles to Sun Harbor Road. Turn north and follow signs about 2 miles to the park.

5 Fishhook Park ★ ★ ★

SITES	RESERVATIONS	CONTACT
🏕️ 🚐	(877) 444-6777 or www.recreation.gov	U.S. Army Corps of Engineers (509) 547-2048
	OPEN	
61 sites, 41 water/electrical hookups, RVs to 45 feet	May to early September	

Like its big brother, Charbonneau, forty-six-acre Fishhook Park is an Army Corps of Engineers site off State Route 124 northeast of Pasco, with good access to the Snake River's Lake Sacajawea, behind Ice Harbor Dam. It's a better campground for tenters. The campground is in a wooded area that provides some shade; many of the utility sites are pull-throughs. The twenty non-hookup sites are walk-in tent spaces. Facilities include flush toilets, showers, water and electrical hookups, a playground, a swimming area, a boat launch and moorage, and an RV dump station.

Getting there: From Pasco, drive about 5 miles southeast on U.S. Highway 12 to SR 124, turn northeast and proceed 18 miles to Fishhook Road. Turn left and continue about 4 miles to the park.

Other Tri-Cities-Area Campgrounds

The keeper of local waterways, the U.S. Army Corps of Engineers, allows camping at non-designated sites near many of its public day-use areas and boat launches on Lakes Wallula and Sacajawea (try to whip out those names with a mouth full of peanut butter). Some riverfront parks with "primitive" (read: parking-lot style, or sandbar tent sites) camping include **Madame Dorian Memorial Park** and **Sand Station** on Lake Wallula; and **Big Flat**, **Lake Emma, Matthews, Walker,** and **Windust Park**, all on Lake Sacajawea. Contact the corps' Ice Harbor Project office in Pasco, (509) 547-7781; or, better yet, click the "recreation" button on the agency's extensive Internet website, found at www.nww.usace.army.mil.

6 Lyons Ferry Park ★ ★ ★ ◀

SITES	RESERVATIONS	CONTACT
  52 sites, no hookups, RVs to 45 feet	None **OPEN** March 15 through September	Lyons Ferry Park (509) 399-8020

It's as rich in history as it is hot and dry. And out here, that's saying something. Lyons Ferry, which sits on a point at the confluence of the Palouse and Snake rivers, is much like Central Ferry, another former state park farther upstream (east) on the Snake. As at Central Ferry, the boat that crossed the river here for 108 years—very often with skipper Dan Lyons at the rudder—long ago was replaced by a bridge. Unlike Central Ferry, however, the Lyons Ferry, which operated on river current alone, is still here, tied up on shore, where it serves as a fishing pier and historical display. The park lies on either side of the north end of the Lyons Ferry Bridge on State Route 261. On the west side is a plain, poorly landscaped campground. Not exactly a garden spot, but it'll do for an overnight spot, particularly if you're in an RV. The campground has an RV dump station and coin-op showers.

In addition to the old ferry, the much nicer day-use area features a long spit of land (a ridge top, before dams flooded the valley) that juts into the lake, providing

Don't turn your back on your lunch.

a wealth of good waterfront picnic spots. Farther south are more picnic grounds, a swimming beach, a bathhouse, and a boat launch. At the north end of the day-use area, a trail leads about a mile up a bluff to a canyon overlook, where you'll find historical information about Marmes Rock Shelter, an ancient Palouse Indian burial cave below here, now flooded by the lake waters. Before the flooding, archaeologists discovered human remains carbon-dated to 10,000 years ago. For a time, they were considered the oldest human remains on the continent. Other evidence showed this was a Native burial site for many, many centuries, most recently for the Palouse tribe. About 400 graves were unearthed and moved before the valley was flooded by Lower Monumental Dam.

Getting there: Lyons Ferry is at the confluence of the Palouse and Snake Rivers, 8 miles northwest of Starbuck on State Route 261.

Palouse Falls in February (Photo by Dan A. Nelson)

7 Palouse Falls State Park ✦ ✦

SITES	RESERVATIONS	CONTACT
🏕 🚐	None	Washington State Parks (360) 902-8844
	OPEN	Palouse Falls State Park (509) 646-3252
10 sites, no hookups, RVs to 40 feet	Mid-March to late September	

Absolutely do not, under any circumstances, drive all the way here from Bellingham just to camp. The campground at Palouse Falls State Park, which is upstream from Lyons Ferry Park (above), isn't much. The primitive camp, which has pit toilets and an RV dump station but no other amenities, is often used as a day-use area by the many nature lovers who come to see the real attraction: Palouse Falls itself. The 200-foot waterfall is one of Washington's most spectacular natural sights, plunging from the top of a half-circle of wall-like columnar basalt into a deep pool. The falls are at their peak in the spring (usually late March), when the Palouse River is at high flow. The prolific spray at the bottom often forms a rainbow, making this a photographer's dream. The falls are believed to have been formed by the same prehistoric floods that carved other Eastern Washington features, such as the Grand Coulee. Our suggestion: Camp at Lyons Ferry Park, and make this a day trip.

Getting there: The park is 16 miles northwest of Starbuck via State Route 261 and Palouse Falls Road.

8 Central Ferry Park ★ ★ ★ ♦

SITES	RESERVATIONS	CONTACT
🏕️ 🚐	(877) 444-6777 or www.recreation.gov	U.S. Army Corps of Engineers Clarkston office (509) 751-0240
68 sites, 60 full hookups, RVs to 45 feet	**OPEN** Mid-March to mid-November	

Sun-worshippers, unite. You'll see a lot of boat trailers and swim fins at Central Ferry Park, which fronts on the Snake River's 10,000-acre Lake Bryan and draws many boaters and water-sport fans. This is the most developed full-service RV campground in this corner of the state, and the only one within about 20 miles. Spaces here often are reserved well in advance. The park was built specifically to take advantage of Lake Bryan, the large waterway created by Little Goose Dam on the Snake River. Two basins

Palouse Falls gushes on after an early winter snowfall. (Photo by Dan A. Nelson)

were dug to protect moored boats from nasty winds that occasionally whip through the river gorge—often taking haphazardly staked tents with them. (Stake those babies down!) The campground sites, most of which have full hookups, are in six loops located in a flat, grassy area. Loops 2 through 5 are closest to the water. The campground has flush toilets, coin-op showers, an RV dump station, three horseshoe pits, a boat launch and moorage, water-ski launch ramps, a marine sewer pumpout station, a non-patrolled swimming beach and bathhouse, a group camp, and sheltered picnic sites near the river. The eight tent sites are primitive, walk-in spaces. Campsites are $17 to $25 at this writing. Note: This is another park that formerly operated as a Washington State Park until budget cuts forced the state to cancel leases.

Getting there: Central Ferry is 17 miles south of aptly named Dusty and 34 miles southwest of beautiful downtown Colfax. on State Route 127.

9 Wawawai County Park ✦✦✦

SITES	RESERVATIONS	CONTACT
🏕 🚐	None	Whitman County Parks and Recreation (509) 397-6328
	OPEN	
9 sites, no hookups, RVs to 24 feet	Year-round; no water in winter	

Wawawai, aside from setting a record for most *w*'s in one word, is a pretty little getaway set on a small bay off the Snake River at the outlet of Wawawai Creek. The hillside campsites are basic, but nice, with four pull-through sites and two with tent pads. (Use them in the summer, or you'll get sprinkled!) The day-use area is used by boaters and anglers. But the park has other interesting features, including a half-mile interpretive trail and a bird-watching platform. Also of note is an "earth-sheltered" (underground) house built here in 1980; it now serves as the park ranger's house. The park also has a reservable large group shelter for up to 100 people. Campsites were $15 a night at this writing. And, since you had to ask about the name, *wawawai*, (pronounced, "wuh-WAH-ee," sort of like "Hawaii") is said to be a Native word for "council ground."

Getting there: From Colfax, drive 15 miles south on U.S. Highway 195 to Wawawai–Pullman Road 9010, near Pullman. Turn right (west) and proceed 9.5 miles to Wawawai Road 9000. Turn right and proceed 5.5 miles down the canyon to Wawawai County Park.

10 Kamiak Butte County Park ✦✦✦

SITES	RESERVATIONS	CONTACT
🏕 🚐	None	Whitman County Parks and Recreation (509) 397-6328
	OPEN	
9 sites, no hookups, RVs to 18 feet	Year-round; no water in winter	

Kamiak, a simple but pleasant park between Colfax and Pullman, is a great place to stretch your legs and take in some of the rolling, hilly Palouse topography. In fact, it's one of the best ones: The grassy butte within the park is a National Natural Landmark (whatever that is), with a sterling view from more than 3600 feet. The park contains a total of 5 miles of trails, including the scenic Pine Ridge Trail. The campsites are set in trees and are fairly small. The campground has pit toilets and piped water, but no showers or other amenities. Sites were $15 a night at this writing. Note that the park is often closed during the peak fire season in late summer; call before you go.

Getting there: From Pullman, drive 11 miles north on State Route 27 to Clear Creek Road. Turn left and proceed a half mile to Fugate Road 5100. Turn left and proceed a half mile to the park entrance on the left. From Colfax, drive 5 miles east on State Route 272 (Palouse Highway) to Clear Creek Road. Drive 7 miles to Fugate Road 5100, take a sharp right, and proceed a half mile to the park entrance.

ıı Chief Timothy Park ★ ★ ★

SITES	RESERVATIONS	CONTACT
⚠ 🏕🚐 66 sites, 25 full hookups, 8 water/electrical hookups, RVs to 60 feet	(877) 444-6777 or www.recreation.gov **OPEN** Year-round; limited winter facilities	U.S. Army Corps of Engineers Clarkston office (509) 751-0240

Hmm. I think we've seen this theme before. A former state park situated on a Snake River impoundment, popular with boaters and anglers (see Lyons Ferry and Central Ferry, above). Chief Timothy Park, near Clarkston, is another sunny waterworld. It sits on an island of glacial till in Lower Granite Lake, a Snake River dam creation. The proximity of the island to the shore creates a nicely protected waterway—an ideal swimming and water-play area made even better by a broad, flat, sandy beach. The day-use area has eight shaded picnic sites, playground equipment, a bathhouse, coin-op showers, horseshoe pits, four boat-launch ramps, and moorage. You'll also find 2.5 miles of hiking trails. The campground's sixty-six campsites, half with hookups, are split into three camping loops.

A historical display tells of Timothy, a Nez Perce chief, and describes Alpowai, an old Nez Perce village located here long before the old pioneer town of Silcott was built on the same site. Unfortunately, like many other Snake River historical sites, most of it now lies beneath the lake waters.

Getting there: Chief Timothy Park is 8 miles west of Clarkston, just off U.S. Highway 12.

Other Palouse/Snake River Campgrounds

In the Clarkston area, alternate camping is available at **Boyer Park and Marina**; (509) 397-3208. Around Pullman, the city's **Pullman RV Park** (nineteen full-hookup sites; Riverview Road and South Street; call [509] 338-3227 for reservations) has decent RV spots in the summer.

Walla Walla and the Blue Mountains

12 Lewis and Clark Trail ★★★↓ State Park

SITES	RESERVATIONS	CONTACT
🏕️ 🚐	None	Washington State Parks (360) 902-8844
	OPEN	Lewis and Clark Trail State Park
41 sites, no hookups, RVs to 28 feet	Year-round	(509) 337-6457

They came, they saw, they stepped in the ocean—and came back. The latter part is how Lewis and Clark touched this part of Washington—on their return trip east in 1806. Lewis and Clark Trail State Park (not to be confused with Lewis and Clark State Park in Western Washington) is a small place set in a very pleasant forest of big, straight ponderosa pines with a tinder-dry grassy floor. The thirty-seven-acre park, which fronts on the Touchet River (good rainbow and brown trout fishing), is an oasis in this flat, dry area—no doubt one reason the Lewis and Clark Expedition chose it as a picnic spot, of sorts. The park is split by U.S. Highway 12; day-use areas, playfields, and picnic grounds are on the south side, camping on the north. The two riverside loops contain nice, tidy campsites, as well as a fifty-person group camp. In the winter, seventeen primitive sites in the day-use area remain open for camping, and the park provides ample cross-country skiing and snowshoeing trails. Other facilities include flush toilets, piped water, coin-op showers, an RV dump station, and two group sites for up to 100 campers each. The park also has several hiking trails, including a three-quarter-mile designated bird-watching trail and a mile-long interpretive trail. Interpretive programs about the Lewis and Clark Expedition are presented Saturday evenings in the summer. This is a popular camp for hunters in the fall.

Getting there: The park is on US 12, 4.5 miles west of Dayton, 25 miles northeast of Walla Walla.

13 Fields Spring State Park ★★★★

SITES	RESERVATIONS	CONTACT
🏕️ 🚐	None	Washington State Parks (360) 902-8844
	OPEN	Fields Spring State Park
20 sites, no hookups, RVs to 30 feet	Year-round; limited winter facilities	(509) 256-3332

Wouldn't you know it: One of the nicest state parks in Washington, particularly for tenters, is located about as far away from most of the state's population as you can get

A thicket of trees lights up in fall along the Touchet River. (Photo by Dan A. Nelson)

without being in Idaho. Fields Spring qualifies as just that. In fact, it's well worth the long trip for westside campers frustrated by big crowds. This park—located 29 miles south of Clarkston, just north of the Grande Ronde River Canyon, and east of just about everything—lies in a thicket of trees marking the transition from flat plains to the high, dry forests of the Blue Mountains. The park, spread across 4500-foot Puffer Butte above the Grande Ronde, is a lovely spot, rich with wildflower blooms on mountain slopes in the spring, and with wildlife year-round. Don't miss the hiking trail to the grand view atop Puffer Butte, where (legend has it) the first homesteaders would trek every morning and watch for Indians coming up the canyon. The campground is quite pleasant, especially for tenters. It's equipped with flush toilets, piped water, coin-op showers, and an RV dump station. It's also a good spot for RVs, although the 30-foot sites are too short for the larger land yachts. The 800-acre park has a lot more going on than just camping. The park has extensive playfields; a six-person teepee camp; 7 miles of mountain-bike trails; a picnic area with a covered shelter, electricity; and a wood stove, and other day-use facilities. It's also a popular winter hangout, with lighted sledding and tubing runs near the park's twin Environmental Learning Centers and numerous marked cross-country ski routes on local fire roads. All in all, a winner.

Getting there: The park is 29 miles south of Clarkston on State Route 129.

14 Tucannon ★★✦

SITES	RESERVATIONS	CONTACT
▲ 🚐	None	Umatilla National Forest Pomeroy Ranger District (509) 843-1891
	OPEN	
20 sites, no hookups, RVs to 21 feet	Year-round; weather permitting	

Tucannon is the most developed of a half dozen very remote campgrounds in the Blue Mountains of the Umatilla National Forest—and currently the only one to charge a fee. Small local lakes are stocked with trout by the Department of Fish and Wildlife, putting this camp in high demand in the spring. It gets busy again in the fall, during elk-hunting season. But in between, it's one of the most far-out-there places we know of to get away from it all. There's good hiking in the area; you're right at the Wenaha–Tucannon Wilderness. The camp has pit toilets, but no water, garbage service, or other amenities. See below for other Blue Mountains camps.

Getting there: From U.S. Highway 12 about 5 miles west of Pomeroy, turn left (south) on Tatman Mountain Road (signs indicate Camp Wooten), which becomes Forest Road 47. Continue about 19 miles to the National Forest boundary and an additional 4 miles to the campground, at Road 4700160.

Other Walla Walla/Blue Mountains Campgrounds

Five other remote Umatilla National Forest campgrounds (see Tucannon, above) are found in or near the Blue Mountains, in the Wenaha–Tucannon Wilderness. Most of them make excellent jump-off points for wilderness backpacking or fishing treks and are used most heavily in the fall, when elk and deer hunters flock to the wilderness area. All these campgrounds are free and open summers only, and none have piped water. Bring a filter, or pack in your own water. They are **Alder Thicket** (five small sites at 5100 feet, 18 miles south of Pomeroy on Forest Road 40); **Big Springs** (eight small sites for tents only at 5100 feet, 23 miles south of Pomeroy on Forest Road 42); **Teal Spring** (five small sites at 5600 feet, 26 miles south of Pomeroy on Forest Road 40); **Godman**, (eight sites and horse hitching rails and other facilities, on Forest Road 46); and **Wickiup** (five sites, 34 miles southeast of Pomeroy via Forest Roads 40 and 44). For forest maps and other information, contact the Umatilla National Forest's Pomeroy Ranger District; (509) 843-1891.

RATINGS INDEX

American Legion Park, 270
Ballard, 141
Blue Lake Creek, 227-28
Bogachiel State Park, 91
Clear Creek, 119-20
Corral Pass, 192
Goose Creek, 157
Halfway Flat, 201
Kaner Flat, 198-99
Little Naches, 198
Mineral Springs, 177-78
Osoyoos Lake State Park,
    275-76
Palouse Falls State Park, 308-9
Sawmill Flat, 200-201
Shannon Creek, 131
Sherman Pass Overlook, 283
Staysail RV Park, 42
Sugarloaf, 271
Tinkham,168

Crow Creek, 200
Tillicum, 225-26

Other (Including Boat-In, Primitive, Private)

A.J. Pat Kehn, 298
Alder Thicket, 315
Aldrich Lake, 71
Alpine Meadows, 159
American Forks, 202
Antilon, 256
Aqua Barn Ranch, 58
Atkinson Flats, 159
Atkisson Group Camp, 226
Baker Lake Resort, 132
Barnaby Island, 287
Battle Ground Lake State Park,
    237
Bayview Group Camps, 132
Beach 77, 71
Beach 78, 71
Beach 79, 71
Beach 83, 71
Beach 85, 71
Beaver Bay, 220
Beaver Creek, 121
Beaver Plant Lake, 122
Big Beaver, 138
Big Creek (Lake Chelan), 255

Big Flat, 306
Big Springs, 315
Bird Creek, 232
Black Pine Lake, 147
Blind Island, 54
Blue Sky RV Park, 58
Boardman Creek, 121
Boiling Lake, 255
Boulder Creek (Olympic
    Peninsula), 88
Boundary Bay, 138
Boyer Park and Marina, 311
Bradbury Beach, 287
Bridge Creek (Stehekin), 255
Brown Creek, 111
Browns Lake, 295
Buck Creek, 120
Burlington KOA, 52
Buster Brown, 138
Campbell Tree Grove, 98
Camp Cushman, 111
Camp Spillman, 71
Cascade Island, 137
Cat Creek, 232
Cat Island, 138
Chain of Lakes, 232
Chiwawa Horse Camp, 159
Chopaka Lake, 284
Circle H RV Ranch, 266
Clark Island, 54
Clark's Skagit River Resort, 137
Cloverleaf, 287
Coal Creek Bar, 121
Coho, 111
Cold Springs, 284
Coppermine Bottom, 98
Corral Creek, 255
Cottonwood (Middle
    Columbia), 250
Cottonwood (Olympic
    Peninsula), 98
Cottonwood (Stehekin), 255
Cougar, 220
Cougar Island, 138
Cresap Bay, 220
Cub Lake, 255
Cutts Island, 63
Cypress Head, 54
Deep Creek, 159
Deer Camp, 159
Deer Point, 255
Devils Junction, 138
Doe Bay Village Resort, 53
Doe Island, 54
Dolly Varden, 255

Domke Falls, 255
Domke Lake, 255
Dosewallips, 111
Douglas Falls, 295
Dragoon Creek, 298
Dry Creek, 138
Dungeness Forks, 88
Eagle Island, 63
Elkhorn, 111
Ellensburg KOA, 179
Erickson's Bay, 88
Esswine, 121
Excelsior Group Camp, 132
Fall Creek, 63
Finner Creek, 159
Fish Lake, 176
Flat Creek, 255
Flodelle Creek, 295
Foggy Dew, 147
Fort Ward State Park, 71
Fox Creek, 250
Gatton Creek, 98
Godman, 315
Gorge Lake, 137
Graham Harbor, 255
Graham Harbor Creek, 255
Grandy Lake Park, 132
Grange Park, 295
Grasshopper Meadows, 159
Green Mountain Horse Camp,
    71
Green Point, 138
Griffin Bay, 54
Grouse Creek Group Camp, 159
Grouse Mountain, 256
Haag Cove, 287
Handy Springs, 256
Hannegan, 132
Harlequin, 255
Hidden Cove, 138
High Bridge, 255
Hoh Oxbow, 98
Hoh River Resort, 98
Holden Ballpark, 255
Hope Island (Skagit Bay), 54
Hope Island (south Puget
    Sound), 63
Howell Lake, 71
Hozomeen, 138
Hunters, 287
Hutchinson Creek, 52
Icewater Creek, 178
Icicle River RV Resort, 166
Indian Flat, 202
Indian Horse Camp, 179

CAMPGROUND INDEX

ABOUT THE AUTHOR

Washington native Ron C. Judd took his first camping trip in the pouring rain in a big, heavy canvas tent as an infant—the precise age is not known because his mother has blocked it all out. After more than four decades of repeating the act, he's finally getting it right—with some exceptions. A longtime columnist at the *Seattle Times,* Judd writes the weekly "Trail Mix" column about life in the Northwest outdoors, as well as "The Wrap by Ron Judd," a pointed, humorous review of the week's news. He also covers the Olympic Games. He is the author of numerous popular outdoor guides and two works of humor: *The Roof Rack Chronicles* and *The Blue Tarp Bible.* His latest nonfiction work is *The Winter Olympics: An Insider's Guide to the Legends, the Lore, and the Games.* He lives in Bellingham, Washington. To see updates on Judd's work and find updates to this guide, go to www.ronjudd.com.

ACKNOWLEDGMENTS

The author sincerely thanks anyone who's ever stood by and refrained from snickering as he attempted to erect an REI dome tent in a stiff wind. No easy task, for either party. Many thanks also to my best friend, partner, and wife, MJ, for keeping that spirit of adventure alive. Lastly, but by no means leastly, a long-overdue thanks to those fabulous people, whomever and wherever they are, who make big blue tarps, the very fabric of our camping existence.

THE MOUNTAINEERS, founded in 1906, is a nonprofit outdoor activity and conservation club, whose mission is "to explore, study, preserve, and enjoy the natural beauty of the outdoors...." Based in Seattle, Washington, the club is now one of the largest such organizations in the United States, with seven branches throughout Washington State.

The Mountaineers sponsors both classes and year-round outdoor activities in the Pacific Northwest, which include hiking, mountain climbing, ski-touring, snowshoeing, bicycling, camping, kayaking and canoeing, nature study, sailing, and adventure travel. The club's conservation division supports environmental causes through educational activities, sponsoring legislation, and presenting informational programs. All club activities are led by skilled, experienced volunteers, who are dedicated to promoting safe and responsible enjoyment and preservation of the outdoors.

If you would like to participate in these organized outdoor activities or the club's programs, consider a membership in The Mountaineers. For information and an application, write or call The Mountaineers, Club Headquarters, 7700 Sand Point Way NE, Seattle, Washington 98115; 206-521-6001.

The Mountaineers Books, an active, nonprofit publishing program of the club, produces guidebooks, instructional texts, historical works, natural history guides, and works on environmental conservation. All books produced by The Mountaineers fulfill the club's mission.

Send or call for our catalog of more than 500 outdoor titles:
The Mountaineers Books
1001 SW Klickitat Way, Suite 201
Seattle, WA 98134
800-553-4453
mbooks@mountaineersbooks.org
www.mountaineersbooks.org

The Mountaineers Books is proud to be a corporate sponsor of Leave No Trace, whose mission is to promote and inspire responsible outdoor recreation through education, research, and partnerships. The Leave No Trace program is focused specifically on human-powered (non-motorized) recreation. Leave No Trace strives to educate visitors about the nature of their recreational impacts, as well as offer techniques to prevent and minimize such impacts. Leave No Trace is best understood as an educational and ethical program, not as a set of rules and regulations. For more information, visit www.lnt.org, or call 800-332-4100.

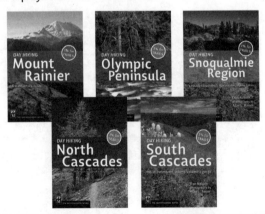
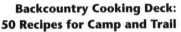